CURRENTS OF REFORM
IN PRESERVICE TEACHER
EDUCATION

CURRENTS OF REFORM IN PRESERVICE TEACHER EDUCATION

Ken Zeichner
Susan Melnick
Mary Louise Gomez

EDITORS

Teachers College, Columbia University
New York and London

Published by Teachers College Press, 1234 Amsterdam Avenue, New York, NY 10027

Portions of Chapter 6 are reprinted from *Teaching and Teacher Education*, Volume 10, Number 3, pp. 319–334. Copyright 1994, with kind permission from Elsevier Science Ltd., the Boulevard, Langford Lane, Kidlington OX5 IGB, UK.

Library of Congress Cataloging-in-Publication Data

Currents of reform in preservice teacher education / Ken Zeichner,
    Susan Melnick, Mary Gomez, editors.
         p.   cm.
    Includes bibliographical references and index.
    ISBN 0-8077-3429-2 (paper). — ISBN 0-8077-3430-6 (cloth)
      1. Teachers—Training of—United States.   2. Educational change—
    United States.   3. Multicultural education—United States.
    I. Zeichner, Kenneth M.   II. Melnick, Susan L. (Susan Lee)
    III. Gomez, Mary Louise.
    LB1715.C856   1996
    370.71'0973—dc20   95-44564

ISBN 0-8077-3429-2 (paper)
ISBN 0-8077-3430-6 (cloth)
Printed on acid-free paper
Manufactured in the United States of America
03 02 01 00 99 98 97 96   8 7 6 5 4 3 2 1

We dedicate this book to our parents:
Marion Butler Gomez and Manuel Gomez
Honee Popiel Melnick and Joseph B. Melnick
Albert Zeichner and Bernice Zeichner

Contents

Acknowledgments

We would like to thank a number of people who contributed to the completion of this book. First, we would like to thank Lois Triemstra of the University of Wisconsin–Madison for her careful preparation of the manuscript. We would also like to thank former and current U.S. Department of Education staff members Betsy Ashburn and Joyce Murphy, who served as project monitors at the U.S. Office of Educational Research and Improvement, for the research reported in several of the chapters of the book that was conducted with funding from the National Center for Research on Teacher Education and the National Center for Research on Teacher Learning. Finally, we would like to thank our editors, Carol Collins and Sarah Biondello, for their support, understanding, and patience when we were forced to ask for several extensions of the deadlines for the completion of the book.

CHAPTER 1

Introduction

Ken Zeichner

Teacher education reform in the United States has probably received more attention in the last decade than in any single decade in its history. Since the widely publicized teacher education reports of the Holmes Group (1986) and the Carnegie Task Force on Teaching as a Profession (1986), which followed the publication of *A Nation at Risk* (National Commission on Excellence in Education, 1983), numerous changes have been proposed in the ways in which teacher education students are recruited and selected, and in the content, organization, and control of teacher education programs.

Both of the major teacher unions (American Federation of Teachers, 1986; National Educational Association, 1982), several consortia of teacher education institutions (e.g., Consortium for Excellence in Teacher Education, 1987; Holmes Group, 1990, 1995; Project 30, 1991; Renaissance Group, 1989), both major professional organizations of teacher educators and teacher education institutions (Association of Teacher Educators, 1986; Pugach, Barnes, & Beckum, 1991), most state departments of education (e.g., California Commission on the Teaching Profession, 1985), and many individual teacher educators (e.g., Darling-Hammond, 1994; Goodlad, 1990; Liston & Zeichner, 1991; Schlechty, 1990) have given their interpretations of the problems in teacher education in the United States and have offered specific scenarios for reform.

Although these proposed changes have spanned the full scope of teachers' careers, the focus in this book is on reform in preservice teacher education. This is a time of increasing cultural diversity and poverty in the United States, of declining resources both in colleges and universities and in the public schools, and of increased external regulation of teacher education programs, and the chapters in this volume are organized in three sections that reflect some of the major issues in contemporary teacher education reform. The chapters in the first section discuss several aspects of standards movements such as national program accreditation and state education department regulation of teacher certification, with a focus on what standard setting and regulation look like at the level of teacher education programs and how faculty and students interpret and

1

give meaning to the various reform efforts. There is also a particular concern in these chapters with consistency among the reforms initiated by different actors.

The second section contains three chapters that describe various aspects of current efforts in the United States to better prepare prospective teachers to teach in our increasingly multicultural and diverse society. Each of these chapters examines the efficacy of specific instructional strategies and programs for developing greater cultural sensitivity and intercultural teaching competence in preservice teacher education. The two chapters in the third and final section of the book discuss the consequences of different approaches to preparing teachers who are reflective about their practice and the contexts in which their practice is embedded. This section includes a discussion of the relationship between teacher reflection and teacher empowerment and the role of field experiences in promoting teacher reflection. Following is a more detailed summary of the major issues that are addressed in each chapter.

SECTION I—REGULATION AND STANDARDS
IN TEACHER EDUCATION

In Chapter 2, "External Influences on Teacher Education Programs: National Accreditation and State Certification," Alan Tom provides a critical analysis over a 30-year period of the standard-setting and enforcement process in teacher education that focuses on the processes of state oversight of teacher certification and teacher education program approval, and the voluntary national accreditation of teacher education programs by the National Council for Accreditation of Teacher Education (NCATE). Tom criticizes these regulatory processes on several grounds: the large number of overlapping and often conflicting standards that programs must meet for state and NCATE approval, the political self-interest that he argues governs the standard-setting process and leads to an unnecessary proliferation of standards, and the failure of this regulatory process to make substantial improvements in teacher education programs. Tom calls for an end to detailed program regulation by both states and NCATE and urges that we adopt more modest expectations about what can be accomplished through regulatory accreditation.

Specifically, he argues that the desire to promote high-quality programming through the regulatory process may be unreasonable, and that we should focus program accreditation instead on the goals of identifying and improving weak programs. Tom also calls for more systematic inquiry into the standard-making and standard-enforcement process in teacher education.

In Chapter 3, "Reforming Teacher Education Through Legislation: A Case Study from Florida," Susan Melnick notes several tensions between regulatory standards and professional judgment in teacher education. Specifically, she analyzes the complex and contradictory effects of three reform initiatives taken by the state department of education in Florida in the 1980s to improve the quality of teaching and teacher education in Florida schools: the Gordon Rule, which mandated course work for all undergraduates in Florida with a specified amount of required writing; the College Level Academic Skills Test (CLAST), which included a test of writing competence; and the Florida Performance Measurement System (FPMS), a classroom observation system that specified criteria for the evaluation of beginning teachers. The focus in this chapter is on how these policies influenced the development of expertise in the teaching of writing in the elementary and secondary English teacher education programs at State University, a major public university in Florida. Melnick argues, based on interviews with faculty and students, that these policies, although well intentioned, promoted rule-bound conceptions of the writing process and a conception of teaching as the mastery of generic skills that conflicted with the predominant views of good writing and good teaching that are indicated by research and held by teacher education faculty. Melnick argues that the main function of these regulatory standards is their symbolic value in assuring the public that beginning teachers have an absolute minimum level of competence, but that the standards have not served to improve the teaching and learning of writing in Florida's public schools.

In Chapter 4, "The Continuing Reform of a University Teacher Education Program: A Case Study," Dorene Ross and Elizabeth Bondy describe the evolution of the elementary teacher education program at the University of Florida (PROTEACH) over a 20-year period. This analysis traces the ideological shifts and changes in program structures in relation to a variety of external and internal factors that influenced program reforms. These factors include the educational orientations of individual faculty members, the reward structure of a research university, the leadership provided by the dean of the School of Education, the support by the central administration of the university, and the national and state climates for teacher education including various initiatives concerning teacher education in the state legislature. Contrary to Alan Tom's claim that teacher educators have largely assumed a passive "meeting-standards" mentality in relation to the increasing external pressures on teacher education programs, Ross and Bondy's case study shows the way in which teacher educators can actively shape these external regulations in ways that allow them to implement a teacher education program that is congruent with their ideological orientations. Even when externally mandated regulations conflict with these orientations, as when the state of Florida implemented a teacher-induction program that reflected a view of teaching different from that of many PROTEACH faculty, the faculty were able to respond to the requirement in a way that met both the need to prepare their students for their evaluation as beginning teachers by the state and enabled the faculty to encourage their preferred view of teaching. Ross and Bondy outline various internal processes and structures that were initiated to sustain program reform such as faculty study groups, team teaching, and conducting research on teacher education. It is interesting to note that although the University of Florida's teacher education programs are accredited by NCATE, this organization is not mentioned at all by Ross and Bondy in describing the reforms in their program. From one point of view, this absence conflicts with Tom's belief that much time is spent by teacher educators in meeting excessive regulations. From another perspective, Tom's position about the lack of connection between meaningful program reform and program regulation is supported.

In Chapter 5, "Traditional and Alternate Routes to Teacher Certification: Issues, Assumptions, and Misconceptions," Trish Stoddart and Robert Floden analyze the trend over the last decade in many states to allow alternate routes to teacher certification, which are developed and administered by state departments of education and/or school districts with relatively little involvement of colleges and universities. While the chapters by Tom, Melnick, and Ross and Bondy are concerned with the nature and effects of the increasing regulation of teacher education by external agencies, this chapter focuses on an opposing trend: the deregulation of teacher education and a challenge to the monopoly that colleges and universities have held over teacher education for most of the 20th century. Stoddart and Floden discuss the reasons for the emergence of the alternative teacher education programs (e.g., concerns over teacher shortages and teacher quality); some of the ways in which alternative programs vary in their purpose, content, and structure; and some of the research evidence that has accumulated about the comparative effects of alternative and traditional teacher education programs on teacher recruitment and the development of teaching expertise. Stoddart and Floden discuss the strengths and weaknesses of both the alternative and the traditional programs and outline ways in which both kinds of teacher education programs can be improved.

SECTION II—PREPARING TEACHERS FOR CULTURAL DIVERSITY

In Chapter 6, "Prospective Teachers' Perspectives on Teaching 'Other People's Children,'" Mary Gomez discusses the growing gap between a predominately white and monolingual teaching force and an increasingly diverse pupil population. She summarizes data related to the perspectives of future teachers toward teaching "other people's children," who may differ from them in factors such as race, social class, language background, and sexual orientation. These data show that many prospective teachers want to teach pupils much like themselves in familiar settings and are reluctant to teach in areas where there is a great deal of student diversity. Gomez also discusses the problems associated with the deficit views that many prospective teachers hold about "Other people's children," which locate problems in student learning outside of the school and do not problematize teachers' beliefs and actions. She criticizes teacher education reform reports for failing to give serious attention to issues of preparing teachers for diversity and then describes a number of programs and courses across the United States that have demonstrated some success in developing cultural sensitivity and/or intercultural teaching competence, including the Teachers for Diversity program at the University of Wisconsin–Madison. Gomez discusses the implications of her analysis for improving the ability of teacher education programs to prepare teachers for diversity and calls for serious attention to issues of recruitment and selection of students and to relationships among schools of education, public schools, and those who provide the liberal arts portion of a teacher's education.

In Chapter 7, "Educating Teachers for Cultural Diversity," I discuss the lack of attention in the United States over the last 30 years to the issue of preparing teachers for cultural diversity. The focus then shifts to a discussion of an emerging consensus in the literature about what teachers should be like, know, and be able to do in order to successfully teach poor ethnic- and language-minority students. This includes the ability to learn about one's own students and their families and to build bridges between the cultural resources that students bring to school and the school and classroom cultures. I then discuss various instructional strategies such as field experiences in culturally diverse settings that have been used in preservice teacher education programs in the United States to develop greater cultural sensitivity and intercultural teaching competence, and the research evidence concerning the efficacy of these various approaches. I conclude that although the literature provides clues about how to conduct teacher education that prepares teachers to successfully teach all students, we don't know very much at this point about the impact of these various strategies on the teaching of prospective teachers, even in the short run. Like Gomez, I call for more attention to selection of candidates for our teacher education programs because of the complexity of the task and the limited time that we have to work with prospective teachers.

In Chapter 8, "The Role of Community Field Experiences in Preparing Teachers for Cultural Diversity," Susan Melnick and I provide a historical analysis of the role of community field experiences in preservice teacher education programs. We describe the different purposes and structures of community experiences that have been used in teacher education programs (e.g., community service, cultural immersion, community study) and research evidence about the efficacy of different approaches. A case study is then presented of the American Indian Reservation Project at Indiana University, which provides prospective teachers with a semester-long immersion experience living and teaching on a Native American reservation in the southwest United States. Data are presented from interviews with program faculty and students and from observations of program activities illuminating the key aspects of this community-based teacher education program that are related to the development of greater cultural sensitivity and intercultural teaching competence. Careful preparation for community experiences, systematic monitoring of student teachers' reflections about their experiences, and the use of Native American consultants as paid part-time instructors are some of the factors that influenced program outcomes.

SECTION III—PROMOTING REFLECTIVE PRACTICE
IN TEACHER EDUCATION

In Chapter 9, "Teachers as Reflective Practitioners and the Democratization of School Reform," I discuss the emergence and growth of the international reflective practice movement in teaching and teacher education—why it has come about and what it represents. I argue that, despite the rhetoric surrounding efforts to help teachers become more reflective, in reality, teacher education has done very little to foster genuine teacher development and to enhance teachers' roles in school reform, and outline several ways in which the slogan of reflective teaching has maintained the subservient position of teachers and created an illusion of teacher empowerment. Following a description of four different traditions of reflective practice in U.S. teacher education, I argue that efforts to prepare teachers who are reflective should recognize the inherently political nature of the reflective process and aim to foster both genuine teacher development and the realization of social justice in schooling.

Practicum, in Chapter 10, "Designing Educative Practicum Experiences for Prospective Teachers," refers to all varieties of observational and teaching experiences in a preservice teacher education program. An "educative practicum" is defined as one that prepares novices for the full scope of the teacher's role, for accomplishing the central purposes of schooling with all students, and that fosters the disposition and ability to learn from further experience. I describe three conceptions of the teacher education practicum (apprenticeship, applied science, and inquiry-orientation) that have been implemented in preservice teacher education programs throughout the world and analyze how each of these conceptions addresses the criteria of an educative practicum and a set of obstacles to teacher learning that have been associated with the practicum for many years. None of the three approaches by itself is found to be sufficient for addressing the criteria for an educative practicum or for overcoming the obstacles to teacher learning. A series of changes is proposed to better address issues of teacher learning in the teacher education practicum, including the negotiation of the practicum curriculum, broadening the scope of the practicum beyond the classroom level into schools and communities, and changing the institutional context of colleges and universities to place a greater value on the practicum. The chapter closes with a critique of the professional development school (PDS) movement in the United States for the apparent lack of attention given in many professional development schools to some of the issues raised in this chapter concerning the quality of student teacher learning.

The effect of these chapters is to explore, from various positions, some of the major issues of curriculum, instruction, and policy currently being debated in the American teacher education community. Whether the topic is program regulation and accreditation, program structure, educating teachers for cultural diversity, or preparing reflective teachers, the authors identify and then analyze different theoretical positions on the issues in focus and examine the available research evidence on the efficacy of different approaches.

A significant dimension of this book is that all of the authors are actively engaged in the design and implementation of preservice teacher education programs. Although only Chapter 4 involves a study by the authors of their own program, all of the chapters are informed by the authors' involvement in the complexities of trying to build high-quality preservice teacher education programs. Many of the reform efforts in U.S. teacher education over the last decade have been designed by those who are not directly involved themselves in administering or teaching in preservice teacher education programs. This volume offers a broad look at some of the most pressing issues of the day from the perspectives of some of those who struggle with the complexities of preservice teacher education on a daily basis.

Several of the chapters in this book are connected to the work of the National Center for Research on Teacher Education (NCRTE) (1985–1990) and the National Center for Research on Teacher Learning (NCRTL) (1990–1995). Both of these centers, housed at Michigan State University, have been funded by the U.S. Office of Educational Research and Improvement of the U.S. Department of Education. The NCRTE conducted a coordinated set of case studies of preservice, in-service, and alternative-route teacher education programs across the United States. Chapters 3, 4, and 5 are based on the NCRTE study "Teacher Education and Learning to Teach" (TELT). Chapters 7 and 8 are based on work Susan Melnick and I did for our NCRTL research project, "Educating Teachers for Diversity."

It is our hope that the chapters in this book will contribute new insights to both policy debates concerning the future of American teacher education and the practices of the thousands of dedicated teacher educators who work, often without adequate appreciation and resources, in the approximately 1,200 teacher education institutions across the United States and in the thousands of elementary and secondary schools that cooperate with these institutions.

REFERENCES

American Federation of Teachers. (1986). *The revolution that is overdue: Looking to-ward the future of teaching and learning.* Washington, DC: Author.

Association of Teacher Educators. (1986). *Visions of reform: Implications for the educa-tion profession.* Reston, VA: Author.

California Commission on the Teaching Profession. (1985). *Who will teach our chil-dren?* California: Author.

Carnegie Task Force on Teaching as a Profession. (1986). *A nation prepared: Teachers for the 21st Century.* New York: Carnegie Corporation.

Consortium for Excellence in Teacher Education. (1987). *Teacher education and the liberal arts.* Author.

Darling-Hammond, L. (Ed.). (1994). *Professional development schools: Schools for de-veloping a profession.* New York: Teachers College Press.

Goodlad, J. (1990). *Teachers for our nation's schools.* San Francisco: Jossey-Bass.

Holmes Group. (1986). *Tomorrow's teachers.* East Lansing: The Holmes Group, Inc., Michigan State University, School of Education.

Holmes Group. (1990). *Tomorrow's schools: Principles for the design of professional de-velopment schools.* East Lansing: The Holmes Group, Inc., Michigan State Univer-sity, School of Education.

Holmes Group. (1995). *Tomorrow's schools of education.* East Lansing: The Holmes Group, Inc., Michigan State University, School of Education.

Liston, D., & Zeichner, K. (1991). *Teacher education and the social conditions of school-ing.* New York: Routledge.

National Commission on Excellence in Education. (1983). *A nation at risk.* Washing-ton, DC: U.S. Government Printing Office.

National Educational Association. (1982). *Excellence in our schools: Teacher education.* Washington, DC: Author.

Project 30. (1991). *Project 30 year two report: Institutional accomplishments.* Newark, DE: University of Delaware, Project 30 Alliance.

Pugach, M., Barnes, H., & Beckum, L. (Eds.). (1991). *Changing the practice of teacher education: The role of the knowledge base.* Washington, DC: American Association of Colleges for Teacher Education.

Renaissance Group. (1989). *Teachers for the new world: A statement of principles.* Cedar Falls: University of Northern Iowa.

Schlechty, P. (1990). *Reform in teacher education: A sociological view.* Washington, DC: American Association of Colleges for Teacher Education.

PART I

Regulation and Standards in Teacher Education

CHAPTER 2

External Influences on Teacher Education Programs: National Accreditation and State Certification

Alan R. Tom

Any teacher education program is subject to many forms of influence external to that particular program. Besides the often-cited reports from the Holmes Group (1986) and the Carnegie Task Force on Teaching as a Profession (1986), there are numerous lesser-known teacher education reports and a significant number of institutional consortia: for example, the Consortium for Excellence in Teacher Education (CETE), a cluster of northeastern elite liberal arts colleges (CETE, 1987; Rothman, 1987); Project 30, a group of 30 institutions in which faculties of education and of arts and sciences are working together to improve teacher education (Project 30, 1991); and the Renaissance Group, a group of eight regional universities whose presidents and deans of education adopted a set of principles to guide program reform (Renaissance Group, 1989; Viadero, 1990). Moreover, the list of groups interested in reforming teacher education is literally endless, including professional societies that recommend revisions in the teacher education curriculum, and educational foundations that use money as a lever to foster a variety of changes in teacher education.

At the same time, these reports and groups are one layer removed from the nucleus of power, since none of them has the power to compel change. Indeed, some of these reports and groups have arisen to counter the influence of those external forces that really do have substantial impact on the direction and substance of teacher education programming: the administrative oversight of teacher licensure by the state[1] and the accreditation of teacher education programs by the National Council for Accreditation of Teacher Education (NCATE). Of these two forms of regulation, state authority is by far the more significant, since teacher licensure—commonly referred to as certification—is controlled by the state. NCATE accreditation is voluntary unless state authorities decide to make such program accreditation mandatory.[2]

Thus I have decided to focus my discussion of external influences affecting teacher education on state oversight of certification and national accreditation of programs, with a 30-year time perspective on both processes. In the analysis that follows I will be stressing several negative aspects of regulation, including the trend toward overlapping purposes for state and national regulation; the tendency for the revision of NCATE standards to reflect the narrow interests of stakeholders; and the failure of so-called Redesign to make major improvements in NCATE. To anticipate my conclusions, I contend that teacher education programs are excessively regulated and that this programmatic regulation often is internally contradictory and overly detailed. In the end we might be far better off if we reduced our expectations for accreditation from the promotion of high-quality programming to the identification and elimination of weak programs.

CERTIFICATION AND ACCREDITATION: TREND TOWARD OVERLAPPING PURPOSES

In theory, state certification standards and national accreditation standards serve differing (and potentially complementary) purposes, as certification (hereafter called licensure) involves whether a particular individual should be given a license by the state while accreditation is a judgment made about the quality of the program in which that person is trained. Thus the unit of analysis differs, with state licensure focusing on the teacher and national accreditation centering on the preparation program. As a result, a division of labor seems to exist between the processes and purposes of state licensure and those of national program accreditation.

However, state licensure policy—initially with emphasis on examinations, as had been the case with 19th century local licensure—moved in the early 20th century away from measuring the competence of licensure candidates through written examinations toward improving the quality of program content (Stinnett, 1968; von Schlichten, 1958). In a sense, the move by state authorities to take control of the licensing of individual teachers away from local officials ultimately evolved into the control of teacher preparation programming (as a proxy for ensuring practitioner competence).

The vehicle for state regulation of the content of teacher education programs became known as the process of "state program approval." Until exit testing for licensure became commonplace during the 1980s, a university that had its program "approved" by state officials was guaranteed that its teacher education graduates would receive licenses to teach in the public schools of that state. Faculty in departments and colleges of education initially were enthusiastic about the policy of approved programs, since such endorsement permitted them to promise every incoming student that program graduation also conferred a state teaching license. In addition, state standards affected professors of education personally since these standards were more likely to regulate the content of professional studies than that of subject-matter preparation. As a result, education professors typically were pleased not only to help implement state program approval policies but also to collaborate on the advisory panels and other mechanisms that astute state commissioners of education periodically used to achieve consensus on any proposed revision of the standards for program approval.[3]

The support by professors of education for the program-approval approach probably can be traced not only to their self-interest in being able to influence the substance of this regulation but also to the tendency during the 1950s and 1960s for program-approval standards to give these professors increasing latitude for designing teacher education programs. As recently as the mid-1960s, Beggs (1965) could say that "the trend is moving away from legislative prescription of the details" of certification requirements and toward giving "partial or even complete autonomy to the state boards, or the departments of education, for establishing requirements" (p. 48). In turn, these state agencies used their greater autonomy to institute the "reduction of specific course requirements. States tend to make fewer specific requirements and to leave this decision to the institutions within the general framework of an 'approved program'" (p. 57).

Note how Beggs (1965) linked certification requirements reciprocally with program approval. A common approach of that era was for state authorities to specify minimum credit hours for both academic and professional study, as well as for the distribution of course work within these two areas (von Schlichten, 1958). Thus program approval came to signify very little about a university's teacher education program other than that the university agreed to follow the minimum course requirements mandated to secure a state teaching license. In the end, the course-work requirements for obtaining a teaching license drove the process of state program approval, and this approval, as recently as the late 1960s, was typically "little more than a formality" (Stinnett, 1968, p. 86).

NCATE Accreditation

The only serious review of programs done at that time was conducted by the National Council for Accreditation of Teacher Education (NCATE), a private organization formed in 1952 with equal representation from public school practitioners, preparing colleges, and state education legal authorities (Stinnett, 1970). For much of its history, NCATE concentrated on evaluating individual teacher education programs (e.g., art education or elementary education), though as part of its recent Redesign (Gideonse, 1992; Roames, 1987) NCATE now accredits the basic "unit" (including all programs for initial teacher preparation) and the advanced "unit" (including programs for the advanced preparation of teachers and the initial and/or advanced preparation of other school personnel). Thus, NCATE has stressed the evaluation of programs, considered either individually or in clusters, with the purpose of assuring "that institutions are accountable for maintaining [the] quality of the professional preparation programs offered by those institutions" (Christensen, 1980, p. 42).[4]

At least in the 1960s, the focus of NCATE differed significantly from that of state program approval, since the latter amounted to little more than loosely specified minimum course requirements for state licensure while NCATE standards regulated the content and structure of teacher education programs in considerable detail (Ladd, 1963; Mayor, 1965). The course work and programmatic foci of state approval and national accreditation respectively were complementary, and an institution generally could address both NCATE's program-oriented standards and the course-work minimums tied to state program approval without encountering state and NCATE standards that conflicted with one another. In some states, such as Missouri, institutions that were NCATE-approved did not even have to go through state program approval; the circular reasoning behind this laxity was that these institutions must already have met Missouri's course-work requirements for a state license by virtue of NCATE's policy that any institution seeking national accreditation must already have secured state program approval.

During the 1970s, NCATE continued to hone its standards, with a major modification in 1970 and a subsequent smaller revision in 1977 whereby institutions were required to include multicultural education in the professional curriculum (National Council for Accreditation of Teacher Education [NCATE], 1977; Roames, 1987). Though this new multicultural standard had a major impact on many institutions, the real action in NCATE during the 1970s involved a successful struggle by the National Education Association (NEA) to gain greater power in the NCATE governance structure and greater representation of K–12 personnel on visiting teams (Christensen, 1980, 1984–85; Cushman, 1977; Roames, 1987).

This shift in power relations corresponded with a dramatic increase in the rate at which institutions were denied accreditation. From 1954 to 1973—the year before NEA achieved parity with the American Association of Colleges for Teacher Education (AACTE) in representation on the council—only 1 in 10 institutions was denied accreditation, but the denial rate rose to nearly 1 in 5 during the remainder of the decade (Wheeler, 1980, p. 3). Both the director of NCATE at the beginning of the 1980s (Gubser, 1983) and his immediate predecessor (Larson, 1979) believed that NCATE's role in the mid-1970s changed from a developmental one in which standards were viewed as desirable goals to a regulatory one in which standards became "rules" in which "sanctions follow . . . if

the conditions are not met" (Larson, 1979, pp. 11–12). The regulatory emphasis persists to this day, with the failure rate under the Redesign standards (in
effect since the fall of 1988) being comparable to the 20% failure rate of the mid-
to-late 1970s (Diegmueller, 1992a; Staff, 1993a; Staff, 1993b; Wise & Leibbrand,
1993).

State Program Approval

At the same time that NCATE was becoming tougher 20 years ago in enforcing its
standards, major changes were also occurring in state program approval. This
approval gradually lost its flexibility and open-endedness during the 1970s and
1980s, and state officials increasingly viewed specifying the titles (and the distribution) of professional courses as an inadequate basis for approving programs.
With substantial variation across states, program approval standards took a
harder and harder look not just at the names of courses but also at the content
of these courses. However, other than war stories from participants in the state
program approval process, we have little systematic information about how state
standards are implemented during institutional reviews. Teacher educators—
ideally situated to document this process—are understandably hesitant to do
so, as these teacher educators know it is not wise to risk alienating the state officials who have the authority to close any program. Nor do we have more than
a handful of studies that analyze how the standards themselves are developed
(for one such study, see Prestine, 1991).

   We do know that by 1984, 29 of the states modeled their state standards
after those of the National Association of State Directors of Teacher Education
and Certification (NASDTEC) or their equivalent (Roth & Pipho, 1990, p. 128),
and that the NASDTEC standards themselves were similar to the standards of NCATE
(Christensen, 1984–1985). Thus state program approval standards by the early
1980s were covering much the same programmatic turf as was NCATE, though
the specific standards promulgated by NCATE and any particular state are not
necessarily the same—or even similar.[5] Moreover, state standards usually are
considerably more detail-oriented than are those of NCATE.

Meeting Overlapping and Often Conflicting Standards

By the 1980s, therefore, the purposes of state program approval and national
accreditation were basically the same—the regulation of programs—while the
standards used to guide these two overlapping purposes were often related but
by no means necessarily identical. Even after NCATE publicly moved away from
the accreditation of individual programs as part of its Redesign in the mid-1980s
(Gideonse, 1992; Gollnick & Kunkel, 1986), its new approach to assessing units
still includes standards that focus on such programmatic issues as design of

curriculum, delivery of curriculum, and content of the curriculum (NCATE, 1990). Under Redesign, moreover, NCATE now approves for the first time the curriculum guidelines of learned societies, another factor that keeps NCATE's attention at the program level (Roames, 1987). Any overlap in program focus between NCATE and state program review has serious consequences for institutions, since over the last 20 years both national and state reviews have become more rigorous processes.

As a result, teacher educators in an institution of higher education often have to try to reconcile their programs with two sets of conflicting program-oriented standards, or with two sets of similar standards at differing levels of detail, each set being strictly enforced. Such an exercise tends not to foster cumulative improvement in teacher education programming. Rather, this balancing act leads to an emphasis on sleight of hand by teacher educators as we attempt to prove that our programs meet numerous and related—but often dissimilar—state and national standards. We become adept at showing how our existing programs, or some modest revision of them, satisfy whatever new standards a state or NCATE can generate. This "meeting-standards" mentality accentuates the passive and conforming role of teacher educators as we scramble to patch together programs in response to often conflicting state and NCATE standards.

NATIONAL ACCREDITATION: POLITICS AND MINIMAL CHANGE

Implicit in parts of the preceding discussion of state and NCATE standards is the idea that these sets of standards not only are overlapping but also are politically derived. While this political grounding is probably as true for state standards as for national standards, I concentrate in this section on NCATE standards. Even though NCATE accreditation is usually voluntary, while state approval is required, I have decided to emphasize national accreditation with the rationale that more public information is available about it and that this level of accreditation is potentially easier to change than are 50 separate systems.

NCATE is political in two senses that are pertinent to its difficulty in fostering cumulative improvement of teacher education programming. First, NCATE's accreditation standards are developed through a politics of consensus among a variety of constituent groups. The result is a hodgepodge of standards (Cruickshank, McCullough, Reynolds, Troyer, & Cruz, 1991), standards that often reflect the narrow interests of these constituent groups. Second, NCATE is political in the sense that this organization typically portrays relatively minor changes in its standards and procedures as major revisions with sweeping implications.[6] The first political theme of "consensus politics" is developed in the following analysis of NCATE's Redesign in the 1980s while the second theme, "magnifying minor changes," is illustrated both by discussion of NCATE Redesign and by a brief review of the content of the several standards, before and after Redesign.

NCATE Redesign: The Politics

The activities characterized as NCATE Redesign occurred between 1984 and 1986, but there were several false starts toward Redesign in the late 1970s and early 1980s. Since Redesign took so long to develop, it was anticipated to be a major reform of national accreditation by literally all participants in the Redesign process.

The Impetus. The first movements toward Redesign were initiated in 1978 when the land-grant education deans threatened to create an alternative accreditation system if NCATE did not make some major changes within five years (Gideonse, 1992; Gollnick & Kunkel, 1986). In the years immediately after 1978, the organization of the land-grant deans—the Association of Colleges and Schools of Education in State Universities and Land Grant Colleges and Affiliated Private Universities (ACSESULGC/APU)—continued to press for changes in NCATE. Among NCATE's weaknesses identified in a 1983 resolution passed by ACSESULGC/APU were the following: lack of clarity in the goals of national accreditation, ambiguity in NCATE standards, the vocational as opposed to intellectual focus of the standards, excessively large and poorly trained visiting teams, redundancy in the roles of state and national accreditation, a focus on minimums rather than program excellence, and the high cost of NCATE (Palmer, 1983). These criticisms overlap those made by Wheeler (1980) in a major study that was commissioned by NCATE itself and are similar to criticisms that I had made as an individual (Tom, 1980a, 1980b, 1981).

Frustration with the slowness of NCATE's internal reform led four land-grant deans—all of them active in the American Association of Colleges for Teacher Education—to seek the support of AACTE's executive director and board of directors for establishing an AACTE committee charged with developing proposals for reforming NCATE (Gideonse, 1992). The Committee for Accreditation Alternatives (CAA) was appointed by the president of AACTE in November 1981 and was composed of the four land-grant deans who originally had made the proposal for such a committee.

An important precipitating event for the creation of the CAA by AACTE was the proposal by the NCATE Council in 1981 to institute a "finance standard," which mandated a maximum 12:1 student-faculty ratio in initial teacher preparation (NCATE UPDATE, 1981; Roames & Dye, 1986). This proposal was disliked by all segments of higher education but was especially feared by institutions that conducted large-scale teacher education programs with relatively small faculties.

Widespread negative reaction to the proposed finance standard delayed and ultimately killed this standard:

> [Final] action on proposed standards on finance . . . , including a controversial proposed student-faculty ratio, has been postponed until the October [1982] meeting of the [NCATE] Council. . . . Over 100 responses to the published standards were received. The prevailing reaction was negative, particularly from institutional organizations and central administrative officers. (NCATE UPDATE, 1982, p. 1)

At that October 1982 meeting, the NCATE Council reversed its earlier support for the 12:1 student-faculty ratio—originally approved by one vote—and rejected that policy.

A case can be made, therefore, that an important factor that pushed AACTE into appointing the Committee on Accreditation Alternatives in 1981 was an attempt to stall and subvert the finance standard by self-interested administrators, despite a growing public recognition that teacher education was underfunded in relation to other undergraduate programs (e.g., Peseau & Orr, 1980). The student-faculty ratio in the finance standard would have put real teeth in the NCATE standards, since many large colleges of education in public institutions subsidize their graduate programs by diverting faculty resources away from undergraduate teacher preparation while many institutions, private as well as public, use the income generated by teacher education enrollments to subsidize other parts of the institution. The proposed NCATE finance standard would have challenged these dubious practices since it required a substantial level of financial support; other proponents of a financial-resources standard were much less explicit in how to operationalize this standard (e.g., Tom, 1981).

Thus a catalyst mobilizing the four deans to propose that AACTE take leadership in redesigning NCATE may have been the potential for NCATE intrusion into the financial affairs of colleges of education and universities. Dale Scannell, one of the four original deans and ultimately the chair of AACTE's Committee on Accreditation Alternatives, subsequently reported that AACTE was moved to action by four NCATE proposals that surfaced in 1981. NCATE had "proposed new standards relating to public disclosure, education for exceptional children, finance, and use of standards developed by professional associations" (Scannell, quoted in Roames & Dye, 1986, p. 21). In addition to the finance standard, the public disclosure of the particulars concerning an accreditation decision and the use of the detailed standards developed by numerous professional associations were potential NCATE policies that could have substantial impact on the programs in colleges of education (Toch, 1982).

Gideonse (1992) has a less self-serving interpretation of the motives of the deans; he maintains that the precipitating event for AACTE's formation of CAA was the failure of the NCATE Council in October 1981 to act on reform proposals that the NCATE staff had derived from Wheeler's (1980) comprehensive study of NCATE. This interpretation is supported by William Gardner (personal communication, May 15, 1992), one of the four deans who initiated the proposal for the Committee on Accreditation Alternatives. NCATE officials indeed were defensive about NCATE's failure to act on the recommendations in the Wheeler study (NCATE UP-DATE, 1982).

The CAA Report. In any case, the final report of the Committee on Accreditation Alternatives was issued after a year of intensive contact among that committee and AACTE's board of directors, the National Education Association, whose interests had been protected through adding a fifth member to CAA, and the three constituent members of AACTE: ACSESULGC/APU (the land-grant deans), TECSCU (the Teacher Education Council of State Colleges and Universities), and AILACTE (the Association of Independent Liberal Arts Colleges for Teacher Education). TECSCU consists of the education deans in public but non-land-grant institutions, many of which had been normal schools but now are multipurpose institutions aspiring to develop a research as well as a teaching mission; their interests are often similar to those of the land-grant deans, but TECSCU deans of education often chafe at the lower status typically accorded their institutions.

AILACTE institutions tend to have a teaching focus and thus naturally possess some interests similar to those of TECSCU institutions. However, the private form of governance and especially the small size of AILACTE institutions often lead to concerns that differ from those of TECSCU and ACSESULGC/APU institutions. In addition, private institutions historically had played a minor role in AACTE affairs—a major reason for AILACTE's creation in the mid-1970s was to increase this role—so that CAA felt no particular need to include ideas of special interest to AILACTE institutions. I do have firsthand knowledge of the reactions of AILACTE institutions to the work of CAA, since I was on the AILACTE Executive Board for much of the 1980s.

Opposing Arguments. Preceded by four drafts and many meetings, the final report of the CAA (1983) attempted to meld the interests of the two most powerful organizations in NCATE: AACTE and NEA (Gideonse, 1992). However, the CAA report did not necessarily treat the interests of the three AACTE constituencies in an equivalent way. Due to my position within the leadership of AILACTE, I focus on concerns that our group raised about two proposals in the CAA report: the plan for changing the fee structure for NCATE-approved institutions and the "critical-mass" component of the proposed faculty standard. Both of these proposals hit a raw nerve among the small teacher education faculties characteristic of AILACTE institutions.

The critical-mass rationale struck AILACTE members as equating faculty size with quality of program. While the authors of the CAA report (1983) granted that it was difficult to determine precisely how many faculty members are needed to offer a program, they continued:

> It is equally true, however, that a critical mass of faculty must be present for a sufficient depth of expertise to be available to students. Those programs with only limited numbers of faculty directly responsible for the preparation of teachers and other educational personnel will need to present compelling evidence that a depth of expertise exists. It is not in the profession's best interest to accredit units that do not have sufficient faculty depth. (pp. 19–20)

Note how the endorsement of specialized expertise and of large-sized faculty fits well with the way ACSESULGC/APU and TECSCU institutions are usually organized. On the other hand, AILACTE institutions typically are staffed with faculty who are routinely expected to teach a variety of courses, a situation that tends to deemphasize the role of specialized knowledge in teacher education but conversely often tends to foster the development of integrated teacher education programs (Goodlad, 1990).

While the CAA report did outline two ways for funding NCATE, it clearly slanted the presentation toward a new dues structure that would assess all institutions the same fee, regardless of the number of programs or the degree levels at which programs are offered. NCATE's outgoing executive director, Lyn Gubser (1983), complained publicly about the "regressive" nature of the AACTE proposal since it imposed "a flat fee . . . for all institutions." (p. 7). In response, Scannell (1983, p. 20) denied that his committee had recommended "flat fee" dues over the then-current sliding-dues structure that took into account the quantity of graduates as well as the number and degree levels of programs. In reality, the CAA report (1983) did recommend that every institution be assessed "one annual accreditation fee . . . without an additional payment for levels and categories [of programs]" (p. 39). Scannell also disputed Gubser's (1983, p. 7) claim that the CAA report includes "variables that equate to size rather than quality" by overlooking the critical-mass phrase and stating that the CAA report "acknowledges that institutions unwilling or unable to provide the support needed for high-quality programs would be denied accreditation—regardless of institutional size" (Scannell, 1983, p. 20).

Reviewing these arguments provides insight into the internal differences among AACTE constituents and makes clear that an attempt was made to mask these differences by claiming they were a misreading of the CAA report. These differences, however, did break into the open at the 1983 annual meeting of AACTE when the opposition of AILACTE members to the CAA report was largely responsible for its being tabled. This opposition angered many of those central to the association's governance structure, and the AACTE president took the proposals from the CAA report to the NCATE Council meeting the following month without the endorsement of the report by the AACTE membership (Gideonse, 1992). The NCATE Council unanimously accepted the report, a clear sign that NEA's participation in CAA paid off for the AACTE leadership (16 of the 21 votes on the NCATE Council at that time were controlled by AACTE and NEA).

AILACTE, however, ultimately succeeded in removing both the critical-mass rationale and the flat-fee dues structure from the final version of NCATE Redesign, though Redesign ended up being grounded in the six principles on which the CAA report was based:

1. Accredit teacher education units, not programs.
2. Replace reaccreditation with continuing accreditation.
3. Articulate national accreditation with state approval.
4. Create a board of examiners skilled in NCATE standards, processes, and evaluation skills, from which to draw visiting teams.
5. Replace six families of standards applied to programs with five unit-focused standards.
6. Expand the annual list to describe the unit and indicate the support level for its programs. (Gideonse, 1992, p. 249)

Thus the basic form of Redesign did embody the agreements forged between NEA and the strongest segments of AACTE, with AILACTE being able to protect the specific interests of small institutions by defeating the attempt to end the sliding-fee structure and by eliminating the argument for correlating faculty size and specialized expertise with program quality.[7]

NCATE Redesign: Minimal Change

The changes made during Redesign are generally viewed as a substantial improvement in the standards and procedures of NCATE (e.g., Gideonse, 1992; Gollnick & Kunkel, 1986). Most frequently cited is the change from program approval to unit approval, the substantial revision of the standards to emphasize knowledge bases, a tougher stance on enforcing the standards, increased articulation of state approval and national accreditation, and the creation of the board of examiners. In reality, however, most of these changes are permutations of earlier NCATE practice. Here I review several of these alleged reforms: the supposed change to unit accreditation, the assertion that the standards have been substantially revised, the claim that the new standards are more rigorous, and the importance of the board of examiners.

Unit Accreditation? While accreditation decisions now pertain to the unit—with all initial teacher preparation programs and all advanced programs being clustered into two units—the standards themselves, under Redesign, con-

tinue to focus on programs. The wording of many current standards clearly indicates their ultimate grounding in programmatic considerations. For example:
"The unit ensures that its professional education programs are based on . . ."
(Standard I.A); "The unit has systematic procedures for monitoring the progress
of education students . . . [during] their professional education programs" (Standard III.B); and: "Resources are available . . . that allow the professional education unit to fulfill its mission and offer quality programs" (Standard V.B) (NCATE,
1990, pp. 45, 53, 58).

Revision of Standards? Equally important, the titles and content of the
standards in the pre-Redesign period (NCATE, 1982) and the period after Redesign (NCATE, 1990) are essentially the same, with the major difference often being
one of emphasis. For instance, the new family of standards entitled "Relationship to the World of Practice" brought together content formerly located in the
curricula, faculty, and evaluation standards. Further, with the exception of the
"Delivery of the Curriculum" standard, the new family of standards "Knowledge Bases for Professional Education" previously comprised the curricula standards. One of the most significant proposed reforms in recent years—a standard on finance—was not included in the Redesign effort and may even have
been a major stimulus for forming the Committee on Accreditation Alternatives
to focus on other reforms. Much of the effort of CAA, as well as the discussion of
its report, appears to have been driven by political struggles among the three
constituents of AACTE.

Tougher Standards and Improved Board of Examiner Teams? In addition,
we have already seen that the tougher stance on enforcing the NCATE standards
has roots going back to the mid-1970s, and that NCATE and state standards overlap in purpose substantially more now than was the case a generation ago. One
major change brought about by Redesign concerns the development of a smaller
group of site visitors—a five- or six-member board of examiners team—who
appear to be better trained than were prior teams (Diegmueller, 1992b; Tom
interview in Watts, 1986). Overall, however, the changes initiated by NCATE
Redesign seem neither extensive nor dramatic and can be seen as the logical
outcome of the consensual politics that characterizes the process by which NCATE
was redesigned.

ARE ANY OF THE STANDARDS VALUABLE?

This analysis does not seem headed toward a happy ending. State and national
regulation have become more prescriptive in recent years, and have increasingly
focused on the same turf. Not only has this convergence led to a network of

detailed and often conflicting standards but in addition these standards frequently reflect the parochial interests of stakeholders in the accreditation process. In this way, state and national standards, already blanketing the same area, tend to betray varied forms of self-interest (state standards are probably influenced as much by a politics of consensus as are NCATE standards, though I examined only NCATE standards). Moreover, NCATE Redesign resulted in minimal change, despite claims to the contrary. Is there nothing right about these redesigned standards?

Multicultural Standard

Two NCATE standards are often cited as having a particularly beneficial impact on programs. One such instance is the multicultural standard, actually a point of emphasis in several standards that focus on curriculum, students, and faculty. Prior to the development of NCATE's multicultural emphasis in 1977, little attention was given to multicultural education by the typical teacher education program, and even during the early 1980s NCATE seemed to have been cautious in its enforcement of its own multicultural requirements. After the implementation of the Redesign standards, however, NCATE came down hard on programs that did not demonstrate compliance with multicultural criteria. Of the first 132 institutions considered under Redesign, more than half were found to have insufficient cultural diversity (Nicklin, 1991), a trend that improved only marginally after 207 institutions had been reviewed (Diegmueller, 1992a). Perhaps due to this tough stance, NCATE's multicultural emphasis continues to be controversial, with some educators seeing it as imposing a narrow political and social agenda on teacher education (e.g., Parker, 1994). Though we cannot tell how much impact NCATE's multicultural emphasis has had on the composition of student bodies and faculty departments—as well as on the content of teacher education curricula—this stress on multiculturalism has applied pressure on institutions of higher education to change.

Curriculum Design Standard

A second NCATE standard often viewed as having a salutary effect on teacher education programming is the modification made in the curriculum design standard at the time of Redesign. Prior to Redesign, NCATE standards required only that program components be based on "objectives that reflect the institution's conception of the teacher's role" (NCATE, 1982, p. 14). As a result of Redesign, the same standard now requires that "research findings" and "sound professional practice" be included in each program, which must be based on "a systematic design with an explicitly stated philosophy and objectives" (NCATE, 1990, p. 45). To clarify this design standard, the term *model* was introduced in the first compliance criterion for this standard: Each program must have adopted "a model(s) that explicates the purposes, processes, outcomes, and evaluation of the program" (p. 45). This approach to curriculum design seems to promote the coherence Goodlad (1990) suggests is often missing in teacher education programming, but faculties of education visited by NCATE are often unclear about just what is meant by basing a teacher education program on a "model" (Staff, 1991b, p. 8). Moreover, the existence of 18 differing standards—each with multiple compliance criteria to help define it—tends to nullify any coherence that might be stimulated by the curriculum design standard.

Summary

Other examples of potentially worthwhile standards could be enumerated, but the issues I have raised in this chapter are not premised on the irrelevant or inconsequential nature of standards, either state or national, even though such a case might be made for many of these standards. Rather, I have emphasized the large number, conflicting character, stiff enforcement, and self-serving origin of the standards (and related procedures) on which we base state program approval and national accreditation. Along with the wheat—and I do endorse such concepts as multicultural education and program coherence—there is an abundance of chaff. Arthur Wise, the president of NCATE, has succinctly stated our problem: "We must climb out of the demotivating morass of regulations and procedures which have become so repressive" (Wise, 1991, p. 1).

A MORE MODEST ROLE FOR ACCREDITATION?

"Regulate, regulate, regulate" in fact does have a consequence, but it is not necessarily the better programs that the proponents of regulation desire. Excessive regulation leads to passivity on the part of those being regulated, as new rules can easily be replaced by old ones; faculty members wonder why they should bother to respond to each new set of standards if yet another new set is just over the horizon (Goodlad, 1990). We need a major simplification of programmatic standards, as well as the end of program regulation by both the states and NCATE. Rigorous enforcement of standards has been common for almost 20 years, to no particular positive effect. Rigor without simplification leads to gridlock.

Stakeholders in the accreditation process have their own special interests to protect. (My own may well be a commitment to multiculturalism and to the design of coherent programs.) While politics can never be removed from the standard-making and standard-enforcement process, we must become much more aware of the extent to which varied forms of self-interest multiply and magnify the standards by which accreditation and licensure judgments are made, as well as divert attention from significant reforms in accreditation. Systematic inquiry into standard-making and standard-enforcement processes is badly needed to expose the complexity, detail, and contradictions of these processes.

Finally, there is the need for much less boosterism in the field of accreditation. Any improvement made in these areas is likely to be incremental, and the current arrangements leave much to be desired. Let us be more modest in our claims and more willing to acknowledge that our approaches are imperfect. Above all, let us be more cautious in what we assert can be accomplished through regulatory accreditation.

Perhaps all that the policing entailed by accreditation can hope to achieve is to forestall or stop "what is regarded as bad" (Ladd, 1963, p. 296). Our taken-for-granted-desire to promote high-quality teacher education programming through accreditation may be an unreasonable expectation for NCATE, or for any other accrediting body. The point at which we advocate for higher quality—be it multiculturalism, coherent programming, or some other goal—is precisely the point at which we must adopt a view of desirable ends, thus bringing into play our personal or our organizational interests. From this starting point, the politics of consensus may be inevitable, creating the need for us to cover up our confusion and disorder by magnifying the importance of whatever minor changes we are able to achieve in accreditation standards. To focus on the modest goal of identifying weak programs and units may not appeal to our desire to mandate excellence in teacher education, but such a goal may well be the proper role for accreditation in teacher education.

NOTES

1. Legislative action at the state level also can have a substantial impact on teacher education; this topic is the focus of Chapter 3 and is not discussed here.

2. Except for a few states that require institutions to be NCATE-approved as a condition for state program approval (Diegmueller, 1991), NCATE accreditation is optional. Less than half—about 500—of the more than 1,300 U.S. institutions preparing teachers are so confirmed (Diegmueller, 1992a). Though many NCATE supporters would like national accreditation to become mandatory, institutions can opt in or out of NCATE at will. Defections from NCATE can be highly visible, as when the four largest institutions in Iowa simultaneously withdrew from NCATE several years ago, while charging that accreditation policies are "too restrictive and expensive" (Staff, 1992, p. A4).

3. While this interpretation is grounded in my personal experience in Missouri in the 1970s and early 1980s, Beggs (1965) notes that by the mid-1960s, 47 states had broadly representative bodies that served as "valuable sounding boards and recommending agencies for the legally constituted [certification] authorities" (p. 57). Among the participants in these bodies were "faculty from the training colleges" (p. 57).

4. There is no adequate history of NCATE, nor of the issues embedded in its his-

tory. One of the better sources, Mayor's *Accreditation in Teacher Education* (1965), is out of date. Other informative, but incomplete, accounts include: Christensen (1980, 1984–1985), Cushman (1977), Gideonse (1992, 1993), Gollnick & Kunkel (1986), Goodlad (1990), Larson (1979), Roames (1987), Roames & Dye (1986), Roth & Pipho (1990), Stinnett (1968, 1970), Tom (1980a, 1980b, 1981), Watts (1983, 1986), Wheeler (1980), and Wise & Leibbrand (1993).

5. The scholarship that would help substantiate these claims has yet to be done. However, the presence of overlap and conflict between state and national standards is common knowledge among teacher educators and was acknowledged organizationally by the creation of a joint committee of NCATE and NASDTEC (Diegmueller, 1992a). The purpose of this committee, as outlined in the BOE *News* (the NCATE publication for site visitors), was to "examine ways that the two organizations can coordinate efforts to eliminate duplication of effort when reviewing school of education programs and units" (Staff, 1991a, p. 1).

However, the only form of concrete cooperation between state licensure authorities and NCATE is the result of another development: the creation of state/NCATE partnerships. In partnership states—about 35 currently exist—NCATE and state review teams visit an institution jointly and typically curtail some of the overlapping aspects of the two forms of program review (Francis, 1993; Williams, 1994).

6. No single reference is adequate here. There is a long tradition of boosterism in national accreditation, and very little serious scholarship in this arena.

7. Several readers of this chapter have concluded that I was particularly interested in defending and justifying the positions promoted by AILACTE 10 years ago. While I do believe that AILACTE's position on the critical-mass issue was reasonable, I also recognize that a good case can be made for either the single payment or the sliding scale approach to dues. Moreover, I am also aware that AILACTE took positions on both of these issues that represented the narrow interests of AILACTE institutions, just as the parochial interests of larger institutions were consistent with the CAA recommendations in support of the critical-mass argument and the single-payment dues structure. Political interests appear to have been a driving motivation for more than one type of institution.

REFERENCES

Beggs, W. K. (1965). *The education of teachers*. New York: The Center for Applied Research in Education.

Carnegie Task Force on Teaching as a Profession. (1986). *A nation prepared: Teachers for the 21st century*. New York: Carnegie Corporation.

Christensen, D. (1980). Accreditation in teacher education: A brief overview. *Journal of Physical Education and Recreation, 51*(3), 42–44, 83.

Christensen, D. (1984–1985). NCATE: The continuing quest for excellence. *Action in Teacher Education, 4*(4), 17–22.

Committee on Accreditation Alternatives. (1983). *A proposed accreditation system (an alternative to the current NCATE system)*. Washington, DC: American Association of Colleges for Teacher Education. (ERIC Document Reproduction Service No. ED 231 801)

Consortium for Excellence in Teacher Education. (1987). *Teacher education and the liberal arts.* Author.

Cruickshank, D. R., McCullough, J. D., Reynolds, R. J., Troyer, M. B., & Cruz, J., Jr. (1991). *An analysis of standards and criteria for compliance since 1957. Fifth draft.* Unpublished manuscript. (ERIC Document Reproduction Service No. ED 339 686)

Cushman, M.L. (1977). *The governance of teacher education.* Berkeley, CA: McCutchan.

Diegmueller, K. (1991, October 9). NCATE to join Fla. agencies to review programs: Pact may lead to set of uniform standards. *Education Week,* pp. 1, 21.

Diegmueller, K. (1992a, February 26). Revamped NCATE posts highs, lows in tides of teacher-education reform. *Education Week,* pp. 1, 12–13, 15.

Diegmueller, K. (1992b, February 26). NCATE examiners in training hone the skill of skepticism. *Education Week,* pp. 12–13.

Francis, S. (1993, December). State/NCATE partnerships streamline accreditation process while promoting national program guidelines. *NCATE Reporter,* p. 8.

Gideonse, H. D. (1992). The redesign of NCATE 1980 to 1986. In H. D. Gideonse (Ed.), *Teacher education policy: Narratives, stories, and cases* (pp. 245–265). Albany: SUNY Press.

Gideonse, H. D. (1993). Appointments with ourselves: A faculty argument for NCATE. *Phi Delta Kappan, 75,* 174–180.

Gollnick, D. M., & Kunkel, R. C. (1986). The reform of national accreditation. *Phi Delta Kappan, 68,* 310–314.

Goodlad, J. I. (1990). *Teachers for our nation's schools.* San Francisco: Jossey-Bass.

Gubser, L. (1983, March 23). No one wants to "pull the plug" on teacher education: A conversation with Lyn Gubser. *Education Week,* pp. 7, 17.

Holmes Group. (1986). *Tomorrow's teachers.* East Lansing, MI: Author.

Ladd, E. T. (1963). The proper place of accreditation. *Journal of Secondary Education, 38,* 296–305.

Larson, R. W. (1979). Examining standards: An important task for those involved in accreditation. *Action in Teacher Education, 1*(3–4), 11–20.

Mayor, J. R. (1965). *Accreditation in teacher education: Its influence on higher education.* Washington, DC: National Commission on Accrediting.

National Council for Accreditation of Teacher Education. (1977). *Standards for the accreditation of teacher education.* Washington, DC: Author.

National Council for Accreditation of Teacher Education. (1982). *Standards for the accreditation of teacher education.* Washington, DC: Author.

National Council for Accreditation of Teacher Education. (1990). *Standards, procedures, and policies for the accreditation of professional education units.* Washington, DC: Author.

NCATE UPDATE. (1981, November 1). Washington DC: National Council for Accreditation of Teacher Education.

NCATE UPDATE. (1982, June 15). Washington DC: National Council for Accreditation of Teacher Education.

Nicklin, J. L. (1991, November 27). Teacher-education programs face pressure to provide multicultural training. *Chronicle of Higher Education,* pp. A1, A16–A17.

Palmer, J. R. (1983, April 13). "Plausible reasons" for not participating in an NCATE review [Letter to the editor]. *Education Week,* p. 20.

Parker, J. K. (1994). NCATE, PC, and the LCME: A response to James Sutton. *Phi Delta Kappan, 75*, 693–694, 705.

Peseau, B., & Orr, P. (1980). The outrageous underfunding of teacher education. *Phi Delta Kappan, 62*, 100–102.

Prestine, N. A. (1991). Political system theory as an explanatory paradigm for teacher education reform. *American Educational Research Journal, 28*(2), 237–274.

Project 30. (1991). *Project 30 year two report: Institutional accomplishments*. Newark, DE: University of Delaware, Project 30 Alliance.

Renaissance Group. (1989). *Teachers for the new world: A statement of principles*. Cedar Falls: University of Northern Iowa.

Roames, R. L. (1987). A history of the development of standards for accrediting teacher education. *Action in Teacher Education, 9*(3), 91–101.

Roames, R. L., & Dye, C. M. (1986, February). *National voluntary accreditation in U.S. teacher education: Development of the NCATE standards, 1954–85*. Paper presented at the annual meeting of the Wisconsin Educational Research Association, Green Bay, WI.

Roth, R. A., & Pipho, C. (1990). Teacher education standards. In W. R. Houston (Ed.), *Handbook of research on teacher education* (pp. 119–135). New York: Macmillan.

Rothman, R. (1987, November 4). Liberal-arts colleges wary of teacher-training shifts. *Education Week*, pp. 1, 22.

Scannell, D. P. (1983, April 13). Gubser's comments give "one-sided view" of important issues [Letter to the editor]. *Education Week*, p. 20.

Staff. (1991a, October). NCATE and NASDTEC joint committee. *BOE News*, p. 1.

Staff. (1991b, October). Weaknesses cited for unmet standards. *BOE News*, pp. 6–9.

Staff. (1992, March 25). Iowa colleges withdraw from accrediting process. *The Chronicle of Higher Education*, p. A4.

Staff. (1993a, June 9). National accrediting group approves 78% of program. *The Chronicle of Higher Education*, p. A14.

Staff. (1993b, December). 40 institutions accredited at UAB meeting. *NCATE Reporter*, p. 2.

Stinnett, T. M. (1968). *Professional problems of teachers* (3rd ed.). New York: Macmillan.

Stinnett, T. M. (1970). Accreditation of teacher education institutions and agencies. *Phi Delta Kappan, 52*(1), 25–31.

Toch, T. (1982, March 17). Accrediting body reverses policy on disclosure. *Education Week*, p. 6.

Tom, A. R. (1980a). NCATE standards and program quality: You can't get there from here. *Phi Delta Kappan, 62*, 113–117.

Tom, A. R. (1980b). Chopping NCATE standards down to size. *Journal of Teacher Education, 31*(6), 25–30.

Tom, A. R. (1981). An alternative set of NCATE standards. *Journal of Teacher Education, 32*(6), 48–52.

Viadero, D. (1990, March 7). Efforts to improve teacher training urged. *Education Week*, p. 12.

von Schlichten, E. W. (1958). The idea and practice of teacher certification in the United States. *Teachers College Record, 59*, 411–426.

Watts, D. (1983). Four views of NCATE's role and function. *Phi Delta Kappan, 64,* 646–649.

Watts, D. (1986). Four educators comment on the redesign of NCATE. *Phi Delta Kappan, 68,* 315–318.

Wheeler, C. (1980). *NCATE: Does it matter?* (Research Series No. 92). East Lansing: Michigan State University, Institute for Research on Teaching. (ERIC Document Reproduction Service No. ED 195 552)

Williams, B. (1994, June). Ask Boyce. *NCATE Reporter,* p. 8.

Wise, A. E. (1991). An invitation to our readers. *Quality Teaching, 1*(1), 1–4.

Wise, A. E., & Leibbrand, J. (1993). Accreditation and the creation of a profession of teaching. *Phi Delta Kappan, 75,* 133–136, 154–157.

CHAPTER 3

Reforming Teacher Education Through Legislation: A Case Study from Florida

Susan Melnick

During the 1980s, the United States experienced a degree of state-initiated education reform unprecedented in the nation's history. Although the 1983 publication of *A Nation at Risk* (National Commission on Excellence in Education [NCEE]) provided a national stimulus, the federal retreat from policy initiation and education spending in the Reagan administration provided the real impetus for state action. Prompted by individual governors, business interests, and the general public, state legislatures enacted legislation, some comprehensive and some incremental, which in turn affected state departments and boards of education, local schools, and colleges and universities responsible for the preparation of teachers.

THE CONTENT OF STATE REFORMS

The basis of much of the state reform activity derived from the national rhetoric of improving the country's competitive edge, economically and militarily, and striving for academic excellence and educational equity. As then Governor Lamar Alexander of Tennessee said in 1986, "Better schools mean better jobs. Unless the states face these questions, Americans will forfeit their high standard of living. To meet stiff competition from workers in the rest of the world, we must educate ourselves and our children as we never have before" (p. 202). Many states viewed the legislation as an opportunity to stimulate "laggard districts" that did not meet minimum requirements, to provide symbolic support for the importance of academic learning, to increase teacher salaries, to improve the quality of teacher evaluations, and to strengthen public support for schools (Fuhrman, Clune, & Elmore, 1988). Since most local districts exceeded compliance with the legislative mandates for minimum standards, members of the

30

education community, despite their secondary role in the policy formulation process, used the opportunity to garner financial and political support for their own initiatives and goals related to such areas as curriculum, testing practices, textbook selection, and teacher certification and evaluation. By the early part of the decade, all of the states had adopted or seriously considered increased curricular and testing standards for minimally competent student performance in elementary and secondary schools (Cooper, 1981). By 1986, 46 states had increased the requirements for assuring teacher quality (Gabrys, 1987; Melnick & Pullin, 1987).

Despite the relative ease with which many local school districts responded to the student minimum standards mandates, the intent and spirit of much of the new legislation addressed such central issues as who will be permitted to teach, and "what shall be taught and in what manner" (Fuhrman et al., 1988). This new thrust, in effect, altered the role of teacher preparation institutions in guaranteeing that their graduates were qualified to teach. While the states traditionally were delegated authority for teacher certification, the process has been largely pro forma, with the state education departments in actuality granting program approval to college and university teacher preparation programs and thereby granting provisional certification to their graduates (Drummond, 1973). The new mandates, however, effected major changes in the certification process and in curricular requirements in colleges and universities, shifting the balance of authority from the teacher preparation institution to the state. Florida, one of the earliest states to enact comprehensive legislative education reform, is a case in point.

According to information from the Bureau of Teacher Certification in Tallahassee, and in contrast to former program approval/certification provisions, requirements for a provisional five-year Professional Certificate in Florida instituted in the early 1980s included a passing score on a statewide writing test; course work requiring a specified amount of writing mandated by the state as a baccalaureate degree requirement; and the completion of an induction year Beginning Teacher Program requiring acceptable evaluation through the use of a state-mandated performance instrument. Applicants for certification were also required to satisfy eligibility for the two-year nonrenewable Temporary Certificate, meet other professional preparation and recency-of-credit requirements, and achieve passing scores on both the Professional Education Subtest of the Florida Teacher Competency Test and the subject area examination for each subject or field shown on the certificate.

This chapter focuses on the first three of these certification requirements— course work, the test, and performance assessment—associated with the relationship between subject-matter knowledge and pedagogical knowledge in learning to teach writing. Writing serves as the focus for two important reasons: (1) During the reform period under scrutiny, it was a school subject that had received much professional attention with respect to recommended changes for teaching writing in both elementary and secondary schools, and (2) Florida had singled out writing for emphasis in both K–12 and higher education reform. Three policies are considered here: the Gordon Rule, the College Level Academic Skills Test (CLAST), and the Florida Performance Measurement System (FPMS).[1] These policies, mandated as part of the comprehensive legislative reform package, were intended initially to influence the quality of preservice teacher education graduates and ultimately, by presumed extension, the quality of instruction in Florida public schools.

In considering the influence of these policies on prospective teachers, the chapter draws on portions of the Teacher Education and Learning to Teach (TELT) study of the National Center for Research on Teacher Education (NCRTE, 1988). The TELT study was concerned in part with what prospective teachers have the opportunity to learn about the teaching of writing in selected preservice teacher education programs. I was a member of the research team that studied the program at State University, a major university in Florida.

Interview data used in this chapter were collected from program faculty and from students at the beginning and end of the first year they were enrolled in the professional education component of a preservice program at State University. During the period of data collection, students completed elementary and secondary language arts methods courses and practicum experiences that provided opportunities to teach writing in elementary and secondary schools.

WRITING INSTRUCTION IN A NATIONAL CONTEXT

Since the early 1970s, there has been a plethora of criticism regarding student writing in both the public press and the professional literature. While there was some evidence of decline in writing ability in the results of the National Assessment of Educational Progress (NAEP, 1980), Scardamalia and Bereiter (1986) described the source of dissatisfaction as an issue of higher expectations rather than of deterioration of existing programs:

> Increasing numbers of low-income and minority students have been entering higher education and seeking entry into middle-class occupations where facility with written language is expected. At the same time, with the trend in occupations toward processing information rather than materials, more and more people find themselves needing to communicate through written language and depending on written communication from others. This situation has created a new emphasis on readability and on the informational adequacy of texts, rather than on technical correctness. (p. 778)

Originally tied to the 1970s criticism about the acquisition of basic skills in general, concern at the beginning of the 1980s centered on the nature of teaching and learning to write. The magnitude of the concern was captured in Florio-Ruane and Dunn's (1987) reactions to NAEP's Third National Writing Assessment (1980), which highlighted the relative achievement of American students:

> [Our] efforts at effective writing instruction seem to yield not technically competent and motivated young people ready to use literacy to enrich their lives but variation in technical skills highly correlated with social class and life chances. Second, we are dismayed at the attitudes of students toward writing after they have been taught in our schools. Apparently even the more successful young writers seem to view the process as difficult, dull, and devoid of meaning. Finally, this profile of school writing seems strikingly similar to our own school experiences. We are left wondering whether this is because, when learning to teach, we were offered so little in the way of systematic, theory-based alternatives to the kinds of writing tasks we experienced as children. (p. 53)

Florio-Ruane and Dunn (1987) go on to explain the basis for the NAEP criticism:

> Teachers tend to plan and teach with neither the limitations nor the guidance of district policy, published materials, or professional training in theories of the writing process. . . . Often teachers respond to their lack of training and support by choosing simply to teach writing as they were taught. . . . Writing is vulnerable in the school learning environment. It is without the kind of curricular support and limitations present in other school subjects. (pp. 53–54)

Many of the same criticisms could be levied against the teaching and learning of writing at the baccalaureate level during this period. Despite the traditional freshman composition course and some upper-level requirements, it was possible for undergraduates to complete their degrees with very little meaningful instruction or experience in writing (American Association of Colleges [AAC], 1985; Boyer, 1987).

In the late 1970s, language arts educators were aware that there was "ample evidence that most teachers from elementary school through university were ill prepared to teach writing, that not much writing was done in schools, and that much of the required writing gave little motivation or scope for the exercise of higher level composing abilities" (Scardamalia & Bereiter, 1986, p. 779). According to Applebee, "Very little direct instruction goes on in the teaching of writing. What little there is is largely confined to teaching conventions—punctuation rules, format conventions, and even then teachers appear to rely mainly on practice and correction" (Applebee cited in Scardamalia & Bereiter, 1986, p. 794).

Lensmire (1994) sketched a dismal profile of writing instruction in the elementary grades at the beginning of the 1980s:

> Typically, children compose very little in schools. The writing that is done is tightly controlled by the teacher who initiates writing tasks; determines audience, purpose, and format for the writing; and acts as the sole audience and evaluator. There is little opportunity for revision, and the purpose of such school writing is often to display academic mastery in evaluative contexts. In such situations, students' technical competence to write, and their motivation to use writing in ways that enrich and transform their lives, suffer. (p. 3)

Despite common practice, however, there was a growing movement to address these shortcomings in the late 1970s and early 1980s. Through the work of Lucy Calkins (1986), Peter Elbow (1981), Donald Graves (1983), George Hillocks (1986), Donald Murray (1968), the Bay Area Writing Project (Camp, 1983), and the National Writing Project (Tiedt, 1989), among other efforts, attention was focused on the writing processes of emerging writers, the ways in which classrooms were organized for elementary and secondary school students, and effective practices for teaching writing as a process (Gomez, 1989). In contrast to traditional writing instruction,

> process writing approaches conceive of writing as a complex cognitive and communicative act, framed by a purpose, and made up of various recursive phases or stages, such as drafting, revision, editing, and publishing . . . Within such approaches, teachers focus on helping children work through the writing process. (Lensmire, 1994, p. 3)

While the effects were not yet widespread, there was the beginning of a national movement to improve how writing was taught in K–12 schools.

THE STATE UNIVERSITY CONTEXT

From the beginning of the 1980s, language arts education faculty at State University actively worked with prospective teachers to help them learn to teach process writing. Professor Smith,[2] a faculty member who was actively involved with local teachers in the activities of the Florida Writing Project, strongly endorsed the process-centered approach:

> [The] Writing Project . . . made me a believer in the whole idea that, first of all, writing can be taught, not just the presentation of giving students an opportunity to write and say, "Do it, kids." Because I did a lot of that in those first nine years of teaching. You know, "Here's the

writing assignment. It's due tomorrow, it's due next week, it's due whenever. Don't bother me with it. Go home, and do it at home, and bring it in." . . . My belief about the teaching of writing [is] that writing is a process, that the process is teachable, that we need to be giving students positive opportunities to experience that process.

Professor Jones was also committed to the process approach and worked with her students to create a vision of a classroom and of teaching that exemplified the approach (McDiarmid, 1989). In a paper she wrote for presentation at the 1987 annual meeting of the National Council of Teachers of English,[3] she talked about her views on teaching writing:

I strongly believe that we teach writing as a way of helping kids learn about themselves. . . . Writing is for learning. It is for discovering ideas and inventing them. It is a way of assimilating ideas and making them your own. The way we learn through writing is by rewriting—again and again.

Both Professors Smith and Jones, like their colleagues, had long-standing commitments to helping teacher candidates learn a form of writing instruction that helped children and adolescents find voice and meaning in school writing. It is within this context that we turn to the three Florida policies related to writing, which conflicted with teacher educator practices that were based on professional judgments about teaching and learning to teach.

THE GORDON RULE

In 1981, in an early effort to address concerns about writing (and mathematics) in the college curriculum, Florida State Senator Jack D. Gordon (1981), Democrat of Miami, sponsored Rule 6 A-10.30 "Other Assessment Procedures for College Level Communication and Computation Skills." Adopted in 1982 and popularly known throughout the state of Florida as the "Gordon Rule," the rule stated:

Twelve semester hours of English, in which courses the student prepares the equivalent of one paper a week, and six semester hours of mathematics shall be successfully completed by a student attending a public community college or university prior to the receipt of an Associate of Arts degree from the attended community college or university or a baccalaureate degree from the attended university. (p. 4)

The legislative amendment was originally offered for two purposes: (1) as an alternative to a test to measure minimum competency in writing and (2) as an inducement to colleges and universities to provide a "broad-based education" for potential "leaders who have intellectual curiosity and a love of learning for learning's sake" (Gordon, cited in Littler, 1987, pp. 31–32). According to Littler (1987), Gordon "stressed the philosophical connection of skill in writing and the concept of a liberally educated person" (p. 27) and "offered the rule . . . on the theory that institutional measurement of writing competencies as accomplished by English faculty's grading their students' papers is as valid a measure as is the [test of writing competence]" (p. 19). In addition, while Gordon strongly supported the regularity of writing in English coursework, his original petition did not specify its most controversial feature, the 24,000-word requirement. The "paper a week" provision came to be interpreted as 6,000 words per course, or a two-page paper of approximately 400 words each week of a 15-week semester. While the chancellor of the State University system argued against the rule's challenge to faculty prerogative in setting curriculum and expressed fears about increased costs for implementation (Littler, 1987), the Gordon Rule became a fact of life on Florida college and university campuses in 1982.

During the TELT interviews with prospective teachers at State University, there was a great deal of comment about the literature and humanities content of college writing courses rather than about the writing process or activities. The rule itself was infrequently referred to and then in oblique rather than explicit terms. Yet there is a disturbing note in some of these references. As Abigail, one prospective secondary teacher, said:

> I learned to write for the professor. I learned, because I probably wouldn't have survived. I knew just what he wanted, and if it wasn't a lot, I didn't give him a lot. Now I gave him what he needed, . . . and if he wanted his opinion regurgitated, I [did]. . . . The ones that caught me off guard were the ones that really wanted my opinion. I had a lot of those Gordon Rule classes. . . . You had to write like, 6,000 words I think, during a course, so there were a lot of those little papers. . . . I've learned to make my writing less personal and more objective . . . I don't have to put myself in there. I don't have to have personal feelings, you know. I keep myself out of the paper. I can, I've learned how to do that.

The concern about what prospective secondary teachers experienced with writing in their college courses was further elucidated by Becky's comment:

> I can't stand writing in college. Because you have to write the way your professor wants you to write. . . . I try to write my own style and I'd always done well in school. I always had As on my papers and right away, I had a C on my paper. . . . So right away I learned that you have

to listen to how your professors feel about the subjects and spit back kind of their style. Like if . . . you have a professor that really loves creative writing. He likes it when you try different things. Then if you like that, it's okay. . . . But if you go and . . . a professor doesn't want any grammar mistakes, no spelling mistakes, he wants just pure information and facts, and he wants it short and sweet, and he doesn't want any of this flowery language, then you have to write that way in order to receive a grade that you want. If you don't want a C or D, you have to try to write the way they want you to.

While faculty memories of prized freshman "creative writing" and students' assessments of their writing "style" can make one less critical than Becky, four concerns about the potential influence of the Gordon Rule as implemented seem warranted.

First, the salience of the quantity dimension is problematic in its own right. Despite the commonsense appeal of the notion that more writing should result in greater fluency, there is no research evidence to support a direct correlation between the amount of writing required of students and improvement in their mastery of the skill (Littler, 1987).

Second, the apparent fact that some prospective teachers of writing in K–12 schools acquired negative attitudes as a result of their college writing courses is disturbing. As Florio-Ruane and Dunn (1987) and Lortie (1975) have pointed out, teachers often teach the way they were taught. Beliefs like Abigail's and Becky's were common among their peers and demanded that faculty pay careful attention to the nature and quality of writing instruction rather than to mere compliance with quantity dimensions (see Gomez, 1988).

Third, it is perhaps notable that none of the students interviewed at State University indicated that they would do things differently in their own teaching of writing from their own experiences in college writing courses. While the evidence suggests that the implementation of the Gordon Rule did not appear to have prompted these teacher candidates to think about their own teaching of writing, questions regarding the extent to which the liberal arts component of the baccalaureate degree contributes to the education of a prospective teacher are clearly warranted. Despite Gordon's initial desires for the influence of his amendment, there was no evidence to suggest that any of the prospective teachers made the connection between learning to write themselves and learning to teach writing as a result of the Gordon Rule.

Fourth, given the prospective teachers' perceptions of emphasis on quantity and compliance with instructors' expectations, there was a clear discrepancy between the way these prospective teachers experienced writing in their liberal arts courses and the language arts faculty's expectations for the way their students would be expected to teach writing to children and adolescents.

THE COLLEGE LEVEL ACADEMIC SKILLS TEST

A passing score on the College Level Academic Skills Test is one of the requirements for an Associate of Arts degree from a Florida community college, admission to the upper division of any state university, the award of some types of
financial aid, and a five-year Professional Certificate for teaching in the state.
Popularly known as CLAST, the test was designed in response to a 1979 legislative mandate to provide a program to test the "Essential Academic Skills" at the
college level. Implemented in 1982, the test is a four-part, 5-hour timed test of
reading, writing, grammar, and computation skills. The test is administered three
times a year at all community colleges and state universities, and some private
colleges. Students may take the test whenever they like and as many times as
they like, either to earn a passing score or to increase a previous score (only one
score is recorded on the student's permanent record).

Designed by a committee of university and community college faculty, CLAST
was developed with the expressed intent of "help[ing] students reach a minimal level of proficiency in communication skills . . . and [having] the potential
for improving student performance in basic reading and writing skills, thereby
preserving the academic integrity of the state system" (Littler, 1987, pp. 17–18).
It was also anticipated that CLAST, in conjunction with the Gordon Rule, would
have "a long-range impact on the [writing] curriculum improving both instruction and student performance" (Littler, 1987, p. 18). Given their expected influence on the development of writing proficiency, two sections of CLAST war-
rant our examination—the grammar test and the essay test. While the actual
items were unavailable due to test security provisions, the "official" preparation guide provides facsimiles.[4]

The Grammar Test

According to Goldfarb and Johnson (1988), authors of the "official" CLAST preparation guide,

> The CLAST Objective Writing Subtest, as it is officially named, measures your abil-
> ity to recognize correct applications of the rules and conventions of standard
> written American English. . . . The CLAST tests your knowledge of a language that
> both *is standard* and *is a standard*. It is standard because it follows the same rules
> of sentence structure, punctuation, and spelling everywhere in the United States.
> It is also the standard by which all writing is judged in every American school and
> business. Term papers and job applications written in standard American English
> communicate clearly because their words and sentences convey the same mean-
> ing to every educated reader. They communicate impressively as well: writers who
> are skillful with standard American English are most likely to earn the "A" and

win the job. The language tested on the CLAST is the measure by which your academic and professional writing will be judged for the rest of your life. (p. 13, emphasis in the original)

The 37-item pretest in the guide tests the following "skill/error categories": wordiness, word choice, modification, subordination, parallelism, comma splice, fragment, fused (run-on) sentence, subject-verb agreement, adjective/adverb, case, verb form, spelling, noun-pronoun agreement, punctuation, and capitalization (Goldfarb & Johnson, 1988, p. 25). Under actual testing conditions, the CLAST grammar subtest is combined with the reading subtest for a 70-minute period. Thirty-five items are scored for the grammar test, and 36 for the reading test. Passing scores are 23 (65%) and 19 (53%), respectively.

In the preparation guide, students are told:

> The better you understand sentence structure, the better you will do on the CLAST grammar test. . . . Learning how sentences work is not the same as learning (or relearning) a long list of grammatical terms. . . . What matters on this and other tests of your verbal skills is not your ability to name language but *to know how it works*. (p. 52, emphasis added)

As a measure of "knowing how language works," students are tested, largely through the presentation of passages, on the "skill/error categories." The test items in Figure 3.1 are illustrative.

What clearly emerges from the sample grammar test and instructions in the preparation guide is a rule-bound conception of "knowing how language works." Given that the preparation guide is based on state testing specifications, it is fair to assume that such mastery depicted on CLAST is what is expected not only of Florida college students in general but also of anyone eligible for a Professional Certificate. But one might ask: mastery of what, to what ends? Some would argue that the test is not a grammar test at all but a test of usage of grammatical principles at best, and of proofreading ability at worst. While common sense tells us that we should attend to the conventions of standard written English, the research evidence suggests that grammar study in isolation has little or no effect on the improvement of writing. Hillocks (1986) notes further that

> The same is true for emphasis on mechanics and correctness in writing. . . . Taught in certain ways, grammar and mechanics instruction has a deleterious effect on student writing. . . . If the study of grammar and mechanics is brought to bear on the composing process at all, it is likely to influence only the most concrete levels, the planning and editing of specific sentences. *But such study would have no effect on the higher-level processes of deciding on intentions and generating and organizing ideas.* (pp. 226–248; emphasis added)

FIGURE 3.1. A sample CLAST test.

I.   DIRECTIONS: Complete each sentence by choosing the most effective word or phrase which conforms to standard written English.

Home at last, Sam was happy to _____ his house.
A.   enter into
B.   make an entry into
C.   enter
D.   proceed ahead into

II.   DIRECTIONS: Choose the sentence that expresses the thought most clearly and effectively and that has no errors in structure.

A.   Speaking from personal experience, the text for the computer course was adequate.
B.   Speaking from personal experience, I found the text for the computer course adequate.
C.   The text for the computer course, speaking from personal experience, was adequate.

III. DIRECTIONS: Each item below may contain an error in sentence construction: a fragment, a comma splice, or a fused (run-on) sentence. Mark the letter which precedes the group of words containing the error. Mark E if there is no error.

(A) All living things adapt to dangers in the environment, each in its own way. (B) A fly moves out of the way of a flyswatter, and an octopus changes color when it feels threatened. (C) While staying alive during bad times, one-celled plants form a hard coat. (D) Living things don't live forever, however, each has a limited life span. (E) No error.

IV.   DIRECTIONS: Mark "A" if the first alternative within the parentheses is correct; mark "B" if the second alternative is correct.

Everybody in the English classes (take, takes) the same final examination.
                                  A   B
Spot was the (smallest, smaller) puppy in a large litter.
              A   B

During the TELT interviews at State University, both language arts faculty and prospective teachers had a view of grammar consistent with Hillocks's (1986) summary of the research. In addition to the nearly universal proclamation of the teacher candidates attesting to their dislike for grammar, they had acquired a more holistic view of its place in the language arts. As one prospective secondary teacher, Becky, said:

I want to teach grammar through writing, through their writing assignments, and work on it that way. Look at what their main problems are.

> Keep a . . . folder for each student, and have them, their peers, . . . read each other's papers and help each other. Just not me standing up there and taking the red pen.

What Becky believed was clearly what Professor Smith intended that his students learn:

> What I have to do in a methods class is I have to train them in terms of teaching English. That is, downplay grammar. . . . They know that I don't want to see them teaching grammar, but recognize that as a student teacher, they may have to deal with direct teaching of grammar in parts of speech and sentence parsing and diagramming and that kind of thing that the research shows doesn't do any good. . . . I have to show them ways to teach reading skills, composing process, speaking, listening, viewing, critical thinking skills. . . . What I try to do is . . . when I'm giving them ideas, I'm trying to get them to think in terms of integrated stuff.

Essentially, passage of the CLAST Objective Writing Subtest serves only to assure the state that students can pass a grammar usage test. Perhaps this should be sufficient consumer protection, but what is troubling here is, once again, the discrepancy between what is considered relevant knowledge for CLAST and for a teaching certificate and how students experienced writing as they were expected to teach it. The following section on the Essay Subtest provides further evidence of the discrepancy.

The CLAST Essay Subtest

Endorsed by the Bureau of Teacher Certification as the sole measure of this provision after July 1, 1988, the CLAST Essay Subtest tests the student's ability to plan, write, and proofread "a logical, specific, and correct composition in standard written English" (Goldfarb & Johnson, 1988, p. 201) within a 50-minute time period. Although the test instructions do not specify length, the preparation guide points out that CLAST "define[s] the standards by which essays are graded. In order to meet those standards successfully, [the] essay should consist of five paragraphs of from three to five sentences each" (Goldfarb & Johnson, 1988, p. 201). Students are expected to write on one of two topics given, for example, "Useful skills you have learned in college," or "Economic changes that have affected the American family." The essays are graded by two readers, usually college instructors, on a scale of 1 (low) to 4 (high); a composite score of 4 is the minimum passing score. The readers' evaluations are based on how well the essay demonstrates skill with nine elements:

1. A definite purpose
2. A clear thesis
3. An organizational plan
4. Well-developed supporting paragraphs
5. Specific, relevant details
6. A variety of effective sentence patterns
7. Logical transitions
8. Effective word choice
9. Correct standard English usage

Legible handwriting in ink is also required.

> The preparation guide notes further that the test is an exercise in time manage-
> ment as much as it is a test of your language skills. It is not a test of your literary
> originality or creativity. If you think of the essay as art, you will either frighten
> yourself or waste time waiting for inspiration. This sort of essay is not created; it
> is constructed. (Goldfarb & Johnson, 1988, p. 204)

The guide goes on to suggest the following format for constructing an appropriate essay:

1. First Stage: Writing the Opening Paragraph—Time: 10 minutes
   Step 1: Read the Two Topics Presented on the Test (30 seconds)
   Step 2: Choose the Topic You Know the Most About (1 minute)
   Step 3: Write Your Thesis Statement (30 seconds)
   Step 4: Plan Your Essay (4 minutes)
   Step 5: Organize Your Plan (2 minutes)
   Step 6: Complete Your Opening Paragraph (2 minutes)
2. Second Stage: Writing the Body Paragraphs—Time: 24 minutes
   Step 1: Write Topic Sentence 1 (2 minutes)
   Step 2: Complete Body Paragraph 1 (6 minutes)
   Step 3: Begin Body Paragraph 2 (2 minutes)
   Step 4: Complete Body Paragraph 2 (6 minutes)
   Step 5: Write a Topic Sentence for Body Paragraph 3 (2 minutes)
   Step 6: Complete Body Paragraph 3 (6 minutes)
3. Third Stage: Writing the Concluding Paragraph—Time: 6 minutes
   Step 1: Refresh Your Memory (1 minute)
   Step 2: Write Your Conclusion (5 minutes)
4. Fourth Stage: Proofreading and Titling—Time: 10 minutes
   Step 1: Proofread for Errors (5 minutes)
   Step 2: Write a Title for Your Essay (1 minute)
   Step 3: Proofread for Improvements (4 minutes)
(Goldfarb & Johnson, 1988, pp. 204–213)

Although the guide's caveats regarding time, creativity, and construction are themselves curious, what clearly emerges from the preparation guide's recommendations for "essay construction" is a linear, rule-bound conception of writing with an emphasis on the final product rather than on knowledge of and facility with the composing process. As Scardamalia and Bereiter (1986) have pointed out,

> Although there is obviously a structure to the composing process, it does not correspond to the traditional textbook picture of collecting material, organizing it, writing it out, and then revising it. Those procedures all occur, but not in such a linear manner. (p. 781)

Despite the obvious concerns about what experienced writers actually *do*, what is perhaps most troubling about the emphasis of the CLAST Essay Subtest is the fact that it contravenes what research suggests about *teaching* writing. For example, Flower and Hayes (1981) found that "product-based" plans such as those required for the essay test were "peculiarly ineffective," because they "appeared to interfere with the normal generating process that occurs during writing" (cited in Hillocks, 1986, p. 228). As Hillocks (1986) explains it further,

> composing is recursive, with writers moving back to what has been written and forward to what has not. Further, we can be fairly certain that the subprocesses of composing interrupt each other. The writer moves from high-level plans to the transcription of words and back to higher-level planning, rereading what has been written, reconstructing plans already made, making new plans, generating new data, or performing editing of some kind. . . . Together, these recursive and bobbing actions present a far different notion of composing than [the traditional one] which . . . assumes that all planning precedes all transcribing and that all editing follows. (p. 60)

Given the expectations for a successful essay, the CLAST Essay Subtest clearly reflects the outcomes of what Hillocks (1986) calls,

> the most common and widespread yet least effective instructional mode . . . [where] the instructor dominates all activity, with students acting as the passive recipients of rules, advice, and examples of good writing . . . with its often arbitrary assignments given with no preparation; with its structure to be learned from rigid models, such as the "five-paragraph theme"; and with its emphasis on the "correctness" of products. (pp. 246–248)

As Myers (1991) reminds us,

> Writing . . . is no longer simply a written product with a clear distinction between right and wrong conventions. It is now also a process, from prewriting to writing

and revising, and it is also a social context in which a set of social relationships are established between reader and writer. . . . In this new understanding of writing, all errors are no longer equal. . . . In this new view . . . the teacher's task is not a simple matter of circling the errors on the error list. . . . Beginning teachers must learn how to transfer the subject they knew as university students into experiences which are valuable for children and adolescents. (p. 399)

While purported ineffectiveness should be sufficient grounds for concern, what is even more pertinent here is the discrepancy between what prospective teachers are expected to demonstrate as writing proficiency on CLAST as a requirement for teacher certification and the predominant view espoused in their teacher preparation programs. Carol, a prospective secondary teacher, said:

> [My instructors are encouraging me to become] a process oriented teacher . . . someone who shows, well, works with his or her students on the whole, looks at writing as a process with the students and says, "okay, you can't just sit down and just write a perfect paper the first shot." That teacher feels that it's important to the students to know this and that there are ways to get started, and there are ways to organize ideas first for writing activities, brainstorming, just rewriting for a little bit, and using what's called a center of gravity statement in writing. . . . You need to let students know that they can always come back to their writing and that that piece can always be improved, and that you're never really finished until you just have lost interest or you think it's going nowhere. . . . And I like the idea [that] they're encouraged to continue writing, whereas if you just say, "Okay, write a research paper, do a little bit of preparation about bibliography . . ." [and] then stamp the grade on the product, . . . many of the kids think that . . . writing their final draft is just the typed up version of their rough draft without any significant revision, and I think that's a misunderstanding. If I can get them to really look at the thought in their paper and see what details might be added or whatever. . . . You might say, "Okay, yeah, that's true, the comma isn't in the right place, but let's talk about the ideas here." And [in class discussions] we think about . . . how this person said this, what might this person have included to make his or her picture real clear, more vivid.

Professor Brown, one of the elementary language arts faculty at State University, clearly intended that her students acquire the understanding that Carol had:

> My course is really a process course more than anything else. I want them to go through the process of teaching and learn to ask questions

about it and be perceptive about teaching. . . . When they leave my
course, I hope they will have a bunch of ideas, . . . but I want them to
have a sound reason why they're doing it, a sound theoretical basis. . . .
The course is a language arts methods course which teaches teachers,
number one, to love and appreciate writing, and number two, to be able
to help kids love to write. That's my goal. . . . So what I try to do is to
help people make kids love to write, because kids who love to write will
write, and kids who do write will become confident, proficient writers.
. . . In the best of all possible worlds, a student would come away from
my class feeling really good about themselves as a writer, . . . feeling really
good about their abilities to get children excited about writing, feeling
really good about their abilities to teach writing in response to what kids
do in a classroom, feeling really good about organizing a classroom and
providing an environment in that classroom that is conducive to promoting literacy, reading, and writing. . . . In order to be responsive to children,
we have to be able to really listen to them, and see where their language is.
. . . Language arts ought not to be a separate subject. It ought to be
integrally interwoven into whatever you're teaching, and that's how you
do it. Just getting kids to write is not a reason to write.

While these views are diametrically opposed to the product-oriented expectations of the CLAST Essay Subtest, it may be that prospective teachers in fact learned
to teach writing in spite of, rather than because of, state mandates. As Diane
said, in talking about goals for her future students:

It's very important for my twelfth grade students to become responsible,
literate citizens when they graduate. And my entire purpose is to get
them to become that. And I will achieve my goals through making them
think, giving them skills which will force them to use their minds. And I
will allow them to write, both practically as well as a five-paragraph
essay they have to do to pass the SAT. I will make them read for pleasure
and for purpose. And I will give them their basic grammar skills that
they'll need to fill out and edit things they might see later. But the most
important [goal] is to make them become responsible, literate adults.

Despite State University language arts faculty members' hopes for the realization of such goals, however, there was also the possibility that what these students had learned would be challenged once they were in their first jobs in secondary schools. As Ellie noted:

Well, definitely in Florida, and in this county with the county curriculum as it is, you have to be a particular kind of teacher, you've got to be

realistic. If you want a job in the public school system, you're going to have to perform [*sic*] to a lot of things.

Professor Jones was also concerned:

> With my students, as with many of the teachers whose classes they observed or shared, the belief in grammar and usage drills dies hard. Or rather they believe they have to teach grammar and usage, especially in basic skills classes, because if they don't, the kids won't pass the state-mandated [competency] tests. They accept what the research of fifty years has shown: teaching grammar and drilling on standard usage will not improve students' writing. . . . Only they don't believe they can get away with not teaching grammar. . . . Grammar lessons are safer . . . I'm not sure my students really believe in the process approach, though they give it lip service. They have had too little experience with it either in high school or college.

While concerns about the impact of teacher education once students are in the field have been documented for a number of years, the discrepancy between what CLAST and State University faculty expect of their graduates who will teach writing is clear. The third policy, the performance assessment, raises similar concerns about discrepancies between state policies and expert judgments about good practice in teaching and learning to teach.

THE FLORIDA PERFORMANCE MEASUREMENT SYSTEM (FPMS)

One major occasion for "performing" in Florida schools occurs during the induction year, when all beginning teachers are evaluated with the Summative Observation Instrument (SOI) on the frequency of appropriate teacher behaviors derived from the *Domains: Knowledge Base of the Florida Performance Measurement System* (Florida Coalition, 1983). Developed by a group of educators under the leadership of B. Othanel Smith and based primarily on process-product research, FPMS was widely viewed as an effort to "translate research on teaching into a practical form for use in training, evaluating, and rewarding teachers" (Macmillan & Pendlebury, 1985, p. 67). According to Macmillan and Pendlebury (1985), FPMS was designed to use relevant research to address the implications of three premises:

(1)   American teachers are not as good as they ought to be;
(2)   Incoming teachers can be trained well only if their attention is focused on what constitutes good teaching; and

(3) If you want to find out what effective or good teaching is, you look at what
     teachers do and correlate their actions with the resulting student achieve-
     ments. If you do enough correlations of such actions with results, you
     should come up with a list of things you could recommend that beginning
     teachers do, or things you could suggest, with good reason, that they not
     do. (pp. 68–69)

In an effort to improve teaching and teacher education, Smith (1985) believed
that "it is the task of research to replace faulty remedies with effective treat-
ments" (p. 685).

FPMS focuses on six areas, or domains, considered important to teaching:
Instructional Planning, Management of Student Conduct, Organizing and Delivery of Instruction, Presentation of Subject Matter, Communication: Verbal
and Nonverbal, and Evaluation of Student Progress. Given our interest in what
prospective teachers were learning about teaching writing, the FPMS treatment
of *Domain 4: Presentation of Subject Matter*, merits our examination.

According to the FPMS authors, teachers must "deal with . . . definitions (concepts), rules as in grammar and mathematics, laws as in natural science, law-
like principles as in social studies, and value statements. These make up the basic
elements of subject matter" (Florida Coalition, 1983, p. 123). The presentation
of subject matter involves the "manipulation of the content of instruction to
induce learning" and includes four "named concepts":

4.1 Presentation of Interpretative (Conceptual) Knowledge
4.2 Presentation of Explanatory (Law or Law-Like) Knowledge
4.3 Presentation of Academic Rule Knowledge
4.4 Presentation of Value Knowledge (p. 122)

The discussion of ways of presenting each of these "basic elements of subject
matter" includes a definition, indicators, and "positive" and "negative" examples,
and is followed by an overarching Principle and Supporting Evidence from the
research literature. Portions of *4.1 Concept: Presentation of Interpretative (Conceptual Knowledge)* are illustrative:

Definition: Presentation of interpretative (conceptual) knowledge = teacher performance involved in analyzing and presenting information to facilitate the acquisition of concepts.
Indicators
4.1.1   Gives Definition Only
     Definition: Gives definition only = teacher utterances that give the verbal
meaning of pivotal terms when beginning a new topic or some new aspect of the
current topic, no analysis or examples being given.
     Example: (Pos.) MS. JACO: A dendron is a nerve fiber that carries the nerve
impulse to the neurons.

Example: (Neg.) TEACHER: Today we are going to study conjunctions. We use a lot of them in speaking and writing. Sometimes we use too many. *And* is one we use too much. Do you know anyone who strings together a lot of unrelated ideas, or even too many related ideas, with *and*? (No definition). . . .
Principle
If concepts are taught by providing definitions, examples and non-examples, and by identifying criterial attributes, then students are more likely to acquire complex concepts than if taught other ways. (pp. 124–126)

While giving a definition alone, without examples, may not be regarded by many as "best practice," presumably the error in the negative example suggests that if the teacher had provided the students with the definition of a conjunction, they would have been "more likely" to have acquired an understanding of the use of the conjunctions in writing. Portions of *4.3 Concept: Presentation of Academic Rules* lend support to this presumption:

Definition: Presentation of academic rules = teacher behavior that facilitates the acquisition of rules and the ability to apply them.
Indicators
4.3.1   Describes the Situation
    Definition: Describes the situation = teacher behavior that analyzes the kind of circumstances to which a rule is applicable
    Example (Pos.): TEACHER: When two or more sentences are related as, for example, "It's a good car and you will like it," a semicolon can be used in place of "and." Example: It's a good car; you will like it.
    Example (Neg.): TEACHER: When we do most computations with whole numbers, we begin at the right. With long division, we begin at the left. (No analysis)
4.3.2   Provides for Application (Practice)
    Definition: Provides for application = teacher gives a number of situations to help students learn to apply the rule.
    Example (Pos.): In case of the rule in 4.3.1, the teacher provides a number of sentences, some to which the rule is applicable and some where it is not, to provide the students with experience in applying the rule.
Principle
If the teacher directs students in using academic rules by describing rule circumstances and by providing rule practice, then students are more likely to comprehend rule situations and follow appropriate rules. (p. 134)

What clearly emerges from the foregoing is a rule-bound generic conception of teaching, one that runs counter to notions about teaching for understanding generally and to the full spectrum of a process approach to the teaching of writing specifically. And an examination of the Summative Observation Instrument suggests that rule-guided teacher behavior is precisely what the observer looks for in the classroom "performance" of the beginning teacher (see Figure 3.2).

FIGURE 3.2. The Summative Observation Instrument.

SUMMATIVE OBSERVATION INSTRUMENT

Intern: _____
Observer: _____   Date: _____

Domain	EFFECTIVE INDICATORS	Freq.	Freq.	INEFFECTIVE INDICATORS
Instructional Organization and Development 3.0	1. Begins instruction promptly			Delays
	2. Handles materials in an orderly manner			Does not organize or handle materials systematically
	3. Orients students to classwork/maintains academic focus			Allows talk/activity unrelated to subject
	4. Conducts beginning/ending review			
	5. Questions: academic comprehension lesson development; asks single factual (Dom. 5) requires analysis/reasons			Poses multiple questions asked as one, multiple response / Poses non-academic questions/non-academic procedural questions
	6. Recognizes response/amplifies/gives feedback			Ignores student or response/expresses
	7. Gives specific academic praise			Uses general, non-specific praise
	8. Provides for practice			Extends discourse, changes topic w/o practice
	9. Gives directions/assigns/checks comprehension of homework, seatwork assign./gives feedback			Gives inadequate directions/no homework/no feedback
Presentation of Subject Matter 4.0	10. Circulates and assists students			Remains at desk/circulates inadequately
	11. Treats concept-definition/attributes/examples/ non-examples			Gives definition or examples only
	12. Discusses cause-effect/uses linking words-applies law or principle			Discusses either cause or effect only/uses no linking words(s)
	13. States and applies academic rule			Does not state nor does not apply academic rule
	14. Develops criteria and evidence for value judgement			States value judgment with no criteria evidence
Communication: Verbal and Non-Verbal 5.0	15. Emphasizes important points			
	16. Expresses enthusiasm verbally/challenges students			
	17.			Uses vague/scrambled discourse
	18.			Uses loud-grating, high pitched, monotone, inaudible talk
	19. Uses body behavior that shows interest-smiles, gestures			Frowns, deadpan or lethargic
Student Mgmt. of Conduct 2.0	20. Stops misconduct			Delays desist/doesn't stop misconduct/desists punitively
	21. Maintains instructional momentum			Loses momentum--fragments non-academic directions, overdwells

Students' Views of the Pedagogic Value of FPMS

During the TELT interviews with prospective teachers at State University, there was extensive commentary about what they had learned about FPMS and their perceptions of its usefulness and value to teachers. All the students understood that it was a state-mandated evaluation system for beginning teachers and had been introduced to the domains and SOI in course work, but what they knew about the system was a function of where they were in their programs. Those who had not yet been observed with the instrument during field experiences seemed to have a vague and generalized understanding. Most students said things like "It's a way they observe teachers. . . . It's telling them what they're doing well and what they need to work on" (Fran, prospective elementary teacher), or "That's how they grade you, observe you. That's how they determine whether you're getting across what they think you should be" (Gina, prospective elementary teacher), or "There are a lot of categories that you've got to cover, and that you've got to get more on the left side than the right side" (Helen, prospective elementary teacher). Julia's comments were a bit more explicit, and her views help to explain why the comments of some students were less so:

> The FPMS is the teaching standard we've been taught, which is the Florida Performance Measurement System, and in fact, if we stay in Florida, there are, [in] first year teaching we'll be observed and be expected to use these practices in the classroom. And there's a list of them. And, um, I couldn't go through them for you, but there are different teacher behaviors and ways of getting student behaviors, everything from starting class promptly, on time, to waiting after a question, and things like that. So specific teacher behaviors. . . . The FPMS has certainly been emphasized, [but] that was before student teaching. I guess at that time it all seemed a little weird to us, not being in a classroom, and it seemed a little rigid and some obvious, but to realize that those are the things that we'll be evaluated on, it's good information to know, and then they're also important and necessary behaviors.

For those who hadn't yet been observed themselves but had practiced with the instrument, there was evidence of both uncertainty and anxiety. Karen's thoughts were typical:

> It puts a lot of fear into you. . . . It's something that you know is there, and you're going to have to do that and go through all those evaluations. But then, on the other hand, it is actually kind of good, too. Well, the fact that you have it and you're being observed, and it will tell you, maybe different areas that you might need to work on and stuff, whereas

I suppose you're not supposed to really look at it as judging you particularly. It's supposed to be helping you and telling you what you need to improve, . . . what's already good. And you're supposedly not supposed to fail it. All you have to do is get more tallies on the left side than the right side. Basically [this semester] we got a list of the 30, I think it's 30, 32 . . . stuff you have to do and we practiced on it. We had to go through it and do it on some teacher or somebody that we could get to do it, and write a paper about it. . . . It's good, but it just seems like it's just an awful lot of pressure on them or on the teacher herself, and there's more, too, to what you're doing than just that particular day. You know, you might have a bad day.

Most prospective teachers echoed Karen's reservations about being observed with FPMS within the context of the realities of daily classroom life. From Becky's perspective, it "stifled" teaching, and, as Diane said, "You're not always afforded the opportunity of teaching that FPMS way."

While we should clearly expect prospective teachers to be uncertain and anxious about being observed, regardless of the instrument used, some students were especially concerned about the fact that being observed with the SOI might not accurately reflect how beginning teachers really teach. As Laura said:

Unfortunately I've learned about [the FPMS] and I've done it on my teachers, and I don't really like it. I've learned that it's something that we're going to have to do whether we want to or not. I've learned how to code and the geography of it, marking and coding, and what they say are the right things to do and what are the wrong things to do. And it's all right to have some checks on the left, I mean the right, as long as you have more on the left. And I've practiced with it and seen what's right behavior and what's wrong behavior, and, . . . I really, I don't like it. I think that when you're going to be observed, you change your teaching practices. You change the way you teach. I don't think that's very reliable because teachers know when this is going to be done, and they change the way they teach. . . . I don't think it's a very good judge of even how well, how good a teacher you are, how effective you are, because it really [doesn't address] how well did you plan your lesson and how well did you execute it. But that doesn't really have anything to do with whether the students responded, because you don't measure how the students respond to it. You can't just evaluate a teacher without considering the students, and I really don't think it takes the students into account. They just say, did the teacher start on time, yes or no. Did she have her materials ready and easily available, yes or no, and did she ask single factual questions, yes or no, or did she pose multiple ques-

tions. I mean, a lot of things like that, and that really doesn't have
anything to do with whether the students understand her or whether she
goes back and explains it to the students. . . . When they know that
they're going to be evaluated, . . . most teachers know what the FPMS is,
and they're going to change the way they teach. I think the way that, the
things that they think are the right things to do, aren't necessarily the
right things to do, that no one thing is going to be right for every single
class, and I really don't think you should be judged solely on the FPMS. I
think there are some good things that, yes, you have to know how to
plan a lesson, and you have to know how to pose a question to a student, but that's not the most important thing.

Laura admitted that she had learned only about Domain 3 (instructional
management) in class and that she might change her mind once she learned
about the other domains. But she had strong principled feelings about what she
knew at that point:

Maybe when I see the whole thing, maybe when I learn about everything, maybe I won't feel this way about it. But the things that I've seen, I
really don't agree with, and the way they're done, I really don't feel
happy about it. I can change the way I teach, [so] that I can pass it, but
that's not something that I'd really like to do. I'd feel kind of fraudulent
if I just stood up in front of the class and did things this way . . . to get a
good grade. What is that showing the kid, that, oh, well, even though
you don't act this way all the time, you put on a show and get by. . . .
And when you stand up there and change the way you teach so that you
won't get sent away, and so you won't lose your job or whatever, I think
that really gives them a wrong message.

The source of Laura's feelings also came from her experience in practicing
FPMS on a teacher of whom she was critical:

I did it twice on my cooperating teacher and she did really well, but I
don't think she's a very good teacher. She's not compassionate at all. She
doesn't care about the kids, and she yells at them. I think you'd have to
be an idiot and an imbecile to not pass it. Terrible teachers do well. It's
obvious that [cooperating teacher] doesn't like teaching, and she did so
well. When I marked her, she had so many tallies in the left hand
column and not very many in the right. . . . And she doesn't usually
praise students at all, and it really disturbed me that she did so well, that
she scored so well on Domain 3 of the FPMS, and here she is, she doesn't
really like teaching . . . I think they need to do other things. I think they

need to observe teachers and students, how they interact. Not just in the classroom but in the lunchroom, I mean. I think a good teacher takes time to stop and talk to her students and listen to her students, his or her students, and find out what they're all about, and I don't think that they just see them in the classroom. I think when they stand on the playground with them, that they don't ignore them and say go away, that they talk to them, and I really think that they should be seen doing everything with their students, not just teaching a lesson for a couple of hours in the morning.

Some of Laura's opinions may strike us as naive and unfairly judgmental, yet she clearly pointed to the signal danger of using any unidimensional evaluation system—that it can influence practice when required and does not necessarily reflect how teachers teach on a day-to-day basis. In addition, while all of the prospective teachers expressed reservations about FPMS in some general, and perhaps more personal, way, Laura's concerns touch on a critical question related to any criterion checklist used to assess teaching: By focusing on selected indicators based on generic teaching behaviors, do observers look for evidence of expertise in teaching within the contexts of particular learners and subject matter and the realities of daily classroom life? According to Kerr (1981), observable behaviors aid us in understanding phenomena for the purposes of prediction, but they fail to "augment our understanding of the practice of teaching for purposes of improving the actions that constitute that practice" (p. 80).

Our concerns about the FPMS focus in general and the lack of attention to subject matter specifically were further supported by Abigail's observation experience. She concurred with Julia's view that the system was taught "out of sync" with her experience in the classroom: "We had it drilled into us for however many weeks it was, and this semester I found myself forgetting a lot of it. . . . When we learned that, it was too far removed from anything I knew." When it came time for her observation, she recalled that, although FPMS had been "stressed for an entire semester . . . , [she had] forgotten a lot. I had to go back. I was evaluated by an administrator. I asked him to come into my class, and he evaluated me on the FPMS, so the night before I crammed again. Now, what is it we're supposed to be doing?"

Abigail described the observation as an "eye-opening" experience:

It was incredible, but his interpretation of the FPMS, it was an eye-opener. . . . [You know], where you ask the question, you wait, you have your wait time, then you call on the student, but you give him time to think about it? I did this. He wrote that I should do it, call on the student and ask the question, and he had the number of times I should have done that. And I did that twice. I called on the student, and both times I

thought, what am I doing? I need to be asking the question, and let them
think about it, and then calling on [them]. . . . He said I did it right.
Now this was his own interpretation, and he wasn't using [the check-
list]. He just wrote notes. He didn't like to use the actual paper that had
all these little charts on it from the FPMS. A lot of classroom management
skills were solved with [the fact that] I had a quiet class. . . . But I just
didn't feel like I was, he did [say] that I had three activities, that that was
good. I think that was a really positive thing to say, but I thought, this is
really interesting because it's not at all what, he didn't go into indepth
about my content, to see if I had his value knowledge, to see if I could
find terms, to see if I do any of these things, in what was it—Domain 1?
And it was mostly classroom management that he wrote down about,
and it was different than what I thought it would be. So that was an eye-
opener.

Given the observer's focus and the surprising discrepancies Abigail sensed, her
views reflect legitimate concerns about what a beginning teacher would be expected to demonstrate during the induction year and what dimensions of the
practice of teaching may never receive attention.

Despite the reservations and concerns expressed above, all of the prospective teachers agreed that knowing FPMS was valuable. Many regarded the domains
as "a flexible framework" or "useful guidelines" to "create a more productive
environment," or "to help the teacher guide the class, . . . some rules that will
work and will elicit the students' behavior." For Carol, a prospective secondary
teacher, the system provided both guidance and choices:

We were told it was useful in just sharpening your skills, making good
teachers better. If you follow through, some of these things will really
help you to sharpen your teaching, and I guess that was their main
point, that it can help you. Just little things, and especially if you have
problem areas, discipline in this and that. . . . And if you use certain
methods, these are options, they are not the be all and end all, at least I
don't think. There are ways to approach things . . . that they feel are
effective. I would tend to try out those methods before I would try and
drum up some unusual idea on my own, because they seem to be based
on experience and watching . . . effective teachers in action.

Its greatest value, however, seemed to lie with its "commonsense" appeal and
knowing what would be expected during the first year of teaching. The views
of Becky, another prospective secondary teacher, were typical:

A lot of it is just common sense. I think I knew a lot of it beforehand,
where you have to start promptly, and you have to review and consis-

tently test, but I think the only way it's going to help me is because my career depends on it. As a beginning teacher you're gonna be evaluated, and now I know exactly what they're gonna look for, and some of the things, like multiple questions, I never, I ask some of those when I'm teaching, and now I'm aware of it, and the three minutes, seconds, pause. That was important, because a lot of times I'd just go on. I think it's just going to help me knowing the FPMS when it comes time for my first year, to get through it and know what I'm supposed to be doing according to Florida, even though I think I would do those things anyway, and I do.

In spite of the universal agreement about the value of knowing FPMS in anticipation of induction-year observations, some students were nonetheless ambivalent about the amount of time devoted to learning it. As Julia said:

In the beginning, it all seemed a little silly. It all seemed kind of either too obvious, or not practical, or something, and I was surprised when I actually got in and started teaching. Yeah, these things are there and knowing about them beforehand, I think, gave me an advantage. I mean, I think too much time is spent on that. I don't know. They could have done it in a lot shorter time. We spent a whole semester on this, and . . . it was too drawn out. In the fall I . . . moaned and groaned a lot about it, because I felt that it was wasting my time then, and I still think that we wasted a lot of time. I think it's a fine tool, and it's something that we should have and know about, but it doesn't need to be drawn out like it was.

And some students, like Martha, had mixed feelings, which came from her perceptions of what it takes to develop as a secondary teacher. She agreed that FPMS is "a good guide, and it gives you a certain amount of confidence when you're first dealing with material [on] how to present things." But she also felt that it was only a beginning for the beginning teacher: "You should go beyond that and develop beyond it."

Concerns Raised in the TELT Study

FPMS was not considered a major agenda item in the preservice programs at State University when compared with all other topics and foci emphasized. Nevertheless, the foregoing comments raised a number of concerns regarding messages that prospective teachers got from or about FPMS.

First, despite their perceptive reservations about whether SOI takes into account the whole of teaching, it's clear that what the instrument emphasizes is a fragmented view of teaching and an instrumental focus on classroom interaction. As Kennedy (1987) points out, this "technical skills" view of teaching expertise assumes that constituent skills can be identified, that the skills can be taught to prospective teachers, and that they can be appropriately drawn on in practice. Such a view not only lacks attention to other necessary components of professional expertise, such as theories and principles of teaching and learning or an analytic capacity, but also ignores the uncertainties of teaching (Cohen, 1988; Jackson, 1986) and the decisions professionals make about *whether* and *when* to employ a particular skill. In short, definitions of expertise that focus on segments of observable behavior "miss the intentionality of practice" (Broudy, 1984; cited in Kennedy, 1987, p. 6).

Second, while one-sixth of FPMS is designed to focus on the presentation of subject matter, there was little hard evidence to suggest that Domain 4 was of major import in learning FPMS for the prospective teachers in the TELT study. In fact, as Abigail noted about her observation, there was no attention given to the content of her lesson. In addition, there was no evidence suggesting that they learned anything about teaching writing from FPMS. While the apparent absence of attention to Domain 4 may be a function of a particular observer during a particular lesson, the overall appearance of the diminution of the importance of subject matter may more likely be the result of an instrument that is based primarily on process-product research. As Shulman (1986) pointed out:

> Each extant research program grows out of a particular perspective, a bias of either convention or discipline, necessarily illuminating some part of the field of teaching while ignoring the rest. The danger for any field of social science or educational research lies in its potential corruption (or worse, trivialization) by a single paradigmatic view. (p. 4)

The influence of the process-product paradigm on FPMS resulted in an emphasis on generic behaviors focused on the relationship between teacher behavior and student achievement (see, for example, Brophy & Good, 1986). Zumwalt (1982) argues that such an emphasis not only "misses the central core of teaching" (p. 286; cited in Kennedy, 1987) but also limits the usefulness of the instrument to teacher educators because of its narrowness and fragmentation. In addition, the relegation of subject matter to a position of at least apparent lesser importance ignores the fact that "the general public and those who set educational policy are in general agreement that teachers' competence in subjects they teach is a central criterion of teacher quality" (Shulman, 1986, p. 25). Finally, focusing on generic teaching behaviors simply cannot help prospective teachers think about teaching specific subject-matter content or about other subject-matter related issues.

Third, the issue of time, both in learning FPMS and in being observed with SOI, raised concerns about a precious commodity. In effect, relatively little time is actually available to help students learn from and about teaching during preservice teacher education and during the induction year. The use of a criterion checklist like SOI not only limits what is noticed and evaluated in a lesson (Hoover & O'Shea, 1987; Sergiovanni, 1986) but also delimits the focus of discussions about teaching following observations. While we have known for some years that prospective teachers are inclined to develop instrumental perspectives toward teaching during field experiences (see, for example, Goodman, 1985; Hoy & Rees, 1977; Tabachnick, Popkewitz, & Zeichner, 1979–1980), the focus on generic teaching behaviors such as those emphasized on SOI may not only promote minimally competent teaching behavior as recognized by the state but also shape beginning teacher's emerging theories about instruction and notions of requisite expertise that would ultimately run counter to excellence in teaching, the very thing FPMS was purportedly designed to address.

THE TENSIONS BETWEEN REGULATORY STANDARDS AND PROFESSIONAL JUDGMENTS

The foregoing examination of three state policies in Florida raises a number of questions regarding the mismatch between legislative intentions and the nature, quality, and outcomes of the implementation of state mandates. While the states have historically helped to shape the education of prospective teachers through certification requirements, the legislative reform of the 1980s more centrally addressed issues of who would be certified to teach and what they would be expected to teach in public schools and in what manner.

Seen in that light, the contributions of the Gordon Rule, CLAST, and FPMS to prospective teachers' learning to teach writing suggest, at best, a discrepancy between compliance with the mandates and what research on teaching in general and on the teaching of writing in particular require. It is clear that teacher educators in the TELT study promoted a process approach to writing (see McDiarmid, 1989), suggesting more specific goals for writing instruction and qualitatively different views of teaching and writing expertise than the mandates required. Yet the actual and respective influences of the mandates and the teacher preparation programs on the soon-to-be beginning elementary and secondary teachers in our study are unknown. The extent to which the implementation of the Florida Writing Project, the Writing Enhancement Program, and whole-language teaching throughout the state influenced their beliefs about and practices of teaching writing are also unknown.

While the three mandates considered here may have reinforced prior school experiences of these prospective teachers, their university teacher preparation programs worked actively to change prior erroneous beliefs about what it means to be a writer in a school setting. At best, these legislative mandates may have had no deleterious effect on the prospective teachers' teaching of writing in K–12 schools, since the mandates were inimical to what they had learned about a process approach to teaching writing and what they said they had come to believe constitutes good writing. Their sole benefit may simply have been a symbolic gesture to assure consumer protection against the absence of absolute minimum competence in beginning teachers. At worst, however, the mandates could have driven a rule-bound curriculum in writing and fostered discrete generic teaching behaviors that fail to promote the acquisition of subject matter knowledge in general and writing competence in particular.

Two things are known, however. One is that the prospective teachers in the TELT study clearly sensed the tensions between the requirements of the three mandates and the programs's messages about the teaching of writing. The second is that these mandates, despite the good intentions of the Florida legislature, ignored or contravened what we know about what it means to know something and what it takes to teach worthwhile content to students at all levels of schooling. Such tensions between regulatory standards and professional judgment characterized many of the 1980s reforms and may, ultimately, be the most prominent—and troubling—legacy of the reform period.

NOTES

1. A fourth policy, the Writing Enhancement Program (WEP), is not considered here, since the majority of the prospective teachers in our study had little experience in the field and little or no influence of WEP could legitimately be expected.

2. All names used in this chapter are pseudonyms. In an effort to make the original pseudonyms less confusing, since all began with the letter "S," pseudonyms have been assigned alphabetically. For persons interested in comparisons with data using the original pseudonyms, the following key is provided: Brown=Sharleen, Smith=Slade, Jones=Sage, Abigail=Shirley, Becky=Sophie, Carol=Scarlett, Diane=Sena, Ellie=Stella, Fran=Shelly, Gina=Stacey, Helen=Sylvia, Julia=Sheila, Karen=Susan, Laura=Sonya, Martha=Samantha.

3. In keeping with a promise to guarantee confidentiality, the author is unable to give credit for this work in the references.

4. The CLAST *Preparation Guide* states: "The following pre-test, as well as the two other complete grammar tests in this book, are accurate simulations of the test you will see on CLAST day. They are not copies of previous tests, because, unlike other testing agencies, Florida does not release actual test questions. The state does, however, provide exact descriptions of skills tested, sample questions, and the wording of directions used on the CLAST. Carefully following the state's specifications, the questions and format presented in this book are as close as possible to the real thing. Students who have recently taken the state test have been unable to tell the difference between Florida's CLAST and the tests in this book" (Goldfarb & Johnson, 1988, pp. 15–16). The CLAST *Preparation Guide* is recommended by the Office of Teacher Certification.

REFERENCES

Alexander, L. (1986, November). Time for results: An overview. *Phi Delta Kappan, 68*(4), 202–204.

American Association of Colleges. (1985, February). *Integrity in the college curriculum: A report to the academic community.* Washington, DC: Author.

Applebee, A. N. (1981). *Writing in the secondary school: English and the content areas.* Urbana, IL: National Council of Teachers of English.

Boyer, E. (1987). *College: The undergraduate experience in America.* New York: Harper & Row.

Brophy, J., & Good, T. L. (1986). Teacher behavior and student achievement. In M. C. Wittrock (Ed.), *Handbook of research on teaching* (3rd ed., pp. 358–375). New York: Macmillan.

Broudy, H.S. (1984). The university and the preparation of teachers. In L. Katz and J. D. Raths (Eds.), *Advances in teacher education* (Vol. 1, pp. 1–8). Norwood, NJ: Ablex.

Calkins, L. M. (1986). *The art of teaching writing.* Portsmouth, NH: Heinemann.

Camp, G. (Ed.). (1983). *Teaching writing: Essays from the Bay Area Writing Project.* Montclair, NJ: Boynton/Cook.

Cohen, D. K. (1988). *Teaching practice: Plus ça change.* East Lansing: National Center for Research on Teacher Education, Michigan State University.

Cooper, C. (Ed.). (1981). *The nature and measurement of competency in English.* Urbana, IL: National Council of Teachers of English.

Drummond, W. (1973). Role of state departments of education. In D. J. McCarty (Ed.), *New perspectives on teacher education* (pp. 84–99). San Francisco: Jossey-Bass.

Elbow, P. (1981). *Writing with power: Techniques for mastering the writing process.* New York: Oxford University Press.

Florida Coalition. (1983). *Domains: Knowledge base of the Florida Performance Measurement System.* Chipley, FL: Panhandle Area Educational Cooperative.

Florio-Ruane, S., & Dunn, S. (1987). Teaching writing: Some perennial questions and some possible answers. In V. Richardson-Koehler (Ed.), *Educators' handbook: A research perspective* (pp. 50–83). New York: Longman.

Flower, L. S., & Hayes, J. R. (1981). Plans that guide the composing process. In C. H. Frederiksen & J. F. Dominic (Eds.), *Writing: The nature, development, and teaching of written communications* (Vol. 2, pp. 39–58). Hillsdale, NJ: Lawrence Erlbaum Associates.

Fuhrman, S., Clune, W. H., & Elmore, R. F. (1988). Research on education reform: Lessons on the implementation of policy. *Teachers College Record, 90*(2), 237–257.

Gabrys, R. E. (1987). State reaction to national teacher testing and certification issues. In *Trends in teacher certification testing* (pp. 25–29). Amherst, MA: National Evaluation Systems.

Goldfarb, R. L., & Johnson, B. E. (1988). *Cliff's CLAST preparation guide.* Lincoln, NE: Cliff Notes.

Gomez, M. L. (1988, April). *Prospective teachers' beliefs about good writing.* Paper presented at the annual meeting of the American Educational Research Association, New Orleans, LA.

Gomez, M. L. (1989, March). *Learning to teach writing: The graduate year of teacher preparation.* Paper presented at the annual meeting of the American Educational Research Association, San Francisco, CA.

Goodman, J. (1985). What students learn from early field experiences: A case study and critical analysis. *Journal of Teacher Education, 36*(6), 42–48.

Gordon, J. D. (1981, April). Petition to initiate rulemaking pursuant to Section 120.54(5) Florida Statutes.

Graves, D. H. (1983). *Writing: Teachers and children at work.* Exeter, NH: Heinemann.

Hillocks, G., Jr. (1986). *Research on written composition: New directions for teaching.* Urbana, IL: ERIC Clearinghouse on Reading and Communication Skills and the National Conference on Research in English.

Hoover, N. L., & O'Shea, L. J. (1987, April). *The influence of a criterion checklist on supervisors' and interns' conceptions of teaching.* Paper presented at the annual meeting of the American Educational Research Association, Washington, DC.

Hoy, W. K., & Rees, R. (1977). The bureaucratic socialization of student teachers. *Journal of Teacher Education, 28,* 23–26.

Jackson, P. W. (1986). *The practice of teaching.* New York: Teachers College Press.

Kennedy, M. M. (1987). *Inexact science: Professional education and the development of expertise* (Issue Paper 87-2). East Lansing: National Center for Research on Teacher Education, Michigan State University.

Kerr, D. H. (1981). The structure of quality in teaching. In J. H. Soltis (Ed.), *Philosophy and education: Eightieth Yearbook of the National Society for the Study of Education* (pp. 61–93). Chicago: University of Chicago Press.

Lensmire, T. J. (1994). *When children write: Critical re-visions of the writing workshop.* New York: Teachers College Press.

Littler, F. A. (1987). *The impact of the Gordon Rule on student writing in Florida colleges and universities.* Unpublished doctoral dissertation, Illinois State University.

Lortie, D. C. (1975). *Schoolteacher: A sociological study.* Chicago: University of Chicago Press.

Macmillan, C. B. J., & Pendlebury, S. (1985, Fall). The Florida Performance Measurement System: A consideration. *Teachers College Record, 87*(1), 67–78.

McDiarmid, G. W. (1989, March). *Opportunities for learning to teach writing in preservice teacher education programs.* Paper presented at the annual meeting of the American Educational Research Association, San Francisco, CA.

Melnick, S. L., & Pullin, D. (1987). Testing teachers' professional knowledge: Legal and educational policy implications. *Educational Policy, 1*(2), 215–229.

Murray, D. M. (1968). *A writer teaches writing: A practical method of teaching composition.* Boston: Houghton Mifflin.

Myers, M. (1991). Issues in the restructuring of teacher preparation. In J. Flood, J. M. Jensen, D. Lapp, & J. R. Squire (Eds.), *Handbook of research on teaching the English language arts* (pp. 394–404). New York: Macmillan.

NCRTE (1988). Teacher education and learning to teach: A research agenda. *Journal of Teacher Education, 39*(6), 27–32.

National Assessment of Educational Progress. (1980). *Writing achievement, 1969–79: Results from the third writing assessment* (Vols. 1–3). Denver: Education Commission of the States.

National Commission on Excellence in Education. (1983). *A nation at risk*. Washington, DC: U.S. Government Printing Office.

Scardamalia, M., & Bereiter, C. (1986). Research on written composition. In M. C. Wittrock (Ed.), *Handbook of research on teaching* (3rd ed., pp. 778–803). New York: Macmillan.

Sergiovanni, T. (1986, April). *Theories and models as metaphors: Building a science of supervision*. Paper presented at the annual meeting of the American Educational Research Association, San Francisco, CA.

Shulman, L. S. (1986). Paradigms and research programs in the study of teaching: A contemporary perspective. In M.C. Wittrock (Ed.), *Handbook of research on teaching* (3rd ed., pp. 3–36). New York: Macmillan.

Smith, B. O. (1985, June). Research bases for teacher education. *Phi Delta Kappan, 66*, 685–690.

Tabachnick, B. R., Popkewitz, T. S., & Zeichner, K. M. (1979–1980). Teacher education and the professional perspectives of student teachers. *Interchange, 10*, 12–29.

Tiedt, I. M. (1989). *Reading/thinking/writing: A holistic language and literacy program for the K–8 classroom*. Boston: Allyn & Bacon.

Zumwalt, K. K. (1982). Research on teaching: Policy implications for teacher education. In A. Lieberman & M. W. McLaughlin (Eds.), *Policy making in education: Eighty-first Yearbook of the National Society for the Study of Education* (Part 1, pp. 215–248). Chicago: University of Chicago Press.

CHAPTER 4

The Continuing Reform of
a University Teacher Education Program:
A Case Study

Dorene Ross
Elizabeth Bondy

Schools, like other organizations, have an underlying culture involving shared values, rituals, norms, and ceremonies that reinforce existing patterns of behavior (Deal, 1987). Because the organizational culture sustains the ideological perspective of participants, most efforts at reform have a limited effect on the behavior and values within the organization. Goodman (1988) notes that change efforts seldom influence the social norms of the institution and thus have little impact on the "the underlying layer of meaning that includes the assumptions, predispositions, and values about an organization's purpose, and definition of . . . work" (p. 46).

This chapter examines the context and process of reform in elementary PROTEACH, a 5-year teacher education program at the University of Florida. This change is characterized as an ideological evolution that occurs as faculty collaboratively define program purposes and content. First we describe the changes that have occurred. Then, we describe the contextual factors that have supported and influenced the change process.

AN IDEOLOGICAL EVOLUTION: FROM CEP TO PROTEACH

If change has occurred in teacher education at the University of Florida, there should be evidence of an ideological shift by faculty reflecting altered assumptions and beliefs about the purposes and processes of teacher education.[1] To provide evidence of this shift, we present brief portraits of this teacher education program over time, beginning with the teacher education program immediately prior to PROTEACH.

The Childhood Education Program (CEP)

In the mid-1970s, the University of Florida had a well-publicized elementary teacher education program based on the assumption that "teachers must be educated in the same kind of supportive and stimulating environment that they were expected to provide for children" (Liston & Zeichner, 1991, p. 21). Grounded in the work of Art Combs (Combs, Blume, Newman, & Wass, 1974), the program applied the basic concepts of perceptual psychology to teaching. The good teacher was defined as an artist who selected and adapted teaching methods as necessary.

> [The teacher's] methods must fit the goals he [sic] seeks, the children he is working with, the philosophy he is guided by, the immediate conditions under which he is working to say nothing of his own feelings, goals and desires. (p. 7)

Program developers believed that students must feel a need to know before learning can occur, and that this need emerges naturally within an environment that encourages experimentation and eliminates competition and pressure (Combs et al., 1974). To prepare teachers capable of tapping the motivation of their students, teacher educators created a program focusing on the development of self-concept and self-adequacy. Program developers believed that teachers committed to their own continuous growth would nurture that orientation in their students; thus they focused on the development of the teacher as a person.

Educational processes within the program were oriented around choice, freedom, communication, personal discovery, experimentation, and the development of self. Students determined their need for information, when to complete projects, whether to attend lectures and help sessions, how quickly or slowly to proceed through the program, and in what order to complete program requirements. Faculty provided educational assistance and encouraged personal discovery through means such as meeting individually with students to plan and monitor their progress, providing assistance and redirection until students demonstrated competence on assignments, deemphasizing external evaluation by making all courses pass/fail, and writing detailed assessments of student progress. Instructional experimentation was encouraged by the provision of early, continuous, and ungraded field experience accompanied by a seminar designed to help students make sense of their experiences. Each seminar group included students from all levels of field experience and students remained in their group throughout the program. Seminars were collaboratively designed by the leader and the group and "experienced" students assumed the role of mentor for less experienced students. The seminar group and leader were considered central in facilitating personal growth in students. In an effort to recognize the instructional expertise of classroom teachers, direct student teaching supervision was done by classroom teachers rather than university faculty. Evaluation of the program was ongoing, and faculty frequently met to discuss problems and to identify new directions for action. Faculty perceptions of problems and beliefs about teaching and teacher education guided these efforts at revision.

Elementary PROTEACH

Elementary PROTEACH has a broader theoretical and research base than CEP. In fact, the foundations of PROTEACH have been expanded and adjusted over time as the faculty have studied teacher education in general and their own efforts in particular. Ongoing study has led to continuous refinement of the program. As a result, PROTEACH in 1995 is markedly different from the program adopted in 1983. Analyses of our evolution (Ross & Bondy, 1993; Ross, Johnson, & Smith, 1992) have helped us to identify three distinct stages in the development of PROTEACH. Here we review briefly the first two stages and describe in more detail stage three, the one in which we currently work.

Stage One: The Science of Teaching. Program development efforts during the early 1980s were driven by the college leadership's goal of tying teacher education content to the burgeoning research literature on effective teaching. College and university leadership moved the entire College of Education into the restructuring of teacher education with a clear focus on research-based knowledge about teaching and content-area expertise. Consequently, in their program development efforts, faculty drew on research in areas such as effective teaching, cognitive psychology, and subject area learning.

Previous articles have described key programmatic features of elementary PROTEACH (Ross, 1989; Ross, Johnson, & Smith, 1992; Ross & Krogh, 1988; Smith, Carroll, & Fry, 1984). Briefly, the structural features include:

- The provision of a five-year program
- An increase in the length and quality of study of liberal arts and science content
- Expansion of foundational and clinical studies
- An emphasis on research-based knowledge about teaching and learning
- Development of professional expertise in elementary education and a second professional area
- An increase in admission and retention requirements

The themes of the science of teaching and content-area expertise defined the program at this early stage in its evolution. This version of PROTEACH lasted for about two years.

Stage Two: Reflective Teaching. In stage two PROTEACH, the previous themes of the science of teaching and content-area expertise became subsumed under a program theme—reflective teaching. This theme was not entirely "new," as the faculty had guided students in a critical approach to the study of research on teaching from the beginning (see Ross & Kyle, 1987). Nevertheless, helping students to understand what reflection looks like, to learn how to be reflective, and to value reflective teaching became a programmatic focus. Reading and discussing the literature in the areas of teacher reflection, teacher learning, teacher socialization, and action research moved PROTEACH from stage one to stage two. The major focus with students was to clarify the nature of reflection and to find ways to help students become more reflective. At this point in program evolution, the faculty defined reflection as "a way of thinking about educational matters that involves the ability to make rational choices and to assume responsibility for those choices" (Ross, 1989, p. 26).

The faculty introduced students to reflective teaching in their first semester by teaching them about the attitudes and abilities of competent reflection and examining examples of reflective teaching. To support the development of reflection throughout students' programs, faculty used a variety of strategies, such as reflective writing, curriculum development and analysis, development of action research projects, and faculty modeling. Additional program features supported the focus on reflective teaching: use of collaboratively developed core courses to increase programmatic coherence, provision of training for supervisors of field experiences to foster coherence between course work and field experience, and the provision of ongoing support to program graduates (e.g., helping graduates establish a network to support one another and conducting a yearly conference for program graduates). An additional strategy used was the creation of rites and ceremonies to increase the connection graduates and faculty felt to the program. One example is the yearly conference for graduates. Another is a rite of passage in which graduating students present their research at an action research symposium. The development of traditions that reinforce program values and help students and teachers feel they are part of a distinctive group helped to develop program cohesion (Conway, 1990; Owens, 1987).

A final key element of PROTEACH is a commitment to ongoing evaluation of the learning and experiences of program participants and graduates. Ross, Johnson, and Smith (1992) stress the importance of this element:

> This knowledge [derived through evaluation] leads to faculty growth, to clarification of their goals, and to changes in instructional strategies. It is this recursive, reflective process that is the core of PROTEACH. (pp. 24–25)

During stage two PROTEACH, there was so much talk about reflection that faculty and students often joked about the "R" word, while some rolled their eyes when the topic was brought up. When one of the faculty members had a baby, a group of students presented the newborn with a T-shirt that announced in large letters, "Reflective Baby."

Stage Three: Reflective Teaching for What? In recent years, PROTEACH has evolved to a third stage. Although the prior focus on research and reflection remains, program themes have been refined and elaborated. In the spring of 1993, the faculty defined their current shared assumptions:

1. Effective teachers are reflective; that is they draw on research, practical knowledge, and theoretical knowledge to make and evaluate rational and ethical decisions about the aims and practices of education.
2. Effective teachers are committed to educational equity and student empowerment.
3. Effective teachers believe that knowledge is constructed by students.
4. A teacher's classroom practices are developed through the dynamic interaction among three factors: a teacher's perspectives, past experiences, and the unique context of teaching.

These assumptions represent the evolution of many faculty members' understandings about reflection and the purposes of PROTEACH. Faculty have refined their understandings of reflection, in particular by recognizing its moral and ethical basis. They have come to see reflection as linked to the aim of empowering all students to be active and critical citizens in a democratic society and to develop the skill and commitment to make society a better place for all people. This way of thinking about reflection has helped the faculty to focus more intently on the children their students will teach, hence the attention to constructivism and equity.

It would be naive to think that the faculty share a common understanding of these assumptions or a common approach to communicating them to students. Nevertheless, the faculty have accepted them as fundamental guiding principles of PROTEACH. More important than voicing support for the assumptions is the work the faculty do to develop shared meaning. To this point, the faculty have discussed the meaning of reflection and constructivism. In these discussions (and in the many discussions that lie ahead) the faculty clarify their thinking and work toward a shared understanding of these complex concepts.

At this point, most faculty believe that learning to teach is a complex process involving collaborative effort by students and faculty. To help themselves better prepare teachers, several faculty continue to study the learning of their teacher education students and program graduates. From this work and the work of other teacher educators, they have learned that teaching practices are influenced by a variety of factors, including:

entering perspective, personal learning history, theoretical knowledge base, faculty mentors, peers, cooperating teachers, university supervisors, children within classrooms, student teaching experiences, image of self, perception of efficacy. (Ross et al., 1992)

Many faculty recognize that students enter teacher education with implicit beliefs about the purposes of schooling, and about teaching and learning, that have a pervasive influence on what and how they will teach. Growth as a teacher requires that students confront and begin to question their entering perspectives.

Students also enter with ideas about where they will teach and the kind of students they will teach. Like most prospective elementary teachers, the majority expect to teach white, middle-class children in communities similar to those where they grew up (Ross & Smith, 1992). Given the changing demographics of the country and the programmatic commitment to educational equity, faculty also work to help students confront their entering beliefs about diversity and to help them develop multicultural rather than monocultural perspectives.

Stage three PROTEACH is characterized by attention to students' entering perspectives about teaching and diversity, a constructivist orientation to teaching and learning, and the development of the habit of reflection as a means of empowering all children as learners and socially responsible citizens in a democratic society. The thematic focus of the program is supported by many of the program features from stage two. Additional features that support program themes include students' guided intensive analyses of their images of teaching at the beginning and end of the program, participation in a tutoring project in which students work with youth who live in local public housing, in-depth study of cultural diversity and culturally responsive teaching strategies in at least four required courses, and ongoing experimentation to develop alternatives to an apprenticeship model for student teaching.

Has Change Occurred?

The differences between CEP and stage three PROTEACH demonstrate an evolution in beliefs and assumptions. At the core of both programs is commitment to the teacher as a lifelong learner, to the development of decision-making skills, to teacher autonomy, to the importance of creative and analytic thought, and to teacher and student collaboration in learning. Beyond these similarities, however, there are several key differences. At the heart of CEP was a belief that the purpose of teacher education was to facilitate the growth of the teacher as a person, using noninterventionist instructional strategies. The teacher educator's role was to provide an intellectually and creatively challenging environment. Given this environment, faculty assumed student teachers would flourish and that graduates would be able to recreate such environments in their own classrooms.

At the heart of PROTEACH is a more complex view of the teaching/learning process. Faculty recognize that changing teachers' perspectives is hard work that requires teacher educators to study and constantly refine their instructional skills. Additionally, they recognize that constructivist, reflective teaching is not the norm in schools and that without support, many graduates will be socialized into a technical approach to teaching. Compared with CEP developers, PROTEACH faculty attach much more importance to developing substantive knowledge, structuring and evaluating students' educational experiences, confronting and challenging students' entering perspectives about teaching, increasing student's commitments to educational equity and to multicultural education, providing support to help program graduates sustain commitment to program goals, and collecting evidence about the impact of the program. These changes reflect an evolution in the definition of both the purposes and processes of teacher education.

The contrast between CEP during the 1970s and PROTEACH during the 1990s suggests that significant changes have occurred. A key question for educational reformers is why change occurred. What forces encouraged teacher educators to attempt change and sustained them in their efforts? In answering this question, we consider the impetus for change during and since the development of the program.

REFORM IN TEACHER EDUCATION: GETTING STARTED

From spring 1980 until spring 1983, faculty at the University of Florida worked to develop a written description of a teacher education program. Ross and Krogh (1988) characterize that period as a time of collaboration across departments—to develop the various task force reports and literature reviews required by the reform effort—but also of "high stress, tension, and conflict" (p. 26) over the need for change, the direction of change and the nature of the change process. Why would faculty in a widely publicized teacher education program take part in a major reform effort that had the potential to throw them into conflict?

In reality the faculty had no choice. Forces within the nation, the state, and the college had converged to create a context in which change seemed necessary for survival. Let's consider the context in which the reform effort began.

The Context for Change

A variety of external factors combined to create a context in which change seemed essential:

- An increasing national and state perception that the quality of teaching and particularly of teacher education was low

- National and state attention directed at the expanded knowledge base for teacher education (i.e., teacher-effects research), which had not been incorporated into teacher education programs
- A legislative push for reform including recurrent state legislation to abolish colleges of education in Florida's state universities and consideration of changes in certification policies
- Declining enrollments in the College of Education
- Support for teacher education reform from leaders of state educational organizations (Ross & Krogh, 1988; Smith, 1984)

In addition, factors within the college created a context that supported change. During the 1960s and 1970s, the University of Florida had two dynamic leaders on the faculty, Ira Gordon and Art Combs. Around these leaders, faculty factions representing intellectual differences of opinion formed. These differences reflected national differences about the relative importance of developmental versus empirical and behavioral perspectives. Although the faculty interacted well together, intellectual discourse at times was difficult. In the late 1970s both leaders left the college; no one stepped forward to fill the void, yet the divisions within the college remained. Some faculty believed a college-wide reform effort was the appropriate vehicle to unite the faculty.

A second factor was the growing feeling of concern among the faculty about teacher education. An increasing number of faculty were expressing reservations about the quality of the student pool in teacher education, and an in-house study, comparing student perceptions of CEP with the program's goals, indicated the program was falling short of the goals it had set for itself.

The future of the college in 1979 seemed tenuous. The faculty was not united. Student enrollment was declining. The state legislature was actively considering abolishing teacher education at the state universities and the national scene was ripe for a major assault on teacher education. University administrators, concerned about how to respond to the state-level threats against the college, encouraged the dean and the faculty to do something proactive, to initiate reform. Within this context, Dean David Smith began a major reform effort.

The Context of Development

The development of PROTEACH was guided by Dean Smith, who monitored and directed its forward momentum. Another important factor in the program's success was the support of the Vice President for Academic Affairs, who encouraged the restructuring of teacher education. The mechanism for program development was a steering committee that developed tasks to be accomplished. Faculty were involved in tasks at every phase of development, but some expressed concern that they had no power to direct the course of the change. Some were concerned that the development of a 5-year program would mean the death of the college because students might choose to enroll in teacher education programs where they could graduate in less than 5 years. Others, who nevertheless actively contributed to PROTEACH development efforts, had argued for change of a different kind. Many CEP faculty were in this latter group of "friendly resistors."

The first phase of development was a statewide conference to identify what beginning teachers needed to know and be able to do. The second phase was a 2-year process of developing literature-review documents related to the components of teaching (e.g., observation, planning, lesson development, management). The charge to each cross-departmental task force was to review research literature, define key terms, and develop behavioral indicators of competencies and skills to be developed in teachers. This task created dissonance for CEP faculty, who rejected the assumption that teaching any specific set of behaviors to students would produce excellent teachers. They viewed this approach to teacher education as overly technical and simplistic.

Task force committees approached their work in varied ways. Some committees conformed to the task as presented, that is, to develop behavioral indicators of essential teaching competencies. Others deemphasized the development of competencies and behavioral indicators and stressed the complexity of teaching and learning to teach and the multiple possible interpretations of research. All reports were accepted by the steering committee and used in the third phase, the creation of a written document describing the PROTEACH programs in elementary, secondary, and special education.

Amid turmoil and tension, the program described in the written document passed by secret ballot in spring 1983. This document reflected commitments to the science of teaching and to the teacher's role as a subject matter specialist (Liston & Zeichner, 1991). Yet, at its passage, the elementary faculty was firmly committed to the view that teaching and teacher education should be student-centered, based on the learner's understandings, interests, and concerns. Their commitment to this developmentalist perspective (Liston & Zeichner, 1991) had been strengthened during conflict over the PROTEACH program. Faculty within the college who were committed to a developmentalist tradition in teacher education were concerned that a technical program was being imposed on them, despite administrative assurances to the contrary. As Ross and Krogh (1988) note, the faculty effort to communicate their perspectives prior to the adoption of the PROTEACH document was a creative force: "Our concern forced us to clarify what was important to us. Our priorities in teacher education did not change, but we were forced to express those priorities and perhaps, in the process, we strengthened our commitments" (p. 28).

In the spring of 1983, a program existed on paper, but not in reality. As faculty developed the details of program sequence and content, they realized that, in fact, a program had not been imposed on them.

THE IMPLEMENTATION YEARS

Once the program was approved by the faculty, the nature of debates and of program development processes changed. The leadership up to that point had focused on getting the program approved. Once this happened, that leadership fell away and faculty, largely the friendly resistors of the past, stepped in to develop the details of PROTEACH. Small departmental and cross-departmental groups of faculty began to meet to develop courses and to talk about how to prepare teachers to make pedagogical decisions. Given the parameters of PROTEACH, a 5-year program with increased emphasis on liberal arts and science, research-based knowledge, and professional expertise, they began to construct a teacher education program that would help students learn to make learner-centered pedagogical judgments based on teacher knowledge of subject matter, teaching strategies, and learners' understandings, interests, and concerns. These faculty groups had some significant problems to confront.

Implementation Problems

One problem faculty faced was that the state initiated an induction program that included the use of an observation instrument based on teacher effectiveness research that was in conflict with the faculty's developmentalist philosophy. Confronted with the need to prepare graduates to succeed in the induction program, and the emphasis on the behavior-oriented research on teaching evident in the PROTEACH program document, faculty had to incorporate the research emphasized in the observational instrument into the program. However, their concerns about the limitations of this research prohibited them from simply teaching the skills it identified.

A second problem was that faculty morale and energy were low. Some faculty thought that they had spent much time and energy developing the program and were not sure that students would enroll because of its length. At the same time they were aware that a great deal of work still lay ahead.

A third problem was the unease created for faculty by teacher socialization research, which indicated that teacher education often did not challenge the perspectives of preservice teachers. Instead, teacher educators often unintentionally encourage teachers to conform to the traditional technical practices of current elementary classrooms (Goodman, 1982; Tabachnick, Popkewitz & Zeichner, 1980; Zeichner & Tabachnick, 1981). These research studies convinced several faculty members that increased structure, sequence, and coherence were needed in both course work and fieldwork. The research helped to clarify and strengthen faculty beliefs that the development of the teacher as a person was insufficient preparation for teaching excellence.

The first and second problems proved the easiest to solve. To incorporate the teacher-effectiveness research into the program, a small team of faculty created a course to introduce the research to students within a decision-making framework. In the course, Research in Elementary Education, students learn that the teacher-effectiveness research supports an instructional model that is appropriate for teaching low-level cognitive skills to low-achieving students. To achieve other goals with all students, and for high-achieving students, teacher education students are encouraged to seek alternative instructional strategies (Ross & Kyle, 1987).

The problem of faculty morale was solved by the entrance of the first group of PROTEACH students.

> When these students decided to enroll, they believed they were beginning a new, improved program. They were excited and motivated. Their expectations clearly influenced the faculty. The elementary faculty had historically been a student-centered faculty. Now we had to deliver a good program because the students expected so much. (Ross & Krogh, 1988, p. 29)

Efforts to resolve the dilemmas created by the third problem have been ongoing. Solving this problem has required the faculty to continually ask four questions:

1. What are our goals?
2. Are our goals worthwhile?
3. Is our program structured in ways that seem likely to achieve our goals?
4. Is there evidence to suggest we are accomplishing our goals?

As PROTEACH began, the faculty had no mechanism in place to help us address these questions. Dialogue about these questions began as they created new courses, planned content for the courses, and developed a course sequence. However, when the faculty stopped planning courses and began teaching them, the need to meet no longer existed. So for over a year, these central questions went unasked and unanswered. However, the questions remained and, in time, they resurfaced. A changing context for teacher education at the University of Florida helped refocus attention on these questions.

A Changing Context for Teacher Education

Beginning in 1985, several things happened that changed the context for teacher education at the University of Florida and enabled faculty to initiate an active line of inquiry about teacher education. First, people within the state and the nation perceived that Florida had taken a proactive and positive stance to enhance the quality of teacher education. Florida was no longer on the defensive; we were operating from a position of strength.

Second, the faculty in the areas of early/elementary education, secondary education, reading, and media were combined into one department. The new chair, Margaret Early, was instrumental in securing the Becoming Teachers grant, three years of funding for program development and evaluation efforts. These funds enabled the faculty to develop an evaluation program, initiate the annual conference for program graduates, and hire graduate assistants to conduct literature reviews.

Third, enrollment declines began to abate. Because of this and faculty retirements, the department began to add new faculty members. By making an effort to recruit faculty who shared the emerging philosophy of the program, the core of faculty interested in teacher education research began to grow. The socialization of these new faculty members into PROTEACH has been a way to help establish a norm of doing research related to teacher education (Owens, 1987).

Program Development and Evaluation

The changed context, and the seed money provided by the Becoming Teachers grant, renewed faculty interest in program development. One result of this interest was a brown-bag lunch seminar, initiated and run by faculty on a voluntary basis.

In the fall of 1986 a cross-departmental group of elementary and foundations faculty began meeting to talk about teaching and teacher education. Early discussions were shaped by literature reviews in the areas of teacher reflection and socialization. During that year, faculty developed a definition of reflection and strategies for fostering reflection in PROTEACH students. The brown-bag seminars continued for 3 years; faculty shared instructional strategies, course syllabi, the results of their teacher education research, and relevant articles from the growing teacher education literature. These lunch meetings "helped to create greater coherence in the program and more knowledge about ourselves as teacher educators" (Ross & Krogh, 1988, p. 31). Essentially, they were a forum for faculty development. Goodman (1988) has noted that the professional perspectives of teacher educators are a key component in any change process. Brown-bag seminars provided faculty with a way to challenge their own perspectives about teacher education.

By the spring of 1987, a small group of faculty were working to develop a longitudinal evaluation plan for PROTEACH, and the first study of student learning in PROTEACH was completed (Ross, 1989). The evaluation and program revision cycle begun in 1987 has fueled the process of continual renewal within the program. That is, the process itself has become a force that sustains program evaluation.

Sustaining Program Development

Several features of PROTEACH, including the evaluation cycle, help to sustain reform. Program evaluation contributes in several ways. First, collecting data about our students' learning convinces faculty of the difficulty of teacher education and motivates us to improve our teacher education efforts.

> [Our research has convinced us that] helping students change their perspectives is slow, difficult, and time consuming work. Each study conducted refines our knowledge about what is involved in learning to teach and leads to program revisions . . . [such as] increasing the emphasis on the ethical component of reflection, requiring students to clarify and analyze a personal theory of teaching . . . and placing increased attention on the nature . . . of beginning teaching contexts and the development of micropolitical skills that will empower teachers. (Ross et al., 1992, pp. 19–20)

Second, faculty who are involved in teacher education research and program development approach the literature and conferences such as the annual meeting of the American Educational Research Association (AERA) looking for research and for ideas that will further their efforts as teacher educators. For example, Ross and Bondy (1993) and Ross and colleagues (1992) describe the evolution of instructional strategies in two courses as a result of previous PROTEACH research, and studies on teacher development through narrative inquiry conducted by Butt and Raymond (1989), Bullough and Gitlin (1989), and Clandinin (1986). Similarly, the idea to create a conference for graduates was sparked by a session attended by some faculty at the annual meeting of the American Educational Research Association. The feedback from graduates at this PROTEACH Revisited conference has been a major impetus for program revision. In particular, responses from graduates have encouraged the faculty to focus more attention on preparing students to teach a diverse pupil population.

A third way the evaluation process leads to evolution in the program is that faculty present their work at conferences and in journals for others to critique. For example, comments by Joe Vaughan at the 1988 Florida Conference on Reflective Inquiry and by Sharon Feiman-Nemser during a 1989 AERA session encouraged faculty to address the question "reflection for what?" They helped faculty consider whether reflection in and of itself was a sufficient goal. In addition, comments by Jesse Goodman and Ken Zeichner have encouraged faculty to attend more seriously to the work of critical theorists and have led to increased emphasis on the ethical commitments of teachers within a democratic society. Friendly critiques of the faculty's work stimulate further exploration, examination, and clarification of PROTEACH purposes and content. The faculty continue to ask questions about their goals for students and their strategies for achieving these goals. This collective wondering stimulates program development.

Two additional features of PROTEACH have sustained its evolution: the team teaching of three core courses and the assignment of a faculty member to a quarter-time role as elementary program development and evaluation coordinator. Each semester multiple sections of three core courses are offered, and a team of instructors works together to plan the course, monitor its evolution during the semester, and critique it at the end of the semester. As Ross and Bondy (1993) have explained, "the teaching team is a mini community that plays an important role in our learning" (p. 19). As colleagues work together to teach and improve their course, they develop new and deeper understandings of their work. Teaching teams construct ideas for research studies and course and program revision. Faculty collaboration within these teams fuels program reform.

Although PROTEACH had a coordinator for some time, the coordinator's role was defined in terms of program management. In 1992, a second coordinator position was created to focus on issues of program development. The new coordinator convenes monthly meetings of the elementary faculty to discuss program purposes, content, and structure.

Faculty committees are sometimes formed to develop plans to bring back to the group for discussion. Committees have worked to plan a faculty retreat to examine issues related to preparing students to teach a diverse pupil population, to develop alternatives to the current system of field experiences, and to design a portfolio assessment system for student teachers. The elementary area group is an essential feature of PROTEACH because it provides a place for faculty to think together about the program. The existence of such a structure ensures the continued evolution of PROTEACH.

KEY CONTEXTUAL FEATURES
OF TEACHER EDUCATION PROGRAM REFORM

For 11 years, PROTEACH has been in the process of becoming. It has been constructed over time by the students and faculty who have worked in it in response both to external pressures and to the priorities of program faculty. Our approach to teacher education reform has been similar to the "evolutionary planning process" Louis and Miles (1990) describe in their study of urban high schools. We have not followed a rational model of "plan and then do," but rather we have taken a collaborative journey better characterized by "do, then plan, and then do some more" (Fullan & Miles, 1992). Our journey has not been without direction; however, we continue to clarify our direction as we become more knowledgeable.

When we examine the evolution of elementary teacher education at the University of Florida, we can identify several features of our work context that have contributed to the ongoing reform of our program. These features have implications for reform efforts at other institutions.

Enabling Leadership

According to Rallis (1990), leadership entails "drawing members of an organization together to build a culture within which they feel secure enough to articulate and pursue what they want to become" (p. 186). Leadership is not the domain of an individual, but is the quality of an action. Leadership is enabling when it brings people into "continuing and unrepressed communication about existent school conditions and possibilities for change" (Foster, 1986, p. 167). In CEP and throughout the development of PROTEACH, enabling leadership has promoted faculty dialogue about the purposes and practices of teacher education. This leadership has not resided in an individual, but has occurred when individuals and groups have facilitated communication about program issues. What is important about these "leadership acts" (Foster, 1986) is that they promote communal examination of the program, the raising of questions, and the consideration of solutions.

Norms of Collaboration and Continuous Improvement

Linked to enabling leadership are norms of collaboration and continuous improvement. Although in the 1970s faculty were divided along ideological lines, the college-wide restructuring effort forced cross-departmental groups to work together to complete specified tasks. The intense discussions, though stressful, forged alliances and brought more faculty into the collaborative network. Through open communication, the faculty have built some coalitions among subject-area specialists, a feat that Lanier (1984) has described as "rarely . . . possible, since the various actors share little mutual interest and trust" (p. 2). Community dialogue has rallied some specialists around the common interest of teacher education. Evidence that the norm of collaboration is in place is found in the recent efforts of cross-departmental groups of faculty to design and implement inclusive teacher education programs in early childhood and elementary education that give more sustained attention to issues of diversity.

The norm of continuous improvement or self-study has been in place for many years. The results of a study of students' experiences in CEP led many faculty to consider the need for substantial restructuring of that program. The Becoming Teachers grant launched a number of studies by PROTEACH faculty (see Ross et al., 1992). The annual conference for program graduates also contributes to the ongoing self-study effort because the graduates provide feedback about their teaching experiences that has implications for program reform. Self-study keeps the faculty alert to the details of the program and to students' experiences. We actively monitor the program, identify problems, take steps to cope with problems, and monitor the results of our coping efforts.

Fullan and Miles (1992) argue that this kind of self-examination is essential to successful change.

Norms of collaboration and continuous improvement have been fueled by structures such as team teaching and the elementary faculty group meetings that engage faculty in the collective analysis of PROTEACH. Another supportive force was the Becoming Teachers grant, which required the faculty to develop a program evaluation plan and report the findings.

Expectations of a Research Institution

The faculty, particularly untenured junior faculty, are acutely aware of the expectations for them to conduct, present, and publish research. Doing research quickly becomes part of one's professional identity, and faculty begin to see fascinating research questions around every corner. The expectation for doing research keeps us asking questions, collecting data, sharing findings internally, and venturing out into the larger community of teacher education researchers to get feedback on our work.

Shared Decision Making

Berman and McLaughlin (1974, 1978) identified teachers' participation in decision making as a facilitator of school change. Perhaps this is because shared decision making helps teachers "feel . . . that they own and are in control of the problem of change" (Ruddick, 1991, p. 31). During the three years in which PROTEACH was planned, faculty did not see themselves as controlling the direction of the changes. However, when the shell of the program was turned over to the entire faculty to develop the details, control of the program moved into their hands. Through intensive, ongoing, and shared decision making, the faculty created "local meaning" (Ruddick, 1991) for an abstract program shell.

Shared decision making reinforces a faculty's belief that they are responsible for a program. Fullan (1991) argues that for continuous renewal to occur, "individuals . . . cannot wait for or take as sufficient the actions or policy decisions of others" (p. 353). Instead, he said, "we must first count on ourselves, but do so through constant interaction with others in order to broaden the range of ideas and influence" (p. 352).

Because of the early PROTEACH task force committees, the brown-bag lunches, teaching teams, and the faculty study group, the faculty have had many opportunities for sustained, intense discussion. According to Fullan (1991), "we cannot develop institutions without developing the people in them" (p. 349). At the heart of all of the factors that have influenced the evolution of PROTEACH is the development and stimulation of the faculty.

NOTE

1. When we talk about faculty beliefs and actions, we obviously are not speaking about *all* faculty. Our faculty are diverse and hold many, and often conflicting, beliefs about appropriate purposes and processes for teacher education. However, over time faculty have become more unified in their perspectives. Our program clearly is not coherent and consistent, but we are constantly moving in the direction of greater coherence and consistency. In this chapter, when we speak of "faculty" we are using the term generically and are describing the direction in which most faculty are moving.

REFERENCES

Berman, P., & McLaughlin, M. W. (1974). *A model of educational change*. Rand Change Agent Study, Vol. 1. Santa Monica, CA: Rand Corporation.

Berman, P., & McLaughlin, M. W. (1978). *Federal programs supporting educational change*, Vol. VIII. Santa Monica, CA: Rand Corporation.

Bullough, R., & Gitlin, A. (1989). Toward educative communities. *Qualitative Studies in Education, 2*(4), 285–298.

Butt, R. L., & Raymond, D. (1989, February). Teacher development using collaborative autobiography. Paper presented at the international/invitational Conference on Teacher Development, Ontario Institute for Studies in Education, Toronto, ON.

Clandinin, D. J. (1986). *Classroom practice: Teacher images in action*. Philadelphia: The Falmer Press.

Combs, A. W., Blume, R. A., Newman, A. J., & Wass, H. L. (1974). *The professional education of teachers*. Boston: Allyn and Bacon.

Conway, J. A. (1990). Organization rites as culture markers of schools. *Urban Education, 25*(2), 195–206.

Deal, T. E. (1987). The culture of schools. In L. T. Sheive & M. B. Schoenheit (Eds.), *Leadership: Examining the elusive* (pp. 3–15). Alexandria, VA: Association for Supervision and Curriculum Development.

Foster, W. (1986). *Paradigms and promises*. Buffalo, NY: Prometheus Books.

Fullan, M. (1991). *The new meaning of educational change*. New York: Teachers College Press.

Fullan, M., & Miles, M. (1992). Getting reform right: What works and what doesn't. *Phi Delta Kappan, 73*(10), 745–752.

Goodman, J. (1988). University culture and the problem of reforming field experiences in teacher education. *Journal of Teacher Education, 39*(5), 45–53.

Goodman, J. H. (1982). *Learning to teach: A study of a humanistic approach* (Doctoral dissertation, University of Wisconsin, 1982). *Dissertation Abstracts International, 43*, 3295.

Lanier, J. (1984). *The future of teacher education: Two papers* (Occasional Paper No. 79). East Lansing: Michigan State University, Institute for Research on Teaching.

Liston, D., & Zeichner, K. (1991). *Teacher education and the social conditions of schooling*. New York: Routledge.

Louis, K. S., & Miles, M. B. (1990). *Improving the urban high school: What works and why*. New York: Teachers College Press.

Owens, R. G. (1987). The leadership of educational clans. In L. T. Sheive & M. B. Schoenheit (Eds.), *Leadership: Examining the elusive* (pp. 16–29). Alexandria, VA: Association for Supervision and Curriculum Development.

Rallis, S. F. (1990). Professional teachers and structured schools: Leadership challenges. In B. Mitchell & L. L. Cunningham (Eds.), *Educational leadership and changing contexts of families, communities, and schools. Eighty-ninth yearbook of the National Society for the Study of Education, Part II* (pp. 184–209). Chicago: National Society for the Study of Education.

Ross, D., Johnson, M., & Smith, W. (1992). Developing a PROfessional TEACHer at the University of Florida. In L. Valli (Ed.), *Case studies and critiques of reflective teacher education programs* (pp. 24–39). Albany: SUNY Press.

Ross, D. D. (1989). First steps in developing a reflective approach to teaching. *Journal of Teacher Education, 40*(2), 22–30.

Ross, D. D., & Bondy, E. (1993, April). *Learning from our students and each other: A story of changes in content and practices in teacher education*. Paper presented at the annual meeting of the American Educational Research Association, Atlanta, GA.

Ross, D. D. & Krogh, S. L. (1988). From paper to program: A story from elementary PROTEACH. *Peabody Journal of Education, 65*(2), 19–34.

Ross, D. D., & Kyle, D. W. (1987). Helping preservice teachers learn to use teacher effectiveness research. *Journal of Teacher Education, 38*, 40–44.

Ross, D. D., & Smith, W. (1992). Understanding preservice teachers' perspectives on diversity. *Journal of Teacher Education, 43*(2), 94–104.

Ruddick, J. (1991). *Innovation and change*. Philadelphia, PA: Open University Press.

Smith, D. C. (1984). PROTEACH: Teacher preparation at the University of Florida. *Teacher Education and Practice, 1*(2), 5–12.

Smith, D. C., Carroll, R. G., & Fry, B. (1984). PROTEACH: Professional teacher preparation at the University of Florida. *Phi Delta Kappan, 66*(2), 134–135.

Tabachnick, B., Popkewitz, T., & Zeichner, K. (1980). Teacher education and the professional perspectives of student teachers. *Interchange, 10*(4), 12–29.

Zeichner, K., & Tabachnick, B. (1981). Are the effects of university teacher education "washed out" by school experience? *Journal of Teacher Education, 32*, 7–11.

CHAPTER 5

Traditional and Alternate Routes to Teacher Certification: Issues, Assumptions, and Misconceptions

Trish Stoddart
Robert Floden

INTRODUCTION

Traditionally, the authority to educate and recommend teachers for credentialing has been vested in colleges, which certify to state credentialing agencies that candidates have successfully completed an approved program of teacher education and met state licensing requirements. Recently, however, states have begun to create routes to teacher certification—so-called alternate routes—that do not involve enrollment in a college-based program. Typically developed and administered by state departments of education or school districts, these alternate-route programs give college graduates a short period of preservice training, then provide continued training and support during their first year on the job. At the end of the training period the state agency or school district recommends the candidate for credentialing. Alternate routes to teacher certification have proliferated in recent years. The number of states allowing such programs more than doubled from 18 in 1986 to 40 in 1992 (Adelman, 1986; Feistritzer, 1985, 1990, 1993).

Alternate-route programs give school districts a choice between hiring teachers with two kinds of qualifications: those with academic and professional credentials and those with academic credentials alone. In almost every state, existing provisions, in the form of emergency credentials, allow school districts to hire unlicensed individuals for a period of years, provided they can demonstrate that no regularly licensed teachers are available (Feistritzer, 1993). Such provisions have been widely used to deal with teacher shortages. The difference in the current situation is that alternate certification laws permit those without college-based teacher preparation to gain a permanent teaching credential. What began as a short-term measure to deal with teacher shortages is now becoming an institutionalized alternative to college-based teacher education.

TWO WORLDS OF TEACHER EDUCATION

Alternate certification, therefore, represents a radical departure from the current norm of teacher preparation in the United States. It eliminates the virtual monopoly of teacher education held by colleges, shifting responsibility for the professional education of teachers to school districts and state education agencies. It is also changing the demographics of the teacher pool by recruiting into the profession individuals who are older and more likely to have worked in other jobs than the traditional teacher education population (Darling-Hammond, Hudson, & Kirby, 1989; Stoddart, 1992). Haberman (1986) has argued that we are seeing the creation of two worlds of teacher education. In one world, the college-based programs are increasingly characterized by higher admission standards, higher SATS, higher GPAS for entering and exiting the programs, extended programs of 5 and even 6 years, and a multiplicity of state mandates regarding specific content and courses that must be included in these programs. In the other world, college graduates (or, as in Texas, anyone with "some" college) can simply find a district to hire them.

These two approaches to teacher education are based on very different assumptions about what is involved in learning to teach. Proponents of alternate-route programs believe that individuals with subject-matter expertise can learn to teach on the job provided they are given some in-service training and support. In contrast, supporters of university-based training believe that becoming a teacher requires several years of preservice professional training and supervised practical experience prior to assuming full-time teaching responsibility. Candidates entering the profession through these different routes go through programs that place different amounts of emphasis on preparation in subject matter, pedagogy, and the role of personal experience in learning to teach. These different routes into teaching, therefore, are likely to produce teachers with different kinds of expertise.

Proponents of both alternate and traditional approaches to teacher preparation argue that they are producing competent teachers, but there is little information currently available on what is involved in learning to teach in any kind of teacher education program and how such outcomes relate to pedagogical knowledge and skill (Feiman-Nemser, 1990). The differences in program content and context apparent in these two approaches to teacher preparation give us an opportunity to examine some of the fundamental questions about learning to teach and the role various factors, including teacher education, play in developing the expert practitioner. In this chapter we examine some of the key assumptions underlying traditional and alternate approaches to teacher education: the difference between knowing your subject and teaching it, the difference between learning to teach on the job and learning to teach under the aegis of a college program, and the influence of prior work and life experiences on becoming a teacher. This analysis of the issues underlying alternate approaches to teacher preparation can inform policymakers, university teacher educators, and state and school district personnel in their efforts to raise standards in teaching.[1]

DEREGULATION OF TEACHER EDUCATION

The movement toward school district–based teacher education followed a decline in the public's confidence that colleges can recruit and adequately prepare enough effective teachers. Critics argued that teacher education programs had little substance and that their lack of rigor and low academic standards actually discourage talented individuals from entering the teaching profession (see Roth, 1986; Sikula & Roth, 1984). From this perspective, college-based programs of teacher preparation are viewed as barriers to raising professional standards in teaching and should be bypassed. Alternate-route programs are designed to provide an alternative means of entry into teaching for individuals who do not wish to take the college route and to offer school districts the freedom to recruit, hire, and train teachers.

Field-based routes to teacher certification are not new. Originally, school districts devised their own systems for training and certifying teachers. In the 19th century, many large urban school districts developed "normal schools" to train their own teachers. These normal schools subsequently became teachers colleges (Haberman, 1986; Lutz & Hutton, 1989). It was not until early in the 20th century that teacher education became primarily the responsibility of higher education. Under the aegis of the teachers colleges, the field-based assessment system was replaced with an institution-based, college-credit system. Throughout this century the trend has been toward formalized college-based preparation for teachers and increased state regulation. This trend continued through the last decade, with several projects and reports such as *Tomorrow's Teachers*, a report of the Holmes Group (1986) consortium of schools and colleges of education, which called for more extended and rigorous college-based teacher education.

The move toward alternate routes represents a countervailing trend. Alternate certification programs move toward less professional education and toward the deregulation of teacher education. This move sets teaching apart from other professions—such as law, medicine, and psychology—where completion of an approved program of professional training from an accredited college is a mandatory prerequisite to professional licensing. Teaching is, for example, moving in the opposite direction from nursing, which is shifting away from on-the-job hospital-based training toward college-based training in nursing with supervised internships. This movement associates teaching more with trades—

such as carpentry, plumbing, electrical work—where on-the-job training in the form of apprenticeships is the norm.

Estimates of the relative merits of these two routes to teaching depend on judgments about what teachers need to know in order to be effective instructors and about where and how they can best acquire that knowledge. Proponents of college-based education argue that teachers need an extended pedagogical education and guided practical experience before they begin teaching. Proponents of alternate certification, in contrast, argue that individuals with a college degree can pick up what they need to teach on the job—and should be allowed to do so.

There is little information currently available, however, on the consequences of these different approaches to teacher preparation. Research from the field of vocational education, which has had alternate certification since 1917, is inconclusive about the effectiveness of teachers without traditional teacher education degrees. Because vocational education teachers vary widely in experience and training, links between preparation and performance have been difficult to discern (Erekson & Barr, 1985). Researchers have found, however, that individuals brought into vocational education through nontraditional routes have abnormally high turnover rates as compared with other subject-matter teachers (Lee, 1978; Nasman, 1979), indicating that alternate certification may not be effective as a recruitment device.

Most recent research comparing alternate and traditional forms of teacher preparation has focused on program requirements and demographic characteristics of teacher candidates, not on the effects of professional training (Adelman, 1986; Darling-Hammond et al., 1989; Feistritzer, 1990; Stoddart, 1992; Stoddart & Floden, 1989). This research indicates that alternate routes can be effective in recruiting a diverse group of individuals to teach in hard-to-staff schools, but does not tell us whether they stay in teaching or what kind of teachers they become.

Despite this lack of information, alternate routes into teaching are proliferating. Two-thirds of the states have already dispensed with the approved program requirement as a prerequisite for professional licensing for teachers; several others have legislation pending (Feistritzer, 1993). These initiatives will institutionalize still untested assumptions about the professional training of teachers: that teachers, unlike other professionals, do not need university-based professional training; that teachers' knowledge and skills develop in simple ways—through knowing their subject, through learning to teach on the job, or by being a "natural teacher."

This move toward deregulation in the professional education of teachers comes at a time when schools of education are making fundamental reforms in the preparation of teachers and when the "cognitive revolution" has led to significant advances in our understanding of the learning and teaching of school subjects. (See, for example, Anderson & Pearson, 1984; Bruner, 1985; Putnam, Lampert, & Peterson, 1990; Resnick, 1986; Shulman, 1986.) The education community stands at a crossroads where the choice lies between investing in an extended professional education for teachers based on an established pedagogical knowledge base and returning to an apprenticeship system.

SOURCES OF PRESSURE FOR CHANGE IN TEACHER EDUCATION

Two factors that have contributed to the current press for change in teacher education are concerns about teacher shortages and worries about the quality of newly entering teachers. Alternate routes are seen as ways of increasing the supply of new teachers. Doubts about the value of teacher education programs have led some to think that doing without college-based professional preparation would do no harm, and might even increase the capacities of those entering teaching.

Teacher Shortages

The impetus to bypass the college route has been increased by continuing and growing teacher shortages (Carnegie Forum on Education and the Economy, 1986; Center for Education Statistics [CES], 1985, 1987). School districts unable to recruit sufficient qualified teachers hire uncertified teachers, assign teachers out-of-field, cancel course offerings, and expand class sizes. Nationwide, large numbers of schoolchildren are receiving inadequate instruction in the fundamental disciplines of mathematics, science, history, and English because there are not enough qualified teachers to instruct them (Council for Basic Education [CBE], 1986; National Center for Education Statistics [NCES], 1990).

The situation is complicated by the fact that teacher shortages tend to be localized in specific subject areas, grade levels, and geographical contexts. The situation in urban education is chronic. Throughout this century there has been a shortage of professionally educated teachers in the major urban areas no matter how many teachers were being prepared nationally (Haberman, 1986). Teacher shortages in high-demand subjects, such as mathematics and science, have been acute for at least two decades (Cagampang & Guthrie, 1988; Darling-Hammond et al., 1989; National Council of Teachers of Mathematics, 1982).

There is little hope of quickly improving this situation through traditional sources of teacher supply. The most common route into teaching has been through an undergraduate teacher certification program. This path has typically been followed by college students who decide as sophomores to become teachers. Those wishing to teach elementary school often major in education; those wishing to teach secondary school major in a subject field and complete a series of prescribed courses in education. The 18- to 21-year-old cohort, which forms the traditional college-age population, is declining, and a smaller proportion of this cohort is entering teacher education. Between 1975 and 1984 the proportion of college students majoring in education declined from 21% to 9% and the number of newly qualified teachers dropped by more than 50%—from 261,000 to 105,000 (Carey, Mittman, & Darling-Hammond, 1988; CES, 1987; NCES, 1990). Universities are not recruiting sufficient teachers from the undergraduate populations to meet current or future demand. Although in recent years there has been an upswing in recruitment into teacher education programs (American Association of Colleges for Teacher Education [AACTE], 1989), the increase may not be sufficient to meet demand. Carey and colleagues (1988) estimated that, in the 1990s, the supply of new teachers from traditional sources may constitute less than two-thirds of the number needed. Whether or not that dire prediction will be fulfilled on an overall basis in the remainder of this decade, shortages will continue in particular geographic and subject-matter areas.

General policies that aim to relieve the teacher shortages by making the teaching profession more attractive (e.g., increases in teachers' salaries, career ladders) are often not effective in recruiting teachers in areas of the greatest need. Raising the beginning teacher salary may encourage a new graduate to train to teach history in a suburban school, but is unlikely to encourage a new math and science graduate to consider a career as a teacher in an inner-city school. The inner cities have, and in the foreseeable future will continue to have, chronic shortages in all fields and at all levels. The typical teacher education graduate prefers to teach in a suburban rather than an urban school (Feistritzer, 1993; Haberman, 1988; Stoddart, 1992). In every state the urban areas rely on uncertified teachers or teachers teaching outside their subject area, whereas neighboring suburbs have up to 500 applicants for each job (Haberman, 1988).

This is a serious problem in itself, and is exacerbated by a decline in the number of minorities entering teaching. The importance of teachers as role models for children has long been recognized, especially when the teacher is a member of the students' own cultural group (Middleton, Mason, Stilwell, & Parker, 1988). Increased opportunities for minorities in more lucrative and higher prestige professions have resulted in a dwindling supply of minority teachers (Darling-Hammond, 1984; Feistritzer, 1985; Post & Woessner, 1987; Smith & Welch, 1986). Projections suggest that minorities will constitute only 5% of the teaching force by the year 2000, while the minority student population will expand to 33% (Smith, 1984). By the year 2020, about 40% of the K–12 population will be students of color (Pallas, Natriello, & McDill, 1989), with little expectation for a parallel increase in teachers of color (see also Banks, 1991; Zeichner, 1993).

Haberman (1990) has argued that different kinds of individuals should be recruited—in particular, older individuals who are likely to have the personal maturity and commitment necessary to work in difficult school environments. If a new population of individuals is to be recruited into teaching, entry into teaching will have to be made more flexible. Proponents of alternate certification argue that teacher certification regulations should be restructured to expand the recruitment population beyond the traditional undergraduate cohort and to make entry into the profession easy for individuals at other ages and stages in their careers.

Early in the 1980s, several national reports included recommendations aimed at attracting outside experts into mathematics and science teaching (Boyer, 1983; National Commission for Excellence in Teacher Education, 1985; National Science Board, 1983). These reports suggested that having qualified scientists and mathematicians assist in developing and delivering instruction would improve school instructional programs. Others have argued that eased entry into teaching should be provided for mature individuals willing to transfer into teaching from other professions. These might include early retirees, including technical experts from the armed services, homemakers who wish to reenter the work force, and bright young graduates of the arts and sciences who are undecided about their career direction and who will devote a few years to teaching (Gray, 1987; Wimpelberg & King, 1983).

Under traditional certification standards, potential teachers in all these groups would have to complete professional education college course work before they could be granted a standard teaching credential and be allowed to assume full-time paid teaching jobs. Proponents of alternate certification believe that most of these individuals will be unwilling to take college-based course work or assume the educational costs of becoming a teacher. The requirements of traditional teacher education programs, therefore, are viewed as barriers that prevent qualified individuals from entering the profession. An article in *Newsweek* magazine (Alter, Wingert, & McDaniel, 1989), for example, decries the fact that "right now NASA scientists aren't allowed to go to teach science in the public schools without going back to school" (p. 56). Proponents of alternate certification argue that teacher education requirements should be waived so that any academically qualified individual is allowed to teach.

The Issue of Teacher Quality

Over the past 20 years, concern about the academic quality of individuals entering the teaching profession has grown. Studies conducted from the 1960s through the 1980s showed that teacher education students were among the least academically able of all college students (Carnegie Forum, 1986; Koerner, 1963; Vance & Schlechty, 1982; Weaver, 1979). As a group, undergraduates aspiring to the teaching profession ranked at the bottom of the American College Testing Program (ACT) and Graduate Record Exam (GRE) distributions. Lanier and

Little (1986) concluded that although many talented people become and remain teachers, teachers are underrepresented in the upper quintile of academic talent and overrepresented in the lower quintile.

On the basis of such findings, policymakers tend to blame teacher education programs for failing to recruit academically superior teachers. National reports such as *A Nation at Risk* (National Commission on Excellence in Education, 1983), and *High School* (Boyer, 1983), emphasized the need to recruit more academically able teachers. Underlying this admonition is the assumption that improving teachers' academic qualifications will improve the quality of teaching. Policymakers may even assume that recruitment of candidates with higher SAT scores is the best route to improving US schools. These reports influenced the climate of opinion regarding the autonomy of college-based teacher education and the relative importance ascribed to subject matter and pedagogy in teacher preparation and certification; they set the stage for the development of alternate certification programs.

Altering Certification Requirements. The first important step in the development of alternate routes was to modify teacher certification procedures by adding a test-performance requirement to the requirement for graduation from an approved program. Policymakers, concerned that the approved program method of teacher certification might be failing to ensure the academic competence of beginning teachers, began to introduce teacher-testing legislation. A university's recommendation for teacher certification was no longer deemed a sufficient guarantee of teacher competence; in order to be granted a teaching credential candidates now also had to pass a subject-matter or basic-skills test. Only a few states required tests of teacher competence in the 1970s. By 1984, all but nine states had such testing in place, were adopting such tests within 3 years, or were at least considering their use (Plisko & Stern, 1985). Acceptable performance on a state teacher test became a required indicator of teachers' competence.

The added test-requirement step was a shift in substance as well as in governance. Adding the test typically shifted the focus of certification from pedagogical competence to general academic competence. Teacher-testing programs often assume a strong relationship between academic quality—as defined by the use of such measures as GPA, test scores, and basic skills—and good teaching. Hyman (1984) summarizes the logic of teacher testing as: "Those who pass the test will be more effective teachers than those who do not" (p. 14). The implications of this assumption are spelled out by Nelson and Wood (1985):

> If prospective teachers are recruited from among the academically best of high school graduates; if they perform well in college courses; if they possess basic skills competency and are educated extensively in their academic disciplines; and if they

are placed in schools under the guidance of master teachers, highly competent teachers will emerge. (p. 46)

The logical extension of this increased emphasis on general academic performance would be to abandon college-based professional training for teachers. If knowing one's subject is a sufficient qualification to begin teaching, passing a subject-matter exam might be a sufficient guarantee of teacher competence. These views are represented in most alternate-route programs, which require individuals to pass tests that demonstrate their competence in basic skills and subject matter; give them an orientation to state or school policies, procedures, and practices; and allow them to begin teaching with support and guidance from a mentor teacher or administrator (Adelman, 1986; Feistritzer, 1990).

Reforming College-based Programs. A different approach to enhancing teacher recruitment as well as teaching quality would be to build on current efforts to improve college-based programs. Not surprisingly, those associated with college-based programs frequently suggest that alternate routes are *not* the option of choice. A position statement issued by the American Association of Colleges for Teacher Education (AACTE, 1986) argues that improving the quality of instruction requires that professional education and certification standards for teachers be strengthened, not diluted. While recognizing the need to increase the teacher supply and diversify the teacher pool, AACTE cautions that certifying large numbers of inadequately prepared teachers could negatively affect the quality of instruction in the public schools for decades.

AACTE (1986) contends that the teacher shortage could be used as an opportunity to improve schools by introducing a new generation of highly skilled professionals. The report points out that college-based teacher education programs have developed a number of successful alternative training models designed for a population different from the usual 18- to 24-year-old undergraduates (e.g., MAT [Master of Arts in Teaching] programs, Experienced Teacher Fellowship Programs, Teacher Corps). Such programs provide alternative training with the same standards and expectations of competence as a traditional teacher education program. They propose that universities (in partnership with school districts) develop alternative training programs that meet the following criteria:

1. Selective admission standards including but not limited to (a) a baccalaureate degree, (b) assessment of subject matter-competence, (c) assessment of personal characteristics, and (d) assessment of communication skills.
2. A curriculum that provides candidates with the knowledge and skills essential to the beginning teacher.

3. A supervised internship in which candidates demonstrate pedagogical competence.
4. An examination that assures competence in the subject field and in professional studies.

AACTE argues that entry into teaching can be made more flexible within the college framework without lowering standards.

AACTE is not the only organization proposing reforms in teacher education. The Holmes Group, for example, is working to implement dramatic reforms in the structure of programs in its member institutions, reforms that may lead to an increase in the quality of teachers completing such programs. The Holmes Group was founded in 1985 by a group of deans concerned about the current state of teacher preparation. It now includes deans and chief academic officers from about 100 research universities across the 50 states, whose institutions have formed a consortium intended to improve teacher education and upgrade the profession of teaching.

Tomorrow's Teachers (Holmes Group, 1986), the group's first report, contains proposals that respond to most of the criticisms of teacher education discussed above. To improve the academic quality of teacher candidates, the group has called for the design of more coherent undergraduate majors and greater emphasis on subject-matter preparation for teachers. Since publication of the report, colleges of education in many Holmes Group institutions have been working with liberal arts and science departments to improve the academic preparation of teachers. For example, at Michigan State University, education faculty collaborated with faculty in the Department of Mathematics in the development of a sequence of three mathematics courses required for all prospective elementary teachers (Schram, Wilcox, Lanier, & Lappan, 1988). To facilitate better articulation between subject matter, pedagogy, and practice in the training of teachers many universities are collaborating with school districts in setting up Professional Development Schools, analogous to teaching hospitals, as sites for the demonstration of exemplary practice (Holmes Group, 1990; Stoddart, 1993a).

Advances have also been made in establishing a professional knowledge base for teaching. The cognitive revolution has led to significant advances in understanding the acquisition of knowledge in content areas such as mathematics, reading, writing, and science. These advances have been used to develop more effective instructional practices (see, for example, Anderson & Pearson, 1984; Resnick, 1986; Resnick & Ford, 1981; Schoenfeld, 1987). This work has stimulated research by Shulman and his colleagues, in a project funded by the Carnegie Task Force on Teaching as a Profession, which focused on the development of teachers' subject-specific pedagogical understandings (see, for example, Grossman, 1988; Grossman, Wilson, & Shulman, 1989; Shulman, 1986,

1987a, 1987b; Wilson, Shulman, & Richert, 1987; Wilson & Wineburg, 1988). This pedagogical content knowledge underlies the ability of effective teachers to develop instruction that is responsive both to the structure of the subject matter and to the developmental and learning needs of individual students. In an organizational position statement, AACTE (1986) has argued that this new knowledge about learners and teachers can form the basis for the education and building of a teacher force of highly skilled professionals. Building on the work of Shulman and others, the National Board for Professional Teaching Standards is developing examinations that will certify advanced competence of teachers in particular grade levels and subject areas (National Board for Professional Teaching Standards, 1990).

MISCONCEPTIONS ABOUT ALTERNATE ROUTES

The development of alternate routes to teacher certification is often portrayed as a move to eliminate the professional education of teachers. The public discussions about alternate routes to teacher certification often give the impression of a single basic model, which dispenses with all "professional" course work (e.g., teaching methods, educational psychology, social foundations). This impression is wrong. Alternate routes take a variety of purposes and forms, but usually include some professional course work or its equivalent (Stoddart, 1992). The choice between a traditional program and an alternate route is not a choice between some professional preparation and no such preparation, but a decision about the timing and institutional context for teacher preparation, and about the mix of professional knowledge and skills to be acquired.

Even a cursory examination of alternate certification programs would show that they vary widely in purpose, content, and structure (Darling-Hammond, 1992; Zumwalt, 1991). Programs have been developed in a variety of policy contexts and by different agencies—school districts, state departments of education, state legislatures, and universities (Bliss, 1992; Natriello & Zumwalt, 1993; Stoddart, 1992; Zumwalt, 1991). Because the development of the various alternate-route programs has been driven by differing policy considerations (Zumwalt, 1991), the purpose of alternate-route programs varies. For example, the California and Texas programs were driven by the urgent need to recruit teachers to meet the demands of urban multicultural school districts (Lutz & Hutton, 1989; Stoddart & Floden, 1989). The Connecticut program, on the other hand, focused on improving the quality of the teaching force and was developed in a state with a teacher surplus (Bliss, 1992).

The content taught in alternate-route programs varies widely in quantity and quality (Feistritzer, 1990). Some programs offer full certification on the basis of transcript and resumé analysis while others require individuals to complete the equivalent of a traditional approved program of teacher preparation.

The role of higher education in the development and implementation of these programs also varies. In New Jersey, the alternate-route program is run almost exclusively by teacher education faculty from local colleges and universities (Zumwalt, 1991). The Connecticut and Texas programs are collaboratively staffed by local school district personnel and university faculty (Bliss, 1992; Lutz & Hutton, 1989). In California, the school district–developed programs are staffed almost exclusively by district employees—both teachers and administrators (Stoddart & Floden, 1989).

A common misconception about alternate routes to certification is that they are not programs of teacher education but shortcuts that allow unqualified individuals to receive a teaching credential. It is widely believed, for example, that teacher candidates in alternate programs receive little or no pedagogical preparation (Gideonse, 1984; Watts, 1986). Most alternate-route programs, however, do provide some form of teacher education (Adelman, 1986). Although such programs vary from state to state, many resemble traditional teacher education programs in content, rigor, and expected outcomes. They depart from traditional preparation by focusing on a different source of trainees, emphasizing somewhat different procedures, and compressing the schedule for preservice training (Smith, Nystrand, Ruch, Gideonse, & Carlson, 1985).

A key difference between alternate and university-based programs is the context and focus of the training. Typically, undergraduate university teacher education programs provide preservice liberal arts subject-matter and professional education at the university site, interspersed with short periods of supervised teaching practice in schools. In contrast, alternate certification programs provide in-service professional education while candidates are engaged in full-time teaching responsibilities. Alternate certification programs, therefore, generally require fewer hours of formal education course work than are required under regular certification standards but typically require more hours of supervised field experience as a full-time teacher (Darling-Hammond et al., 1989). They focus more on teaching methods and classroom management than on subject matter because candidates are screened for subject-matter competence before admission (Darling-Hammond et al., 1989; Stoddart, 1992).

An emerging pattern in alternate-route training is the model used by the Los Angeles Unified School District (LAUSD) and State of New Jersey programs. In each of these programs, teacher candidates who have completed a baccalaureate degree and demonstrated subject-matter competence in the area in which they seek certification are given a short period of full-time preservice training before they assume full-time teaching responsibilities. They then continue to take professional training courses while they teach. In LAUSD, teacher candidates go through a 15-day program that focuses on the district's policies, practices, and procedures and then take a further 2 years of course work and a week of multicultural education at a district training center (Stoddart, 1992). In New Jersey, teacher candidates spend 20 days working in a classroom with an experienced teacher and gradually assume teaching responsibilities followed by 20 weeks of professional education at a state regional training center (New Jersey State Department of Education, 1984).

Alternate-route programs, therefore, tend to focus on the pragmatic aspects of teaching—what to do tomorrow and how to survive one's first year of teaching—more than on the theoretical or philosophical aspects of teaching and learning (Stoddart & Floden, 1989). This practical emphasis is supported by the important role ascribed to practicing teachers in the education and induction of alternate-route candidates. In programs such as the LAUSD District Intern Program, courses are taught by practicing teachers and administrators who provide practical examples of instruction and classroom management drawn from their own experience (Stoddart, 1992). Most alternate-route programs provide mentor teachers to support and guide candidates in their first year of teaching. Such mentors help teacher candidates negotiate with the school system and provide feedback on instructional practice (Feiman-Nemser & Parker, 1990, 1992).

This difference in emphasis is also apparent in the evaluation procedures used in university-based and alternate-route teacher education programs. In most university programs, recommendation for a teaching credential is based on successful completion of university course work—based on academic criteria of written essays and examinations—and positive evaluation from a university supervisor of approximately 10 to 16 weeks of supervised student teaching. In most alternate-route programs, the main criteria for being recommended for a teaching credential is a positive evaluation from the school principal based on one or two years of full-time teaching.

The difference between alternate-route and traditional programs of teacher education, therefore, lies not in the presence or absence of a professional training program but in the content and focus of such programs, which are based on different assumptions about what it means to learn to teach.

THE ASSUMPTIONS UNDERLYING REFORM DIRECTIONS

Those in favor of each of the two competing efforts to reform teacher education—alternate certification and reform of college-based programs—make different assumptions about what knowledge teachers need. Supporters of alternate routes assume that anyone with subject-matter expertise and some support can begin teaching without professional education. In contrast, defenders of college-based teacher education programs assume that becoming a teacher requires subject-matter knowledge, professional education, and guided practice prior to assuming full classroom responsibility. Supporters of alternate routes assume that individuals can develop a full range of professional practices by learning to teach within the specific context and using the curriculum of an individual school district. Supporters of college-based programs of teacher education believe that developing professional expertise requires exposure to a range of theory and research-based curriculum and instructional practices. Finally, proponents of alternate-route programs argue that different groups of people must be recruited into teaching—people who are more mature and have a wide range of life experiences. Proponents of college-based programs assume that sufficient numbers of high-quality teachers can be recruited from the undergraduate college population.

To date, few research or evaluation studies have explored the implications of these assumptions for the professional development of teachers and for the kind of instruction offered in the public schools. Once again, a radical educational reform is being rushed into place without thoughtful research and analysis.

Assumption One: If One Knows a Subject, One Can Teach It

Few would disagree with the assertion that in order to teach effectively, teachers must understand their subject matter. Past efforts to show a relationship between teachers' content knowledge and their teaching have, however, been largely unsuccessful (Ball, 1988a, 1988b). Begle (1979) demonstrates that the number of credits in college math is positively associated with student achievement only 20% of the time, and is actually negatively associated with student achievement 15% of the time. Ball (1988a) shows that teacher candidates with extensive course work in the subject they will teach still have difficulty explaining basic concepts, and that few could give explanations for basic principles and meanings. Such findings raise questions about the relationship between "knowing" one's subject and teaching effectively. Someone who "knows math" may be able to solve problems and do well in math courses, yet not be able to explain concepts to others. Personal knowledge of mathematics may not be the same as knowing how to teach it.

Research in cognitive psychology indicates that in-depth knowledge of subject matter may actually impede effective communication of concepts. As individuals develop expertise in a subject, they develop a "technical shorthand" of concepts and terminology (Chi, Glaser, & Rees, 1982). This technical shorthand is not easily understood by novices. Effective teaching requires the expert to unpack, expand, and simplify personal knowledge. Such pedagogical understandings are not typically acquired with subject-matter expertise but must be developed and viewed as distinct professional knowledge and skills.

Shulman (1987b) describes teaching as an act of pedagogical reasoning:

> As we have come to view teaching, it begins with an act of reason, continues with a process of reasoning, culminates in performances of imparting, eliciting, involving, or enticing, and is then thought about some more until the process can begin again. In the discussion of teaching that follows, we will emphasize teaching as comprehension and reasoning, as transformation and reflection. (p. 13)

He describes pedagogical reasoning as involving a cycle of activities: comprehension, transformation, instruction, evaluation, and reflection. The starting point is comprehension—personal understanding of the concept to be taught—but this is not the end point. Personally understood concepts must be transformed into forms that can be understood by learners. Shulman (1986) calls this pedagogical content knowledge.

University-based teacher education programs assume that pedagogical content knowledge must be developed in a professional program before individuals begin full-time teaching. The assumption underlying alternate-route programs is that teachers' ability to effectively represent and explain content to students can be developed as they teach it.

Assumption Two: One Learns to Teach by Doing It

Proponents of alternate certification argue that formal university-based professional training for teachers is unnecessary in the development of pedagogical expertise, because teaching is a practical skill that is best learned on the job. Lyons (1979) asserts that "since teaching is a pragmatic art best learned by experience, school districts should establish apprenticeship programs for people who can satisfy the literacy requirements and show competence in subject matter" (p. 109). (Some people may not even need the practical experience, because they are "born teachers.") Alternate-route programs, therefore, assume that preservice teacher education courses are unnecessary. Anyone with a baccalaureate degree (to provide a good general education) and grounding in the subject matter to be taught can—with some support—develop teaching expertise through on-the-job training.

What are the consequences of learning to teach by doing it? Recent research on what teachers learn from firsthand classroom experience has shown that it can be miseducative (Feiman-Nemser, 1983; Zeichner, 1986). This research has shown that student teachers and beginning teachers, without proper guidance, often learn lessons from school experience that restrict their ability to explore a variety of instructional practices and undermine teachers' ability to continue to learn from experience over a career (Feiman-Nemser & Buchmann, 1987; Hoffman & Edwards, 1986; cf. Buchmann, 1993). Practical teaching experience, in isolation from professional training, tends to socialize teacher candidates into the prevailing school culture, rather than expanding their awareness of a range of different teaching practices.

By relying on *local* experience, alternate routes may also tend to narrow the range of settings for which teachers are prepared. The state departments of education and the school districts that organize the programs generally aim to educate teachers who can fit in with local policies, curriculum, and instructional practices (Stoddart & Floden, 1989). Typically, programs offer some course work, in the evenings and during the summer, and the support of a mentor teacher. The course work, often taught by local teachers, focuses on implementing the district curriculum and provides practical examples of how to do this (Adelman, 1986; Stoddart & Floden, 1989). Mentor teachers induct teacher candidates into district policy, practices, and procedures and help them function within the system (Feiman-Nemser & Parker, 1992).

College-based teacher education, on the other hand, aims to expand individuals' personal views of pedagogy and to guide students in exploring and questioning a range of instructional approaches. A current trend is to prepare reflective practitioners who critically analyze prevailing instructional practice (Feiman-Nemser, 1990). By helping students to break out of the restrictions of their individual school experience (Floden & Buchmann, 1993), they aim to educate teachers who can take their university-learned pedagogy, teach effectively in any school in any part of the country, and introduce new and innovative practices. College programs, however, place less emphasis on context-specific needs. One consequence of this policy may be the general failure of college programs to produce teachers who are willing to work and capable of working in inner-city schools and with multicultural populations (Haberman, 1986).

Assumption Three: Mature Individuals
with Prior Work Experience Make Better Teachers

One of the key arguments in favor of alternate certification is the need to expand and diversify the teacher pool. The traditional route into teaching has been through an undergraduate major in education. As a consequence, about 80% of teacher candidates are under 25 years of age (Haberman, 1990). The typical teacher education graduates have limited life and work experiences. The majority of their pre-professional lives has been spent in school, and the views they bring to teaching are heavily influenced by their own experiences as students (Lortie, 1975). In addition, the majority of teacher candidates come from rural areas, small towns, or the suburbs (Zimpher & Ashburn, 1992). Limitations in maturity and personal experience may make it difficult for such individuals to relate effectively to a diverse student body. Many preservice teachers have negative attitudes toward individuals who are different from themselves (Law & Lane, 1987). Proponents of alternate certification believe that the teacher pool would be enriched by recruiting individuals with a wider range of life and professional experiences.

There is increasing evidence that personal perspectives, based on prior life experiences, exert a powerful influence on what students learn in teacher education programs and the kind of instruction beginning teachers practice in their classrooms (Britzman, 1986; Bullough, 1989; Connell, 1985; Crow, 1987; Ginsberg & Newman, 1988; Gomez & Stoddart, 1991; Hollingsworth, 1989; Holt-Reynolds, 1992; Knowles & Holt-Reynolds, 1991; Ross, 1987; Zeichner, Tabachnick, & Densmore, 1987). These personal perspectives have been shown to serve as major pedagogical driving forces several years into a teaching career (Crow, 1988). Developers of traditional and alternate routes into teaching differ in their evaluations of the importance of these personal perspectives in learning to teach. In alternate-route programs they seek to build on personal perspectives as sources of knowledge for teaching (Fox, 1984; Gray, 1987). In university-based programs they seek to replace naive views of teaching with a professional pedagogy based on research and theory (AACTE, 1986).

Haberman (1990) has argued for recruiting a greater number of mature individuals into the teaching profession. He believes that college-age students, still in the stages of late adolescence and early adulthood, are not developmentally mature enough to teach in difficult environments. Youth in suburban and urban school districts alike often place incredible demands on the person who would take charge of their learning. To be successful in the job of a teacher an individual must have a strong sense of personal identity, good support systems, and unusually high commitment to the roles and tasks of the job (Wimpelberg & King, 1983).

Citing the work of Erickson (1963), Haberman argues that young adults are self-absorbed, searching for identity—and that it is not until the middle years that a person typically becomes concerned with others beyond his or her immediate family, with future generations, and with the nature of the society and world in which future generations will live. To support his contention he cites Marcia's (1976) studies, which found that only about 20% of college-age students had achieved a strong identity status. The majority were still searching for identity and 24% were in the stage of diffusion, where they had no commitment to anyone, and no commitment to any philosophy or set of beliefs. Haberman (1990) argues that it is unrealistic to expect individuals in this stage of life to be able to identify with and commit to students who come from very different backgrounds from themselves.

It has been suggested that older individuals not only bring greater maturity to the teaching situation but also bring with them the accumulated expertise they have acquired in the work place. They not only know their subject but also know how to use it in the real world. For example, Gray (1987) has argued that we should recruit engineers to teach mathematics or retired technical personnel from the armed forces to teach science. It is assumed that by relating subject-matter knowledge to real-life applications, such individuals will be able to more effectively teach it to students. Individuals with work experience in other fields will also bring with them different views of professional roles and organizational structures. Many traditional teacher education candidates have no institutional experience in organizations other than schools—either as students or as teachers. It may be hard for them to challenge the status quo or conceive of different ways of organizing schools.

The effects of maturity and prior work experience are important issues to explore. Are older individuals more sensitive to issues of multicultural education? Do individuals who have worked in other occupations use more concrete real-life representations of subject matter in their teaching?

CONCLUSION

Learning to teach is a complex process that involves the integration of knowledge, skills, and dispositions shaped by both personal and professional experiences. The diversification of program content and context contained in these different forms of teacher preparation provides a natural laboratory in which to examine some of the key questions about the development of expertise in teaching, and the role various factors, including teacher education, play in developing the expert practitioner. Findings from initial research that compares the outcomes of traditional and alternate routes to teacher certification reveal some clear trends in recruitment patterns but a more confused picture in respect to the development of professional expertise.

Studies of alternate certification programs in California, New Jersey, and Texas demonstrate that the population recruited into such programs differs from the traditional teacher education population on several demographic dimensions (Houston, Marshall, & McDavid, 1993; Natriello & Zumwalt, 1993; Stoddart, 1992). They are older and more likely to be males, from minority groups, and to have transferred from other occupations. They also differ in their prior experience with and dispositions toward teaching in urban schools. The alternate-route teachers have more experience living and working in urban environments, and are more interested in working in the inner cities (Feistritzer, 1993; Stoddart, 1992).

Alternative routes to teacher certification are making a significant contribution to the recruitment of teachers for urban schools. Between 1986 and 1991, over 10,000 new teachers were recruited through alternate routes in nine states in the Southern Regional Board—Alabama, Florida, Georgia, Maryland, Mississippi, North Carolina, South Carolina, Texas, and Virginia (Corbin, 1991). In 1989–1990, Texas alone enrolled 1,064 new teachers in its alternative route program (Texas Education Agency, 1990). Between 1984 and 1990, the Los Angeles Unified School District recruited 1,100 new teachers through the alternate-route program, many of these in the high-need recruitment areas of math, science, and bilingual education (Stoddart, 1992).

Such routes also attract a significant number of minorities into teaching. In Texas, the alternative route to teacher certification is viewed as a primary means of attracting minority professionals into the classroom: In 1989–1990, approximately 50% of the interns were from minority groups and 30% were males (Texas Education Agency, 1990)—this in a Texas teaching force that is 22% male and 22% minority. Over the 6 years from the LAUSD alternate-route program's inception until 1990, one-third of the teachers recruited have been from minority groups. Alternative-route candidates are also more likely to hold high expectations for low-income and minority students than are the college-based teacher candidates (Stoddart, 1992).

The findings of research on the development of professional expertise, however, are not so clear. Researchers from the National Center for Research on Teacher Education found both similarities and differences when they compared the development of pedagogical knowledge and skill in Los Angeles Unified School District alternate-route interns with three groups of university-educated secondary math and English teachers (Ball & Wilson, 1990; Gomez & Stoddart, 1991; Stoddart, 1991, 1993b).

Ball and Wilson (1990), in a study that compared university-educated and alternate-route secondary mathematics teachers, found little difference in the mathematical knowledge or instructional practices between the groups. Both groups of teachers could competently solve mathematical problems for themselves—they knew the correct rules and procedures—but had difficulty explaining the underlying mathematical meaning of the concepts. The majority of teachers in both groups believed that effective teaching involved showing and telling students how to solve mathematical problems and giving them practice. They had difficulty generating concrete examples or activities that would enable students to construct mathematical understanding. These ideas about effective teaching were manifested in their teaching practices (Stoddart, 1991). The majority of novice teachers in both groups used traditional didactic instructional methods in their classrooms—teacher lecture and demonstration of problem solutions on the blackboard followed by individual student work on problems from the textbook with feedback from the teacher. Ball and Wilson (1990) argue that neither group of teachers is being prepared to teach mathematics in a way that will adequately develop students' conceptual understanding. Both the traditional and the alternate routes to teacher education produce teachers who focus on drilling algorithms into students.

In contrast, Gomez and Stoddart (1991) found significant differences in the pedagogical knowledge and instructional practices for teaching writing between novice secondary English alternate and traditional teachers. Both groups of teachers came to teacher preparation with extensive subject-matter preparation—all the candidates had completed a baccalaureate degree with an English major, with a GPA of 3.0 or more—and there were no significant differences in their content knowledge. The university-educated English teachers, however, were significantly more knowledgeable about specific approaches to teaching writing. They had gone through a teacher education program that emphasized the "process" approach to teaching writing, in which students are viewed as "authors" who own the text they are producing and who learn to improve their writing through the processes of drafting, revising, and publishing. The university-educated teachers were extremely knowledgeable about this approach and as part of their professional program had developed an extensive curriculum resource file to draw on in their teaching practice. In contrast, the alternate-route teachers had developed restricted and highly idiosyncratic approaches to instruction that tended to be based on their own learning and life and work experiences.

These findings are supported by Stoddart's (1991) case studies of alternate-route teachers. She also found that novice teachers' prior life and work experiences and the subjects they taught were the dominant influences on their developing professional practice. While the English teachers in these studies developed highly creative approaches to instruction, and the mathematics teachers used standardized didactic models, both approaches were essentially unidimensional. These teachers are "singers with only one song"—they developed a modal approach to practice that they applied and misapplied, with little opportunity to reflect on and critically analyze the consequence of their teaching actions (p. 278).

These case studies of individual teachers are consistent with the conclusion that teachers in alternate routes typically learn how to function in their local context, but do not learn skills designed to be used in varied settings. The studies of mathematics teachers also show that university-based preparation provides no guarantee that teachers will learn what is needed to teach all students in ways that promote understanding.

The interest in alternate routes has grown out of dissatisfaction with the system in place for recruiting and preparing teachers. That dissatisfaction is based on problems that are documented in studies of teachers from all methods of preparation: problems of recruiting teachers to work in areas of continuing need, and problems of helping teachers learn what they need to know to teach subject matter to diverse learners.

The initial years of experience with alternate routes indicate that these routes can get teachers into hard-to-staff schools and help them learn enough to remain there, a least for a while. Alternate routes can provide some support in learning to manage, which is especially needed in some schools. But this emphasis on management is a limited virtue. Throughout this century, higher education has been criticized for failing to help teachers learn to go beyond order and discipline to promote meaningful learning (Dewey, 1904/1965; Feiman-Nemser & Floden, 1986; Fuller & Bown, 1975; Hoy & Rees, 1977). Current alternate routes are not well positioned to prepare teachers for the "break-the-mold" schools some policymakers are currently seeking to create.

College-based programs may be better at providing visions of the possible, but current programs still often do not provide the continuing support or models that would help teachers learn to teach in ways that will enable students to attain the more challenging standards currently being developed at state and national levels.

Both traditional and alternate routes to teacher preparation are in need of improvement. Current alternate routes do not seem to significantly improve teacher learning, but they also may be no worse than many college-based programs. To achieve new goals for increased subject-matter understanding for all students, teachers will have to learn much that they have not previously been asked to know—about the subjects and students they teach, about the connections between schools and other parts of society, and about teachers' own learning. The improvement of teacher preparation will probably require closer work between school sites and colleges, without giving up what either has to offer.

NOTE

1. Work on this chapter was conducted as part of the Teacher Education and Learning to Teaching study of the National Center for Research on Teacher Learning (NCRTL), College of Education, Michigan State University. NCRTL is funded primarily by the Office of Educational Research and Improvement, U.S. Department of Education (OERI/ED). The opinions expressed herein do not necessarily reflect the position or policy of OERI/ED, and no official endorsement by OERI/ED should be inferred.

REFERENCES

Adelman, N. E. (1986). *An exploratory study of teacher alternative certification and re-training programs*. Washington, DC: Policy Studies Associates, Inc.

Alter, J., Wingert, P., & McDaniel, A. (1989, October 2). A Summit for Schools. *Newsweek*, pp. 56, 58.

American Association of Colleges for Teacher Education. (1986). Alternative certification: A position statement of AACTE. *Journal of Teacher Education, 36*(3), 24.

American Association of Colleges for Teacher Education. (1989). *Rate III teaching teachers: Facts and figures.* Washington, DC: Author.

Anderson, R. C., & Pearson, P. D. (1984). A schema-theoretical view of basic processes in reading comprehension. In P. D. Pearson, R. Barr, M. L. Kamil, & P. Mosenthal (Eds.), *Handbook of reading research* (pp. 255–291). New York: Longman.

Ball, D. L. (1988a). *Knowledge and researching in mathematical pedagogy: Examining what prospective teachers bring to teacher education.* Unpublished doctoral dissertation, Michigan State University: East Lansing.

Ball, D. L. (1988b). Unlearning to teach mathematics. *For the Learning of Mathematics, 8*(1), 40–48.

Ball, D. L., & Wilson, S. (1990, April). *Becoming a mathematics teacher through college-based and alternate routes: The relationship between knowing your subject and learning to teach it.* Paper presented at the annual meeting of the American Educational Research Association, Boston.

Banks, J. (1991). Teaching multicultural literacy to teachers. *Teaching Education, 4*(1), 135–144.

Begle, E. G. (1979). Critical variables in mathematics education! *Findings from a survey of empirical literature.* Washington, DC: Mathematics Association of America and the National Council of Teachers of Mathematics.

Bliss, T. (1992). Alternate certification in Connecticut: Reshaping the profession. *Peabody Journal of Education, 67*(3), 35–54.

Boyer, E. (1983). *High school: A report on secondary education in America.* New York: Harper and Row.

Britzman, D. (1986). Cultural myths in the making of a teacher: Biography and social structure in teacher education. *Harvard Educational Review, 56,* 442–472.

Bruner, T. (1985). Models of the learner. *Educational Researcher, 14*(6), 5–7.

Buchmann, M. (1993). Making new or making do: An inconclusive argument about teaching. In M. Buchmann & R. E. Floden (Eds.), *Detachment and concern: Conversations in the philosophy of teaching and teacher education* (pp. 50–65). New York: Teachers College Press.

Bullough, R. V., Jr. (1989). *First year teacher: A case study.* New York: Teachers College Press.

Cagampang, S., & Guthrie, J. W. (1988). *Math, science and foreign language instruction in California: Recent changes and prospective trends.* Berkeley, CA: PACE.

Carey, N. B., Mittman, B. S., & Darling-Hammond, L. (1988). *Recruiting mathematics and science teachers through non-traditional programs.* Santa Monica, CA: RAND Corporation.

Carnegie Forum on Education and the Economy's Task Force on Teaching as a Profession. (1986). *A nation prepared: Teachers for the 21st century.* New York: Carnegie Corporation.

Cazden, C. B., & Mehan, H. (1989). Principles from sociology and anthropology: Context, code, classroom and culture. In M. C. Reynolds (Ed.), *Knowledge base for the beginning teacher* (pp. 47–57). New York: Pergamon.

Center for Education Statistics. (1985). *Projections of education statistics to 1992–93.* Washington, DC: U.S. Department of Education.

Center for Education Statistics. (1987). *Digest of education statistics.* Washington, DC: U.S. Department of Education.

Chi, M. T., Glaser, R., & Rees, E. (1982). Expertise in problem solving. In R. J. Sternberg (Ed.), *Advances in the psychology of human intelligence* (pp. 7–75). Hillsdale, NJ: Erlbaum.

Connell, R. W. (1985). *Teachers' work.* Sydney, Australia: Allen and Unwin.

Corbin, W. (1991). *Facts and figures for South Carolina's critical needs certification program.* Rock Hill, SC: Winthrop College.

Council for Basic Education. (1986, February). The widespread abuse of out-of-field teaching. *Education Digest,* pp. 36–39.

Crow, N. (1987, April). *Preservice teacher's biography: A case study.* Paper presented at the annual meeting of the American Educational Research Association, Washington, DC.

Crow, N. (1988). *A longitudinal study of teacher socialization: A case study.* Paper presented at the annual meeting of the American Educational Research Association, New Orleans.

Darling-Hammond, L. (1984). *Beyond the commission reports: The coming crisis in teaching.* Santa Monica, CA: Rand Corporation.

Darling-Hammond, L. (1992). Teaching and knowledge: Policy issues posed by alternate certification for teachers. *Peabody Journal of Education, 67*(3), 123–154.

Darling-Hammond, L., Hudson, L., & Kirby, S. (1989). *Redesigning teacher education: Opening the door for new recruits to science and mathematics teaching.* Santa Monica, CA: Rand Corporation.

Dewey, J. (1965). The relation of theory to practice in education. In M. L. Borrowman (Ed.), *Teacher education in America: A documentary history* (pp. 140–171). New York: Teachers College Press. (Original work published 1904)

Erekson, T. L., & Barr, L. (1985). Alternative credentialing: Lessons from vocational education. *Journal of Teacher Education, 36*(3), 2–12.

Erickson, E. (1963). *Childhood and society.* New York: Norton.

Feiman-Nemser, S. (1983). Learning to teach. In L. Shulman and G. Sykes (Eds.), *Handbook of teaching and policy* (pp. 150–170). New York: Longman.

Feiman-Nemser, S. (1990). Teacher preparation: Structural and conceptual alternatives. In W. R. Houston (Ed.), *Handbook of research on teacher education* (pp. 212–233). New York: Macmillan.

Feiman-Nemser, S., & Buchmann, M. (1987). When is student teaching teacher education? *Teaching and Teacher Education, 3,* 255–273.

Feiman-Nemser, S., & Floden, R. E. (1986). The cultures of teaching. In M. Wittrock (Ed.), *Handbook of research on teaching* (3rd ed., pp. 505–526). New York: Macmillan.

Feiman-Nemser, S., & Parker, M. B. (1990). Making subject matter part of the conversation in learning to teach. *Journal of Teacher Education, 41*(3), 32–43.

Feiman-Nemser, S., & Parker, M. B. (1992). *Los Angeles mentors: Local guides or educational companions* (Report No. NCRTL-RR-92–10). East Lansing MI: National Center for Research on Teacher Learning.

Feistritzer, C. E. (1985). *The condition of teaching: A state by state analysis.* Princeton, NJ: The Carnegie Foundation for the Advancement of Teaching.

Feistritzer, C. E. (1990). *Alternative certification: A state-by-state analysis 1990.* Washington, DC: National Center for Education Information.

Feistritzer, C. E. (1993). National overview of alternative teacher certification. *Education and Urban Society, 26*(1), 18–28.

Floden, R. E., & Buchmann, M. (1993). Breaking with everyday experience for guided adventures in learning. In M. Buchmann & R. E. Floden (Eds.), *Detachment and concern: Conversations in the philosophy of teaching and teacher education* (pp. 34–49). New York: Teachers College Press.

Fox, J. N. (1984). Restructuring the teacher workforce to attract the best and brightest. *Journal of Education Finance, 10,* 214–237.

Fuller, F. F., & Bown, O. (1975). Becoming a teacher. In K. Ryan (Ed.), *Teacher Education* (74th yearbook of the National Society for the Study of Education, Part 2, pp. 25–52). Chicago: University of Chicago Press.

Gideonse, H. D. (1984). State education policy in transition: Teacher Education. *Phi Delta Kappan, 66,* 205–208.

Ginsberg, M., & Newman, K. (1988). Social inequalities, schooling and teacher education. *Journal of Teacher Education, 26,* 49–54.

Gomez, M. L., & Stoddart, T. (1991). Learning to teach writing: The balancing of personal and professional perspectives. In R. Clift & C. Evertson (Eds.), *Focal points: Qualitative inquiries into teaching* (pp. 39–64). Washington, DC: American Educational Research Association.

Gray, B. P. (1987, March/April). Let scientists teach in the science classroom. *Curriculum Review, 4,* 32–33.

Grossman, P. L. (1988). *Sources of pedagogical content knowledge in English.* Unpublished doctoral dissertation. Stanford University.

Grossman, P. L., Wilson, S. M., & Shulman, L. S. (1989). Teachers of substance: The subject matter knowledge of teachers. In M. Reynolds (Ed.), *The knowledge base for the beginning teacher* (pp. 23–36). New York: Pergamon.

Haberman, M. (1986). Alternative teacher certification programs. *Action in Teacher Education, 8*(2), 13–18.

Haberman, M. (1988). Proposals for recruiting minority teachers: Promising practices and attractive detours. *Journal of Teacher Education, 39*(4), 38–44.

Haberman, M. (1990). The rationale for training adults as teachers. In C. Sleeter (Ed.), *Empowerment through multicultural education* (pp. 275–286). Buffalo: SUNY Press.

Hoffman, J., & Edwards, S. (Eds.) (1986). *Clinical teacher education: Reform and reality.* Austin: University of Texas.

Hollingsworth, S. (1989). Prior beliefs and cognitive change in learning to teach. *American Educational Research Journal, 26,* 160–189.

Holmes Group. (1986). *Tomorrow's teachers: A report of the Holmes Group.* East Lansing, MI: Author.

Holmes Group. (1990). *Tomorrow's schools: Principles for the design of professional development schools.* East Lansing, MI: Author.

Holt-Reynolds, D. (1992). Personal history-based beliefs as relevant prior knowledge in course work. *American Educational Research Journal, 29,* 325–349.

Houston, W. R., Marshall, F., & McDavid, T. (1993). Problems of traditionally prepared and alternatively certified first-year teachers. *Education and Urban Society*, 26(1), 78–89.

Hoy, W. K., & Rees, R. (1977). The bureaucratic socialization of student teachers. *Journal of Teacher Education*, 28(1), 23–26.

Hyman, R. T. (1984). Testing for teacher competence: The logic, the law and the implications. *Journal of Teacher Education*, 35(2), 14–18.

Knowles, J. G., & Holt-Reynolds, D. (1991). Shaping pedagogies through personal histories in preservice teacher education. *Teachers College Record*, 93(1), 87–113.

Koerner, J. (1963). *The miseducation of American teachers*. Baltimore, MD: Penguin Books.

Lanier, J., & Little, J. (1986). Research on teacher education. In M. Wittrock (Ed.), *Handbook of research on teaching* (3rd ed., pp. 527–569). New York: Macmillan.

Law, S. G., & Lane, D. S. (1987). Multicultural acceptance by teacher education students: A survey of attitudes towards 32 ethnic and national groups with 60 years of data. *Journal of Instructional Psychology*, 14, 3–9.

Los Angeles Unified School District. (1986–1987, 1987–1988, 1988–1989, 1989–1990). *Teacher demographics*. Los Angeles: LAUSD Personnel Division.

Lee, J. (1978). *Programs for training vocational teachers in selected areas of teacher shortage*. Mississippi State University, Mississippi State Department of Agricultural Extension Education. (ERIC Document Reproduction Service NO. ED 226217)

Lortie, D. (1975). *School teacher: A sociological study*. Chicago: University of Chicago Press.

Lutz, F. W., & Hutton, J. B. (1989). Alternative teacher certification: Its policy implications for classroom and personnel practice. *Educational Evaluation and Policy Analysis*, 11(3), 237–254.

Lyons, G. (1979, September). Why teachers can't teach. *Texas Monthly*, pp. 122–130.

Marcia, J. (1976). Identity six years later: A follow-up study. *Journal of Youth and Adolescence*, 5, 145–160.

Middleton, E. J., Mason, E. J., Stilwell, W. E., & Parker, W. C. (1988). A model for recruitment and retention of minority students in teacher preparation programs. *Journal of Teacher Education*, 39(1), 14–18.

Nasman, L. (1979). Here's how to fill those vocational education slots. *American School Board Journal*, 66(3), 42–43.

National Board for Professional Teaching Standards. (1990). *Toward high and rigorous standards for the teaching profession* (2nd ed.). Washington, DC: Author.

National Center for Education Statistics. (1990). *New teachers in the market*, 1987 update. Washington, DC: U.S. Department of Education.

National Commission for Excellence in Teacher Education. (1985). *A call for change in teacher education*. Washington, DC: American Association of Colleges of Teacher Education.

National Commission on Excellence in Education. (1983). *A nation at risk*. Washington, DC: U.S. Government Printing Office.

National Council of Teachers of Mathematics. (1982). *Mathematics teacher shortage: The facts*. Reston, VA: National Council of Teachers of Mathematics.

National Science Board Commission on Precollege Education in Mathematics, Science and Technology. (1983). *Educating Americans for the 21st century*. Washington, DC: Author.

Natriello, G., & Zumwalt, K. (1993). New teachers for urban schools? The contribution of the provisional teacher program in New Jersey. *Education and Urban Society, 26*(1), 49–62.

Nelson, B., & Wood, L. (1985). The competency dilemma. *Action in Teacher Education, 7*(1–2), 45–57.

New Jersey State Department of Education. (1984). *Report of the State Commission on Alternative Teacher Certification*. Trenton, NJ: New Jersey State Department of Education.

Pallas, A., Natriello, G., & McDill, E. (1989). The changing nature of the disadvantaged population. *Educational Researcher, 18*(5), 16–22.

Plisko, V. W., & Stern, J. D. (1985). *The condition of education*. Washington, DC: U.S. Department of Education, Office of Educational Research and Improvement, National Center for Educational Statistics.

Post, L. M., & Woessner, M. (1987). Developing a recruitment and retention support system for minority students in teacher education. *Journal of Negro Education, 56*(2), 203–211.

Putnam, R. T., Lampert, M., & Peterson, P. L. (1990). Alternative perspectives on knowing mathematics in elementary schools. *Review of Research in Education, 16*, 57–150.

Resnick, L. B. (1986). The development of mathematical intuition. In M. Perlmuter (Ed.), *Perspectives on intellectual development: The Minnesota symposium on child development* (Vol. 19, pp. 159–194). Hillsdale, NJ: Erlbaum.

Resnick, L., & Ford, W. (1981). *The psychology of mathematics for instruction*. Hillsdale, NJ: Erlbaum.

Ross, E. W. (1987). Teacher perspective development: A study of preservice social studies teachers. *Theory and Research in Social Education, 15*, 225–243.

Roth, R. A. (1986). Emergency certificates, misassignment of teachers, and other dirty little secrets. *Phi Delta Kappan, 67*(10), 725–727.

Schoenfeld, A. H. (1987). Cognitive science and mathematics education: An overview. In A. H. Schoenfeld (Ed.), *Cognitive science and mathematics education* (pp. 1–31). Hillsdale, NJ: Erlbaum.

Schram, P., Wilcox, S., Lanier, P., & Lappan, G. (1988). *Changing mathematical conceptions of preservice teachers: A content and pedagogical intervention* (Research Report 88–4). East Lansing: Michigan State University, National Center for Research on Teacher Education.

Shulman, L. (1986). Those who understand: Knowledge growth in teaching. *Educational Researcher, 15*(2), 4–14.

Shulman, L. S. (1987a). Assessment for teaching: An initiative for the profession. *Phi Delta Kappan, 69*, 38–44.

Shulman, L. S. (1987b). Knowledge and teaching: Foundations of the new reform. *Harvard Educational Review, 57*, 1–22.

Sikula, J. P., & Roth, R. A. (1984). *Teacher preparation and certification: The call for reform* (Phi Delta Kappan Fastback #202). Bloomington, IN: Phi Delta Kappan Educational Foundation.

Smith, A. P. (1984). The critical issue of excellence and equity in competency testing. *Journal of Teacher Education, 35*(2), 6–9.

Smith, D. C., Nystrand, R., Ruch, C., Gideonse, H., & Carlson, K. (1985). Alternative certification: A position statement of AACTE. *Journal of Teacher Education, 36*(3), 24.

Smith, J. P., & Welch, F. R. (1986). *Closing the gap: Forty years of economic progress for blacks.* Santa Monica, CA: Rand Corporation.

Stoddart, T. (1991). Learning to teach English, mathematics and science in an alternative route to teacher certification. *The Curriculum Journal, 2*(3), 259–281.

Stoddart, T. (1992). The Los Angeles Unified School District Intern Program: Recruiting and preparing teachers for an urban context. *Peabody Journal of Education, 67*(3), 84–122.

Stoddart, T. (1993a). The professional development school: Building bridges between cultures. *Educational Policy, 7,* 5–23.

Stoddart, T. (1993b). Who is prepared to teach in urban schools? *Education and Urban Society, 26*(1), 29–48.

Stoddart, T., & Floden, R. E. (1989, March). *School district-based teacher training: An alternative route to teacher certification.* Paper presented at the annual meeting of the American Educational Research Association, San Francisco.

Texas Education Agency. (1990). *Alternative teacher certification in Texas.* Austin: Author.

Vance, V., & Schlechty, P. C. (1982). The distribution of academic ability in the teaching force: Policy implications. *Phi Delta Kappan, 64*(1), 22–27.

Watts, D. (1986). Alternate routes to teacher certification: A dangerous trend. *Action in Teacher Education, 8*(2), 25–29.

Weaver, T. M. (1979). The need for new talent in teaching. *Phi Delta Kappan, 61,* 29–46.

Wilson, S. M., Shulman, L. S., & Richert, A. E. (1987). "150 different ways" of knowing: Representations of knowledge in teaching. In J. Calderhead (Ed.), *Exploring teachers' thinking* (pp. 104–124). Eastbourne, England: Cassell.

Wilson, S. M., & Wineburg, S. S. (1988). Models of wisdom in teaching history. *Phi Delta Kappan, 70,* 90–98.

Wimpelberg, R. K., & King, J. A. (1983). Rethinking teacher recruitment. *Journal of Teacher Education, 34*(1), 5–8.

Zeichner, K. (1986). The practicum as an occasion for learning to teach. *South Pacific Journal of Teacher Education, 14*(2), 11–28.

Zeichner, K. (1993). *Educating teachers for cultural diversity* (NCRTL Special Report). East Lansing MI: National Center for Research on Teacher Learning.

Zeichner, K., Tabachnick, B. R., & Densmore, K. (1987). Individual, instructional, and cultural influences on the development of teachers' craft knowledge. In J. Calderhead (Ed.), *Exploring teachers' thinking* (pp. 1–20). Eastbourne, England: Cassell.

Zimpher, N., & Ashburn, E. (1992). Countering parochialism in teacher candidates. In M. Dilworth (Ed.), *Diversity in teacher education* (pp. 40–62). San Francisco: Jossey-Bass.

Zumwalt, K. (1991). Alternate routes to teaching: Three alternative approaches. *Journal of Teacher Education, 42,* 83–92.

PART II

Preparing Teachers for Cultural Diversity

CHAPTER 6

Prospective Teachers' Perspectives on Teaching "Other People's Children"

Mary Louise Gomez

In this chapter, I depict the perspectives of U.S. preservice teachers—the majority of whom are White, middle-class, heterosexual, and monolingual in English—on diverse students. I show how many prospective teachers think about and act toward "Other people's children"—children who are different from themselves in race, class, sexual orientation, and language background and also different in their motivation and ability to learn. I discuss national reports calling for changes in teacher education with regard to their attention to the teaching of "Other people's children" and review teacher education program efforts at reform for cultural diversity. Finally, I analyze efforts that point the way for further struggles for change.

Two key ideas ground the discussion that follows. I use the idea of *perspectives*—the ordinary ways that people think and act—as a tool to help me analyze how the current cohort group of U.S. teachers consider and behave toward those whom they teach. (See Tabachnick, Zeichner, Densmore, & Hudak, 1983, for discussion of the theoretical roots of the concept of perspective and for discussion of its contemporary usefulness in teacher education.) I employ the phrase *Other people's children* to draw attention to the ways in which many prospective teachers view students unlike themselves in race, class, gender, sexual orientation, or language background as children who are not only different, but deficient learners who are undesirable to teach. For the concept of "other people's children," I am indebted to Grumet (1988), who uses the phrase to heighten our sense of responsibility to teaching all children in the ways that we would teach our own, and to Delpit (1988), who uses it to challenge teachers to acknowledge how their participation in the "culture of power" constrains their understanding and teaching of diverse children.

One Teacher's Dilemma

Yesterday I asked the children in my [first-grade] class what they wanted to learn about when we studied our city. You said that we need to take into account the kids' prior knowledge and interests in our teaching, so I said: "What places would you like to learn about? What buildings would you like to go to in Madison?" And the kids said, "We want to learn about the jail! And we want to go in a police car!" The jail! I sure wasn't prepared for that—I had thought, they'll want to do what I did when I was a kid, go to a fire station, to a bakery, places like that. How can I teach about the jail? We can't go on a field trip there! What would we learn about? What would we do? Where I come from (in the rural midwestern United States), you don't even walk on the same side of the street as the jail; the people in jail aren't people you want kids to see. A jail is no place for kids! There's no way we're gonna study the jail! . . . And now what do I do? (Lucy Jackson, story told in a student teaching seminar, 3/19/92)[1]

Here, prospective teacher Lucy Jackson discloses a dilemma of teaching to her peers. In planning lessons about the community, she had thought about the advice her teacher educators had given—take into account children's interests and prior knowledge—and had looked back to her own childhood for clues as to what children would like to study. But the outcome of her lesson was a surprise. She found that she could not employ her personal experiences as evidence of what her diverse group of students would know about or want to study.

Prospective teachers like Lucy Jackson often turn to stories of the past for clues on how to interpret and how to respond to the contemporary actions of others. They ask: What other cases or stories do I know about and how can I draw on them to help me think about my work? In Lucy's case, she relied on particular personal experiences from her own rural childhood 20 years earlier as directly transferrable to teaching others unlike herself living in another time and place. Lucy Jackson's dilemma highlights a fundamental concern: An increasingly homogeneous population of teachers is instructing an increasingly heterogeneous population of students. The problems this raises for the reform of teacher education are how to select prospective teachers and how to develop campus and classroom experiences for them so that all of our children can be successful in school and outside of school.

PROSPECTIVE TEACHERS IN THE UNITED STATES: WHO ARE THEY AND WHAT ARE THEIR PERSPECTIVES?

Who are U.S. teachers and whom do they teach? There is an undisputed mismatch in racial, social-class, and language background between many teachers and their students in the United States. In 1990, for example, when the K–12 school population of the nation was 40% children of color, nearly 90% of teachers were White (National Center for Education Statistics, 1992). The races of those teaching and those taught will continue to differ in the future as numbers of teachers of color decrease and numbers of school-age children of color increase in the United States (Hodgkinson, 1991).

There are also increasing social-class differences between students and their teachers. In 1989, for example, 15% of White children, 44% of African-American children, and 36% of Latino children lived in poverty and these numbers continue to rise (Children's Defense Fund, 1991, p. 24). Nearly half of all children living in poverty in the United States live in central cities (Children's Defense Fund, 1991, p. 2). In contrast, most U.S. teachers come from lower-middle-class and middle-class homes, and have grown up in rural and suburban areas of the nation (Zimpher, 1989). There are also increasing gaps in language background between U.S. teachers and students. There were 2 million limited-English-proficiency students enrolled in grades K–12 in the United States in 1990. This is a 36% increase from 1986 (Olsen, 1991), yet most teachers continue to be monolingual in English (Zimpher, 1989).

Why is it a problem that representatives of one group—White, middle-class, English-speaking people, most of whom are females—teach everyone's children in the United States? The data presented above show only that teachers and many of their pupils differ from one another. However, when we add to these data findings from large-scale studies commissioned by the American Association of Colleges for Teacher Education (AACTE, 1990; Zimpher, 1989), the Metropolitan Life Insurance Company (Louis Harris & Associates, 1991), and the federally funded National Center for Research on Teacher Education (NCRTE) (Paine, 1989), and a smaller study conducted by Sears (1992), we develop a sharper picture of U.S. prospective teachers.[2] We see how the race, social class, language backgrounds, and sexual orientations of prospective teachers affect their attitudes toward "Others," their willingness to live near and be part of communities with "Others," and to expect that "Others" can learn.

The 1990 AACTE study examined questionnaire responses from 472 prospective teachers (60% White, 40% persons of color) enrolled in the third or fourth year of teacher preparation programs located in 42 AACTE-member institutions. Of the prospective teachers surveyed, over half were elementary education majors, one-quarter were secondary education majors, and 10% were students of early childhood education. Nearly all of the Whites surveyed grew up in White neighborhoods, attended institutions of higher education also mostly populated by Whites, and reported spending most of their time at school with other Whites. Their counterparts who were African-American, Latino, and Asian were more likely to live near, go to school with, and spend time with other people of color—especially those who were members of their racial or ethnic group. English was the native language of nearly all the Whites and African Americans, 50% of the Latinos, and 40% of the Asians surveyed. A majority of the prospective teachers surveyed travelled 100 miles or less from their homes to attend college.

Despite the limitations of their home and school experiences with persons unlike themselves, nearly 100% of African Americans, Latinos, and Asians and over 80% of Whites surveyed felt prepared to work with persons from a cultural background different from their own. But when asked if they preferred a "majority" (White) as opposed to a "minority" or non-White setting in which to teach, 80% of Whites, Blacks, and Latinos and 60% of Asians indicated a preference for a "majority" setting for a teaching assignment.

Zimpher (1989) reported results of an earlier AACTE-sponsored three-phase longitudinal study of teacher education known as RATE (Research About Teacher Education) for which 2,700 prospective elementary and secondary teachers enrolled in 90 institutions preparing teachers were surveyed. Zimpher develops a portrait of a typical teacher candidate from this study: She is White and from a suburban or rural home town; monolingual in English; and selected her college for its proximity to home, its affordability, and its accessibility. She has traveled little beyond her college's 100-mile or less radius from her home and prefers to teach in a community like the one in which she grew up. She hopes to teach middle-income, average (not handicapped nor gifted) children in traditional classroom settings.

The Metropolitan Life Insurance Company commissioned Louis Harris and Associates (1991) to survey 1,007 teachers who in 1991 completed their first year of teaching in the United States. This sample was drawn from public school teachers who graduated from AACTE-member "teaching colleges" in 1990 and taught for the first time in a public school that year (p. 1). Those sampled included teachers of elementary (60%), junior high/middle school (20%), and secondary (20%) school students; 80% were female; over 90% were White. In their initial year of teaching, nearly all of the novices had children of color in their classrooms. Nearly three-quarters of the group taught some children who lived in poverty (pp. 25–26).

Two findings from this study (Louis Harris and Associates, Inc., 1991) are salient for a discussion of the population mismatch of teachers and students. First, over 80% of those sampled strongly agreed with the statement "I can really make a difference in the lives of my students" before they began teaching; 25% fewer strongly agreed after they had taught for one year. Second, half of those sampled strongly agreed with the statement that "many children come to school with so many problems that it's very difficult for them to be good students" before they began to teach; 20% more strongly agreed with this statement after one year of teaching. Blacks and Latinos were as likely as Whites to agree strongly with this statement after one year of teaching. Those new teachers working in inner cities, small towns, and rural areas were more likely to cite influences outside of school as challenging students' ability to learn than were their counterparts teaching in suburbia. Those teachers working with students of color and students from low-income families were also more likely to point to outside-of-school influences as detrimental to students' learning and achievement.

Taken together, these responses from novice teachers indicate that early in their careers, many teachers locate children's problems of learning and achievement not as outcomes of teachers' beliefs about and behaviors toward children in school, but as consequences of children's outside-of-school lives—beyond the purview of teachers, schools, and schooling.

Findings from Goodlad's (1990) study of teacher education in the United States corroborate those from the Metropolitan Life–funded research regarding new teachers' willingness to relinquish responsibility for some children's learning and achievement. Goodlad writes: "The idea of moral imperatives for teachers was virtually a foreign concept and strange in language for most of the future teachers we interviewed. Many were less than convinced that all students can learn. They voiced the view that they should be kind and considerate to all, but they accepted as fact the theory that some simply can't learn" (p. 264).

Paine's (1989) analyses of data from another large-scale study of teachers portray an equally dispiriting picture of prospective teachers' beliefs about "Other people's children." Paine drew on baseline data collected in the National Center for Research on Teacher Education study of teacher education for her examination of prospective teachers' beliefs about diverse "Others." Paine analyzed and categorized the orientations toward diversity of 233 teachers at the beginning of their teacher education programs at the five preservice sites of the NCRTE study (Dartmouth College, Illinois State University, Michigan State University, Norfolk State University, and the University of Florida). This sample of prospective teachers included 174 elementary education majors and 50 English and mathematics major intending to teach in secondary schools (all completed surveys and a 62-person subset was also interviewed about orientations toward teaching diverse students).

Paine (1989) developed four categories of prospective teachers' orientations to diversity: an individual orientation to diversity that draws on psychological and biological explanations for diversity and focuses on how people differ in many ways and on many dimensions; an orientation to categorical difference where patterns of behavior across group members are recognized; and a contextual difference orientation that builds on the first two orientations, but also recognizes that categorical differences are socially constructed and embedded. Paine calls the fourth orientation a pedagogical perspective on diversity, and characterizes it as assuming that "differences are not simply random and interesting; they are understood as having pedagogical implications—consequences for both teaching and learning" (p. 3).

Paine (1989) found that, for the most part, teaching candidates in the NCRTE study were oriented toward students' individual differences (e.g., people are different in size, age, skin color, etc.) and "affirmed the importance of equality in education and rejected certain differences (particularly gender) as important to teachers or as aspects of human diversity that should influence teaching" (p. 5). The teachers identified family background, motivation, student attitudes, and ability as differences that are important for teachers to consider (p. 5) rather than categorical differences (e.g., individuals are categorized by common characteristics, as in race, class, or gender groups). Paine also found that the teachers voiced concerns about equity and justice, but were uncertain about how to operationalize these concerns in the classroom. They often saw diversity as a problem for schools and teachers. Paine writes, "In short, these teachers bring approaches to diversity that have the potential for reproducing inequality and reflect larger social and historical dilemmas" (p. 20).

Sears's findings (1992) concerning the attitudes and feelings of prospective teachers toward gays, lesbians, and bisexuals echo those of Paine concerning their perspectives toward persons differing from themselves in race, socioeconomic status, and language background. The 258 prospective teachers that Sears surveyed and interviewed (in South Carolina) expressed supportive feelings for all students, but Sears believes that their "countervailing expressions of high levels of personal prejudice, ignorance, and fear" (p. 29) about gay, lesbian, and bisexual students make it likely that they will reproduce rather than reform others' treatment of homosexuals.

Sears (1992) found that prospective elementary teachers were more likely to "harbor homophobic feelings and express homo-negative attitudes" (p. 53) than their counterparts preparing to teach in secondary schools. Sears established that those prospective teachers who had a friend who was homosexual in high school or who had received accurate information about homosexuals and homosexuality in a course or workshop had *reduced negative* attitudes and feelings—*not positive* ones—toward gays, lesbians, and bisexuals. Sears concluded that new teachers will probably extend the cloak of invisibility currently shrouding issues of sexuality in schools and, in so doing, become "silent conspirators" in sexual oppression (p. 74).

Summaries and critiques of extant research on teacher education for diversity (Grant & Secada, 1990; Zeichner, 1992) also indicate that the personal characteristics and perspectives of many U.S. teachers can be barriers to the effective instruction of substantial numbers of students. For example, in their summary of research concerning demographic diversity and teacher education, Grant and Secada (1990) point out that young, White, female, suburbanite novice teachers are often assigned to classrooms and schools where their more experienced colleagues do not wish to teach. These are often classrooms populated with children of color and students labeled low-skilled. As the AACTE and Metropolitan Life surveys indicate, these are *not* the children that novices *hoped* to teach. And, as Grant and Secada point out, these are *not* the children that novices were *prepared* by their programs to teach.

In his review of the literature concerning what "teachers need to be like, to know, and to be able to do, to successfully teach ethnic and language minority students," Zeichner (1992) reminds us that little has changed in terms of the population of teachers recruited into teacher education—or the ways in which they are educated once enrolled in programs of preparation—since the 1969 publication of *Teachers for the Real World* (Smith, 1969). In this document (the task force report of the National Institute for Advanced Study of Teaching Disadvantaged Youth), Smith decried the race, class, and gender biases that permeated processes of teacher selection as well as programs of preparation for teachers, and warned that their continuation would reap a bleak harvest for U.S. schoolchildren's learning and achievement.

THE REFORM REPORTS: WHAT IS THE AGENDA?

Nearly two decades after the release of Smith's (1969) report, a number of other calls for the reform of U.S. teacher education and teaching have been issued. For the most part, these reports (AACTE, 1986, 1991; Carnegie Forum on Education and the Economy, 1986; Goodlad, 1990; Holmes Group, 1986, 1990, 1991) locate issues of race, class, gender, and poverty at the margins of their concerns for teacher education.

Early in his text on teacher education reform, Goodlad (1990) cites Edmund Gordon's argument that the United States can no longer focus on educating the few while ignoring the needs of so many learners:

> Edmund Gordon properly stated our challenge: "The national problem posed by a concern with equity is that of making educational and social development, and ultimately, social/political/economic participation and survival, independent of the backgrounds from which differential status group members come." (p. 10)

While Gordon's statement about what school reforms are required is as strong or stronger than that found in most other reform reports, the proposals for the reform of teacher education that Goodlad (1990) presents in subsequent pages have little to say about equity and justice as related to schools, schooling, and teacher education. Of the 19 postulates for reform that he proposes, only one directly focuses on the need to develop teachers who embrace all children's rights and abilities to learn and achieve:

> Postulate Thirteen. Programs for the education of educators must be infused with understanding of and commitment to the moral obligations of teachers to ensure

equitable access to and engagement in the best possible K–12 education for *all* children and youths. (p. 292) (Goodlad's italics)

In a discussion of how teacher educators might respond to such a challenge, Goodlad (1990) acknowledges that past practices of focusing on such issues within single courses are not viable. Rather, his own work with teachers preparing to be school administrators leads him to believe that "carefully prepared case studies [are] necessary, augmented by field observations and by short, student-prepared cases derived from their teaching internships—all accompanied by intensive discussion and relevant reading" (p. 293). Goodlad's work acknowledges the moral imperative of school change for equity and justice, yet says little about how we might act on such a mandate for change.

An AACTE (1991) report, *What College and University Leaders Can Do to Help Change Teacher Education*, echoes a 1986 predecessor issued by the organization's Commission on Excellence in Teacher Education. Both fail to address the need for rethinking teacher education on other than organizational grounds—for example, whether teacher education should adopt a medical education model, in what years of preparation clinical experiences should take place, and so forth. The 1991 AACTE document is essentially a summary of the Goodlad study, yet is remarkable in that it fails to include any of Goodlad's calls for concerns of equity in schooling.

The initial reports of the Carnegie Forum on Education and the Economy (1986) and of the Holmes Group (1986) also lack substantive discourse on and specific proposals for reforming teacher education with regard to effective schooling for diverse student populations. The first Holmes Group report (1986), *Tomorrow's Teachers*, addressed varying facets of the professionalization of teaching, such as the need for differentiated and hierarchical staffing of schools, but none of its five major goals took into account how "intellectually more solid teachers" or more rigorous standards of entry to the profession would change or benefit diverse students' lives. The theme of the Carnegie report (1986) is found in the name of the unit of the Carnegie Corporation sponsoring the report—the Carnegie Forum on Education and the Economy. The emphases of the report are firmly focused on creating schools that can foster a more productive U.S. work force, or in the words of its executive summary, "There is a new consensus [in the United States] on the urgency of making our schools once again the engines of progress, productivity, and prosperity" (p. 2). In this document, the focus is on preparing more knowledgeable teachers in the spirit of an academic tradition of teacher education linked to national industrial and technological prowess. (See Liston and Zeichner, 1991, for a discussion of four traditions of teacher education reform in the United States.)

The three-paragraph section of the Carnegie Forum on Education and the Economy (1986) report devoted to the underclass in U.S. schools concludes that a combination of demographic factors—increases in "permanently unemployed people" and in "poorly educated workers who must be retrained for a technology-based economy" along with a decline in the proportion of the population in "the prime working years"—make it imperative "that those who are able to work make the maximum contribution to the economic well-being of the whole population" (p. 14). Other than calling for the recruitment and education of more "minority" teachers, neither the Holmes Group (1986) report nor that of the Carnegie Forum on Education and the Economy (1986) gives more than lip service to the challenges of preparing teachers to meet the needs of the diverse populations of children enrolled in U.S. schools.

However, more recent reports from the Holmes Group, including *Tomorrow's Schools* (1990), which is focused on conceptions of professional development, and its curriculum committee report (1991), do address the need for teachers to be prepared to meet diverse children's needs. For example, the third of the six principles grounding the *Tomorrow's Schools* report states a goal of working "against the fundamental grain of unequal society, to make teaching and learning for understanding available for everybody's children" (p. 29). Questions concerning the role of schools in creating and perpetuating many children's low achievement, low skills, and bleak economic and social futures are discussed in a section of the report devoted to this principle. Also in this section of the report, teachers are challenged to become "students of their students" and to build on learners' existing cultural capital (p. 11). Absent from the document, however, are discussions of teachers working for change of an unjust social and economic system *with* students or of teachers helping students to become change agents themselves.

Likewise, the curriculum document (Holmes Group, 1991) calls for attention to teaching for diversity in programs of teacher preparation. However, as Delpit (1991) points out in her commentary on the curriculum document in general, two weaknesses stand out: "First, nowhere in the document is there discussed the need to provide students of education a vision of their futures as connected to the futures of the students they teach; and second, I believe the sections are uneven in their attempt to address teaching in our multicultural society" (p. 32).[3]

In fact, both Holmes Group (1986, 1991) documents lack a coordinated vision of how successfully teaching "Other people's children" is tied to all aspects of teacher education—the preparation in liberal arts, professional course work, field experience components, and so forth. The organization of each document exemplifies this point; each is arranged in discrete sections focusing on various aspects of teacher preparation (e.g., reflection and inquiry, curriculum, and leadership). Within each report is one brief section devoted to issues of diversity in teaching; in these are located nearly all commentaries regarding the issues of justice, equity, and diversity covered in the entire set of documents. Further, many of the recommendations within sections of each report are very generally worded. For example, the following statement is located in the section on diversity in the curriculum document: "The issue of school diversity must be attended to in ways that are intellectually sound, programmatically coherent, considerate of the characteristics and requirements in the participants' contexts, and intentional" (1991, p. 25). Specific actions emanating from this or other similar statements in both documents are absent and not easily imagined by readers. The broad and general character of statements in these reports also makes it possible for teacher education program leaders to justify their current practices of teacher preparation rather than reform them.

Given the nature of these reports, equity and justice in schooling for all children become compartmentalized issues to be addressed in discrete portions of reform documents—and, by implication, issues to be addressed piecemeal in discrete components of teacher preparation. As the efforts of the teacher educators discussed in the next sections of this chapter demonstrate, efforts at multicultural education isolated in single courses or field experiences only begin to challenge prospective teachers' beliefs about diverse people; they seldom address the knowledge, skills, and dispositions required to increase diverse children's learning and achievement.

CHALLENGING PROSPECTIVE TEACHERS' PERSPECTIVES ABOUT "OTHERS"

Recently, some researchers and teacher educators (Ahlquist, 1991; Cooper, Beare, & Thorman, 1990; Gomez & Tabachnick, 1991, 1992; Kleinfeld, 1992; Ladson-Billings, 1991; Larke, 1990; Larke, Wiseman, & Bradley, 1990; Murrell, 1992; Noordhoff & Kleinfeld, 1990, 1991) have heeded calls to reappraise the candidates we prepare for teaching and how we do so. They have studied prospective teachers' beliefs about persons unlike themselves and have attempted to modify courses, field experiences, and entire programs of teacher preparation to interrupt, challenge, and change the ways teachers think about themselves and "Others." In these studies of prospective teachers, the researchers looked closely at the views of preservice teachers enrolled in an entire program of teacher education, or in a single course or field experience in which the researchers were also faculty or staff members. The studies were conducted, in part, to better understand the impact of the course, field experience, or programs on their participants and to provide data that would assist program faculty in modifying these to better meet the goals for teacher preparation.

Programs Focused on Diversity

Noordhoff and Kleinfeld (1990, 1991) and Gomez and Tabachnick (1991, 1992) studied the perspectives on teaching diverse students held by preservice teachers enrolled in two different programs of teacher preparation. Each pair of researchers studied the changing perspectives and practices of prospective teachers working across a set of coordinated courses, field experiences, and seminars in a program of teacher education designed for teaching particular populations of learners. Noordhoff and Kleinfeld, co-directors of a teacher education program initially called Teachers for Rural Alaska (at the University of Alaska), studied postbaccalaureate noneducation majors preparing to teach native Alaskan (Eskimo, Indian, and Aleut) peoples in rural secondary schools. In addition to more traditional experiences of teacher preparation like on-campus course work, students in the program are also expected to spend time living and practice teaching in communities of native peoples. The prospective teachers use a three-phase set of classroom and community experiences—"an analyzed apprenticeship"— as well as narratives or cases about teaching in rural Alaska as tools for reflection on what good teaching means for this setting. Noordhoff and Kleinfeld (1990) present the case readings and the field experiences as posing "problems of design" for teaching with the intent that their students will explore "ways of transforming present situations into preferred situations" (p. 167).

Analyses of the changes in the perspectives and practices of the first two cohorts of teachers enrolled in the program show that at its close teachers "began to take more account of a primary facet of the teaching context—their students— in preparing and implementing lessons" (Noordhoff & Kleinfeld, 1990, p. 181). For example, analyses of videotaped teaching samples at the beginning of the program, after the first semester, and at the close of student teaching indicate that more of the teachers took into account "the background knowledge and frame of reference" of their culturally different students at the close of the program than at its beginning (an increase from 28% to 83%). Likewise, the numbers of teachers taking into account students' communication styles rose markedly from the beginning of the program to its close. Noordhoff and Kleinfeld believe that their students initiate shifts in perspective over the year from "seeing instruction as a certain task under their control to viewing teaching as a more uncertain and problematic act that is dependent on contextual factors" (p. 181).

Gomez and Tabachnick (1991, 1992) also used narratives as a means of preparing elementary teachers in the Teachers for Diversity program they co-directed at the University of Wisconsin–Madison. Gomez and Tabachnick asked students in their program to uncover and challenge their perspectives about educating diverse populations of learners by telling one another stories about their teaching, which were then questioned and critiqued by their peers. Students enrolled in the three semesters of professional course work, field experiences, and seminars of the program conducted all field experiences in one of two sets of elementary schools with diverse student bodies—each school enrolls approximately 50% students of color, who, like their White peers, are from varied language, cultural, and socioeconomic backgrounds. Gomez and Tabachnick studied three teachers—Mark, Julia, and Wendy—who were enrolled in the second cohort group of their program.

Mark, Julia, and Wendy are all White, middle-class, heterosexual Midwesterners. Mark and Julia are monolingual in English and Wendy speaks Spanish as well as English. All began their teacher education program with professed positive dispositions toward teaching children of diverse backgrounds, but each had different, particular images of diverse learners and how, as teachers, they might serve these children's needs. The beginning perspectives of each toward diverse children—particularly those of color and those from low-income families—can be characterized as limiting these children's opportunities to learn and achieve in school.

Mark, for example, declared repeatedly in the first semesters of his program that children's skin color—and by implication their culture and background—were not important to him; he aimed to treat all children equally. In the first semester of the program, Julia looked continually for recipe-type solutions to how she should behave with children of color. She complained of confusion when different teacher educators of color whose views she read, or heard on videos or in personal presentations, contradicted one another about the exact role one's culture plays in framing students' learning styles. How was she to teach, she asked, when so-called experts could not agree on effective instructional strategies for African Americans, Asians, and so forth? Wendy experienced a different problem as she struggled to teach an African-American fourth-grader named Nate in her second semester in the program. She puzzled about the roles that she, her cooperating teacher, and the child played in Nate's engagement and learning in school. At first, Wendy saw Nate as the one who must conform to existing school expectations for behavior; later in the year, Wendy began to understand the role she and other teachers had played in constructing Nate as a learner whose behavior interfered with his ability to learn.

Like Noordhoff and Kleinfeld, Gomez and Tabachnick found that changing teachers' perspectives on diverse "Others" is a long and labor-intensive process. They found that only after two or more semesters of carefully coordinated course work, practicums, and seminars did prospective teachers Mark, Julia, and Wendy demonstrate any substantial reconsideration of the ideas about diverse learners with which they had entered the program. Gomez and Tabachnick caution that even in programs expressly designed with a coordinated set of experiences to challenge and/or to enhance prospective teachers' notions about teaching those unlike themselves, such change is difficult to effect.

Individual Courses

Given the concerns of these teacher educators, who are attempting to effect change in preservice teachers' perspectives through a coordinated effort over multiple semesters, it is not surprising that others challenging and studying the perspectives of students enrolled in one or two facets of a program have raised analogous questions about their efforts. For example, Ahlquist (at San Jose State University, California), Ladson-Billings (at Santa Clara University, California), and Beyer (at Knox College, Illinois), have attempted to challenge and to change the perspectives about "Others" of students enrolled in their teacher education courses. They have achieved limited success in their efforts as students often bring to the courses images of "Others"—their accomplishments, needs, and goals—grounded in ignorance, fear, and/or indifference.

Ahlquist (1991), for example, attempted to challenge and interrupt the beliefs about "Others" held by 30 prospective secondary teachers (27 White women, 1 White man, and 2 Mexican-American women) in her Multicultural Foundations of Education course at San Jose State University. Her purpose was to "teach my students to challenge the status quo in the hopes that they, as the teachers of the future, will choose to take a stand in the interests of social justice" (p. 158). Students in the course were curious about multicultural education at the beginning of the course, but soon asserted that sexism and racism no longer existed and that Ahlquist was "utopian and idealistic for advocating cultural diversity" (p. 160).

As the course progressed, the students became more resistant to rethinking their contemporary beliefs about people different from themselves and how one might teach them in ways that were equitable and just. The class then began to focus on whether teachers in general and Ahlquist in particular should take positions on controversial issues; the student consensus was that teachers should remain "objective and neutral" on controversial issues. Simultaneously, Ahlquist became equally resistant to their challenges. The course ended with a stand-off of sorts—both class and teacher were uneasy over the dynamics of their relations. While the prospective teachers left the course acknowledging that racism and sexism continued to operate in the world, they denied responsibility for or engagement in its perpetuation. As Ahlquist (1991) reflects on her experiences in teaching this course, she believes that she may have misunderstood and underestimated the complex dynamics of power and resistance in her classroom. She also believes that she expected too many changes in students' thinking in a brief period of time. "Now I realize that deep understanding of an issue grows out of reflective examination of one's own experience, and true consciousness often comes very slowly" (p. 167).

Ladson-Billings (1991) had goals similar to those of Ahlquist as she investigated the perspectives of preservice elementary teachers enrolled in her undergraduate course Introduction to Teaching in a Multicultural Society at Santa Clara University. Ladson-Billings's desire was to help students "examine critically the ways that culture mediates our ways of knowing the world, the ways that schools structure inequality, and the ways in which they, as prospective teachers, could make a commitment to social justice and social change" (p. 4). Through readings, the viewing of films, class discussion, and a 10-hour field experience in a human service agency (including drop-in shelters, soup kitchens, and child care centers for low-income people), Ladson-Billings attempted to develop in the university students a "critical reflection" or a "critical consciousness" toward societal inequities and injustices. While those enrolled in the course demonstrated new and different understandings of racism and the causes of poverty—as shown in their journals and in class discussions—Ladson-Billings and her colleagues did not find significant differences in the subsequent attitudes and beliefs of preservice elementary teachers who took her course and those who did not.

Beyer's (1991) analyses of how a course he teaches at Knox College affects preservice teachers may provide clues about why Ladson-Billings failed to see large differences between preservice elementary teachers who had taken her course and those who had not. In Beyer's course School and Society, students must engage in community service; each must work 25 hours either in a human service agency or helping out in an individual home. In his assessment of how the course differently affected three preservice teachers, Beyer writes that "an important dimension of this difference involves the previous commitments and consciousness of political, economic, and social issues that students bring with them" (p. 127). He finds that teachers' entering perspectives on diversity and their existing moral commitments play a pivotal role in how they experience and understand the community service in which they engage. In conclusion, Beyer wonders about how moral commitments are formed, how teacher education programs can foster them, and whether, in teacher education, we spend too much time in what he calls "crucial and essential" theoretical analysis and too little time nurturing "the affective, existential quality of moral engagement and commitment" (p. 127).

Field Experiences

Another group of teacher educators have developed field-experience components of programs designed to challenge the perspectives of their students regarding people unlike themselves. Efforts by Murrell (at Alverno College, Wisconsin), Cooper, Beare, and Thorman (at Moorehead State, Minnesota), Mahan (at Indiana University), and Larke and colleagues (at Texas A & M University) differ on a number of dimensions and demonstrate the scope of activity surrounding field experiences as sites for challenging and changing prospective teachers' perspectives.

Murrell (1992) arranges field placements for White, middle-class female teacher candidates in inner-city schools in Milwaukee where their teacher education program is located. In these buildings, the prospective teachers are often in the minority in terms of social class and race. He studied the beliefs about good teaching evidenced by 15 White female prospective teachers enrolled in the seminar that accompanied their 25-hour field placement. Murrell found that once placed in a classroom, prospective teachers accommodate their beliefs to those of their teaching colleagues and to the school culture at large, a phenomenon that works against maintenance of a program-advocated critical stance toward teaching diverse children in an urban setting. His study supports earlier work conducted by Zeichner and Tabachnick (1985) on how novice teachers take from their teacher education programs those ideals most like their own entering beliefs or sharpen their own perspectives via the contrast with those of the program.

While Murrell's location in Milwaukee facilitates the placement of teacher candidates in ethnically, economically, and racially diverse schools, other teacher educators have sought out-of-area placements to provide experiences with diverse learners for their teacher candidates. Cooper, Beare, and Thorman (1990) and Mahan (1982a, 1982b) describe two such efforts. Since 1985, selected prospective teachers enrolled in Moorehead State University have conducted their student teaching in a south Texas community with a prevailing Latino culture. The purpose of this option to the university's traditional student teaching experiences is to "redirect teaching practice from the vantage point of a different cultural setting" (Cooper et al., 1990, p. 2). Once in Texas, student teachers participate in weekly seminars and keep journals of their experiences and observations. Following the student teachers' return to Minnesota, the researchers compared the responses of 18 of the student teachers in one Texas cohort with those of 85 Minnesota student teacher peers via the Self-Assessment in Multicultural Education Instrument (SAME), a Likert-scale instrument. No data on the two groups of teachers' classroom practices were reported, yet results from the survey indicated encouraging differences in the Texas-placed student teachers' attitudes toward the role that race and culture play in classroom interactions and student learning and achievement. A critical component of the power of this particular program to change teacher candidates' perspectives toward "Others" may have been the immersion of the student teachers in a culture in which they themselves became the "Other."

Mahan (1982a, 1982b) reports similar shifts in teachers' perspectives in a program he has directed for two decades at Indiana University; selected prospective teachers leave their White, midwestern campus to become student teachers in one of three sites with populations of people unlike themselves. These student teachers either work with Navajo and Hopi Indians living on reservations, Latinos living in towns on the border of Arizona and Mexico and in the Rio Grande Valley of Texas, or low-income African-American children living in Indianapolis. Prior to leaving for their 16–17 weeks of student teaching, university students enroll in a course focusing on the target cultural group. In addition to traditional expectations for student teaching, all participants must fulfill an additional 15 hours per week of community involvement and service. Those working in Indianapolis and in the Southwest begin their placements with five 40-hour weeks of work in a community service agency serving the people whose children they will teach. Mahan reports that "structured, semester-long field experiences in cultural communities produce a significant positive response from preservice teachers" (1982a, p. 171).

Finally, Larke and colleagues (Larke, 1990; Larke et al., 1990) at Texas A & M University have experimented with a different kind of field experience called the Minority Mentorship Project. This experience is added to more traditional program requirements of practicums and student teaching. Preservice teachers in the elementary education program are paired with an African-American or Latino school-age youngster for a minimum 5-semester period; during this time, they befriend and mentor the child and also attend a one-credit seminar to share and examine their experiences. Pre- and post-test measures obtained via survey of the prospective teachers' attitudes toward persons of color and persons of low income suggest that frequent contact with a culturally different child over a number of months, coupled with opportunities to think and talk about the experience, can influence positively the attitudes of White, middle-class prospective teachers toward "Others."

Changes in teachers' perspectives toward diverse persons as outcomes of the field experiences reviewed here appear to be affected by a variety of factors. These include: the diversity of the student population, the school and community contexts in which the experiences took place, the ongoing support for challenging and changing teacher candidates' perspectives during the field experiences, and the degree of dissonance experienced by teachers as "Others" themselves. Among the most promising practices for challenging and changing preservice teachers' perspectives was their placement in situations where they became the "Other" and were simultaneously engaged in seminars or other ongoing conversations guiding their self-inquiry and reflection.

IMPLICATIONS FOR REFORM

For further clues as to how we might proceed in the reform of teacher education for diversity, I turn to the work by teacher educators reviewed earlier in this chapter. Perhaps the most remarkable outcome of the studies of teacher education courses, field experiences, and programs discussed here is the agreement found among teacher educator authors that their work just begins the critical self-inquiry demanded if prospective teachers are to successfully educate diverse learners. Perhaps their uniformity of response would not be so striking if all of the prospective teachers had, in a sense, unknowingly enrolled in components of programs designed to challenge and change their perspectives, as we are led to believe those taught by Ahlquist, Beyer, Ladson-Billings, or Murrell had done. Yet Noordhoff and Kleinfeld and Gomez and Tabachnick—who educate students competing for limited numbers of places in programs specifically designed for such purposes—also indicate that their students often develop the requisite understandings for successfully teaching diverse students only one-half or two-thirds of the way through their programs, when little time is left to practice implementing them.

Why are the perspectives of prospective teachers so difficult and so slow to alter? And what implication does this have for reform of teacher education? Haberman (1991a, 1991b) highlights the entry point of teacher education—the recruitment and selection processes—as the critical point for reform if we are to achieve different outcomes for teacher education—different commitments, knowledge, and skills in teachers—as well as different results for diverse children—their greater learning and achievement. Haberman makes two arguments. First, he contends that attempting to educate prospective teachers—young people still engaged in the struggle to develop their own identities—lies at the heart of the problem. He dismisses the cohort of young, White, female prospective teachers in the United States as too immature and inexperienced to educate youths facing poverty, racism, and other serious challenges of our world. Haberman argues for the recruitment into teaching of older persons with diverse work and other life experiences as one means of responding to diverse students' unmet classroom needs. Second, he argues that research into how one's values are formed has shown that single course or field experiences in a teacher education program cannot interrupt and change those formed over a lifetime. In particular, Haberman (1991b) maintains that isolated reforms of teacher education programs on campuses and in communities where the majority culture supports distorted images of "Others" are misguided and doomed to failure.

Haberman grounds his arguments regarding the improbability that teacher educators will be able to alter the perspectives of young prospective teachers in a literature concerning the values formation and transformation of college students. Popkewitz (1991) draws similar conclusions regarding the outcomes of such efforts, but he frames the problems differently. Rather than asking how we can alter selection processes or schooling for individual teacher candidates, he asks us to consider how and why we have come to regard grave economic and social problems as being within the scope and responsibility of resolution by individuals. Further, he asks how we have come to regard schoolchildren as the locus of reform and salvation for our nation's woes. Popkewitz questions both the feasibility of teacher educators—working within institutions structured for purposes other than social and economic justice—to solve these problems, and the notion that it is through children that striking societal changes might be effected.

What Can We Do?

I heed the words of both Haberman and Popkewitz in forming the discussion that follows. As a teacher educator engaged in challenging—and attempting to change—the perspectives on "Others" of young, White, monolingual-in-English, heterosexual females from suburbia, I am keenly aware of the difficulties and ironies of the tasks I and my colleagues have set for ourselves. I recognize that it is unlikely that a few semesters in a teacher education program can turn racists or homophobes into teachers who carefully and joyfully educate the children of "Others." I also appreciate the inherent contradictions of participating in an endeavor that focuses its efforts on individual females as change agents in schools where this work contravenes the institution's tacit and explicit purposes, and in a society that devalues the labor of women (who are now and will continue to be the majority of U.S. teachers), particularly when that labor is related to caring for and working with children. Yet, I remain convinced that despite its tensions, the effort to provide a safe, nurturing, and encouraging environment for everyone's children for the 13,000 hours they will spend in school is a worthy one.

Four factors assure me that as teacher educators we will, for some time in the future, continue to educate prospective teachers resembling those in our current cohort. These factors are:

1. The predictions of demographers regarding the characteristics of and numbers of different incoming student populations (see Hodgkinson, 1985, 1991, for discussion of contemporary population trends).

2. The increased pressure from groups within and outside of education for "professionalizing" teaching (e.g., the National Board for Professional Teaching Standards; various state department mandates for selection, credentialing, and licensure) that often result in rejecting or sifting out people unlike those already credentialed.

3. The continuing availability of higher-status, higher-paying positions in professions *outside* of teaching for people of color.

4. The pervasive racism, sexism, and homophobia marking life in the United States that prevents the encouragement and induction of diverse people into teaching.

Given these caveats, I return to the problem at hand: What fruitful options appear likely to challenge and to change the perspective of prospective U.S. teachers, and concomitantly, their classroom practices with and for "Other people's children"? As Haberman (1991a, 1991b) has suggested, the recruitment and selection processes for teaching require reexamination and action. While it appears unlikely that large numbers of diverse persons will enter teaching in the near future, we can, as teacher educators, more carefully select from our existing pool of applicants people with a variety of work and life experiences demonstrating their existing commitment to social and economic justice and equity for "Others." Through interviewing and documenting teacher candidates' prior experiences, and giving greater weight in the selection process to these, we may be able to abbreviate the time required to challenge and alter prospective teachers' perspectives about "Others," and in so doing, maintain more time in teacher education courses and field experiences for crafting excellent, just, and equitable practices of teaching.

Beyond recruitment and selection, questions of teacher education reform lead us to consider what we do and where and when we do it in all facets of a teacher's education. While none of the studies I reviewed here directly spoke to the liberal arts preparation of future teachers, that portion of a teacher's education certainly requires scrutiny if we are to challenge and change candidates' perspectives on "Others." The portrait of our collective history and those who shaped and wrote it presented in the liberal arts can either serve to reinforce the stereotypes and confusion that most prospective teachers bring regarding the contributions of diverse people, or can disrupt and challenge these. Therefore, increased dialogue and collaboration with our colleagues in the arts and sciences is necessary regarding the nature of the courses in which we enroll prospective teachers.

Further, the length, character, and quality of field experiences we require must be examined. As the encouraging work of Larke and her colleagues (1990), Cooper and his colleagues (1990), Mahan (1982a, 1982b), and others shows, positive personal relationships and investments in the lives of "Others" and their futures can occur when prospective teachers are *carefully placed and carefully supervised* in field experiences where they have the opportunity to interact over time and across occasions with people *different* from themselves. (See DeHart's [1992] study of preservice teachers who chose to conduct a field experience in a computer laboratory located in the community center of a low-income African-American neighborhood for further discussion of how preservice teachers' stereotypes of "Others" can be reinforced when they are not challenged to look beyond their surface understandings of events.) The need for both careful placement and careful supervision is highlighted by Beyer (1991) and Ladson-Billings (1991) when they discuss the effects of community-action components in their courses. Clear to both was the tendency for the greatest benefits of these experiences to accrue to those students who came to teacher education predisposed to the reflection-in-action and reflection-on-action required by their courses.

Murrell's (1992) research concerning how mainstream prospective teachers learn to teach in schools with large numbers of "Other" children adds a heretofore missing dimension to this discussion. Murrell found that the perspectives on "Others" as deficient people that preservice teachers brought to their practicum and its accompanying seminar were often reinforced by their cooperating teachers, other teachers, and staff in the schools. As a teacher educator who was also a person of color, he was often a lone, dissonant voice challenging these perspectives in the seminar. Developing relations between programs of teacher education and schools designated as professional development schools may address, in part, the problems Murrell and his students faced in schools where staff members did not necessarily understand or support the intentions and goals of the teacher education program. However, as Winitsky, Stoddart, and O'Keefe (1991) point out, tensions concerning program goals and activities exist between school and university faculties in professional development schools just as they do in traditional teacher education programs. Further, not all professional development school sites are chosen as exemplars of multiculturalism or pedagogical excellence. Rather, some may be chosen as "unfinished schools" where faculties work together to improve children's education and teachers' working conditions, and these also may have problems of program coherence.

Lucy Jackson, the prospective teacher whose words open this chapter, found that her cooperating teacher, and other teachers on the first-grade team in her school, shared her dismay at the children's desires to visit the jail in their community. In an interview one month after she told her story, Lucy commented that her peers in the teacher education program had encouraged her to revisit the topic of going to visit the jail with her first graders and to find out why the children wanted to visit it and what they hoped to learn there. However, lacking encouragement from her cooperating teacher and other teachers on the team, who told her "not to worry, the children will forget that they asked to go to the jail," she did not return to the earlier discussion; instead, she changed the orientation of the lesson.

> We had another kind of brainstorming activity about how they could find out what things were like before they were born and then they talked about pictures and they brought in pictures of the capitol [building] and things like that and looked at them and tried to figure out—it was really interesting because they were looking and they were going "Those trees are so small and there's no cars." And so they made all these lists and they worked in groups to see how much was different between the time of their pictures and now. (Interview, 4/16/92)

So Lucy Jackson and the children studied one community of their city—its public, governmental dimension—and the children enjoyed themselves as they compared one facet of the city in which they now lived with its earlier visage. Yet the purposes that the children had originally invented for the lessons were lost, and Lucy remained puzzled about why they had wished to go to the jail and how she might have used their interests to further the purposes that she had imagined for studying "the community."

CONCLUSION

What do we learn from hearing Lucy Jackson's story, and the stories of teacher educators like Murrell, Ladson-Billings, and others? First, we learn that the problems of educating *all* of *our* children cannot be resolved when we act alone. The reform of teacher education for cultural diversity must take place in partnership with multiple communities within colleges and universities and with our colleagues in public schools, as well as with the various communities from which the children in our schools come. No single activity—reading case studies; conducting community service; living with, tutoring, or practice teaching with people unlike oneself; telling stories of one's teaching; reading about and listening to the stories of "Others"; participating in seminars accompanying practica or student teaching; or being an "Other" oneself—is adequate preparation for teaching "Other people's children." No isolated component, no single course or lone field experience of teacher education, can provide adequate reform. No program of teacher education acting apart from its constituent partners in the college or university and the public school can adequately prepare teachers for classrooms with diverse populations of children. No individual teacher can, working without partners inside and outside of schools, effect the changes our institutions and our society require. To date, no reform report on teacher education nor any teacher education program has adequately addressed the complexity and the urgency of the challenges that lie before us in educating all of our children.

NOTES

1. Lucy Jackson is a pseudonym for a prospective teacher enrolled in an experimental program of teacher education, Teachers for Diversity, that I codirected (1987–1992) with B. Robert Tabachnick at the University of Wisconsin–Madison.

2. Until recently, little information has been gathered by those surveying prospective and novice teachers regarding their perspectives about homosexual and bisexual people. To my knowledge, no questions were asked on any of the large-scale surveys of

teaching candidates reported here regarding prospective teachers' sexuality or their perspectives about the sexual orientations of "Others."

3. Here, Delpit refers to "multicultural education," which holds various meanings for those who use the term. Generally, when these words are used with reference to schooling in the United States, they signal attention to curriculum and instruction that is inclusive of diverse groups of people—for example, persons of color; persons of various social classes; persons who are gay, lesbian, and bisexual; persons who have limited English proficiency, and so forth. For a critique and analysis of various U.S. approaches to multicultural education, see Sleeter & Grant (1987).

REFERENCES

Ahlquist, R. (1991). Position and imposition: Power relations in a multicultural foundations class. *Journal of Negro Education, 60*(2), 158–169.

American Association of Colleges for Teacher Education. (1986). *A call for change in teacher education.* Washington, DC: Author.

American Association of Colleges for Teacher Education. (1990). *AACTE/Metropolitan Life survey of teacher education students.* Washington, DC: Author.

American Association of Colleges for Teacher Education. (1991). *What college and university leaders can do to help change teacher education.* Washington, DC: Author.

Beyer, L. E. (1991). Teacher education, reflective inquiry, and moral action. In B. R. Tabachnick & K. M. Zeichner (Eds.), *Inquiry-oriented practices in teacher education* (pp. 113–129). New York: Falmer.

Carnegie Forum on Education and the Economy. (1986). *A nation prepared: Teachers for the 21st century.* New York: Carnegie Corporation.

Children's Defense Fund. (1991). *The state of America's children: 1991.* Washington, DC: Children's Defense Fund.

Cooper, A., Beare, P., & Thorman, J. (1990). Preparing teachers for diversity. A comparison of student teaching experiences in Minnesota and South Texas. *Action in Teacher Education, 12*(3), 1–4.

DeHart, P. R. (1993). *Dilemma language for our futures: A study of pre-service teachers in a neighborhood center computer lab.* (Doctoral dissertation, University of Wisconsin–Madison, 1992). *Dissertation Abstracts International, 53,* 3175.

Delpit, L. (1988). The silenced dialogue: Power and pedagogy in educating other people's children. *Harvard Education Review, 58*(3), 280–289.

Delpit, L. (1991). A commentary. In Holmes Group (Ed.), *Toward a community of learning: The preparation and continuing education of teachers* (pp. 32–34). East Lansing, MI: The Holmes Group.

Gomez, M. L., & Tabachnick, B. R. (1991, April). *"We are the answer": Preparing pre-service teachers to teach diverse learners.* Paper presented at the annual meeting of the American Educational Research Association, Chicago, IL.

Gomez, M. L., & Tabachnick, B. R. (1992). Telling teaching stories. *Teaching Education, 4*(2), 129–138.

Goodlad, J. (1990). *Teachers for our nation's schools.* San Francisco: Jossey-Bass.

Grant, C. A., & Secada, W. G. (1990). Preparing teachers for diversity. In W. R. Houston (Ed.), *Handbook of research on teacher education* (pp. 403–422). New York: Macmillan.

Grumet, M. R. (1988). *Bitter milk: Women and teaching.* Amherst: University of Massachusetts Press.

Haberman, M. (1991a). The rationale for training adults as teachers. In C. E. Sleeter (Ed.), *Empowerment through multicultural education* (pp. 275–286). Albany, NY: State University of New York Press.

Haberman, M. (1991b). Can cultural awareness be taught in teacher education programs? *Teaching Education, 4*(1), 25–32.

Hodgkinson, H. L. (1985). *All one system: Demographics of education—kindergarten through graduate school.* Washington, DC: Institute for Educational Leadership.

Hodgkinson, H. L. (1991, April 10). Remarks made on a video teleconference, *Who's missing from the classroom? The need for minority teachers.* Washington, DC: American Association of Colleges for Teacher Education and the ERIC Clearinghouse on Teacher Education.

Holmes Group. (1986). *Tomorrow's teachers.* East Lansing, MI: Author.

Holmes Group. (1990). *Tomorrow's schools: Principles for the design of professional development schools.* East Lansing, MI: Author.

Holmes Group. (1991). *Toward a community of learning: The preparation and continuing education of teachers.* East Lansing, MI: Author.

Kleinfeld, J. (1992). Learning to think like a teacher: The study of cases. In J. Shulman (Ed.), *Case methods in teacher education* (pp. 33–49). New York: Teachers College Press.

Ladson-Billings, G. (1991, April). *When difference means disaster: Reflections on a teacher education strategy for countering student resistance to diversity.* Paper presented at the annual meeting of the American Educational Research Association, Chicago.

Larke, P. (1990). Cultural diversity awareness inventory: Assessing the sensitivity of preservice teachers. *Action in Teacher Education, 12*(3), 23–30.

Larke, P. J., Wiseman, D., & Bradley, C. (1990). The minority mentorship project: Changing attitudes of preservice teachers for diverse classrooms. *Action in Teacher Education, 12*(3), 5–12.

Liston, D. P., & Zeichner, K. M. (1991). *Teacher education and the social conditions of schooling.* New York: Routledge.

Louis Harris and Associates, Inc. (1991). *The Metropolitan Life survey of the American teacher 1991. The first year: New teachers' expectations and ideals.* New York: Metropolitan Life Insurance Company.

Mahan, J. (1982a). Community involvement components in culturally-oriented teacher preparation. *Education, 103*(2), 163–172.

Mahan, J. (1982b). Native Americans as teacher trainers: Anatomy and outcomes of a cultural immersion project. *Journal of Educational Equity and Leadership, 2*(2), 100–110.

Murrell, P., Jr. (1992, April). *Deconstructing informal knowledge of exemplary teaching in diverse urban communities: Apprenticing preservice teachers as case study research-*

ers in cultural sites. Paper presented at the annual meeting of the American Educational Research Association, San Francisco, CA.

National Center for Education Statistics. (1992). *American education at a glance.* Washington, DC: Office of Education Research and Improvement.

Noordhoff, K., & Kleinfeld, J. (1990). Shaping the rhetoric of reflection for multicultural settings. In R. T. Clift, W. R. Houston, & M. C. Pugach (Eds.), *Encouraging reflective practice in education* (pp. 163–185). New York: Teachers College Press.

Noordhoff, K., & Kleinfeld, J. (1991, April). *Preparing teachers for multicultural classrooms: A case study in rural Alaska.* Paper presented at the annual meeting of the American Educational Research Association, Chicago, IL.

Olsen, R. (1991). Results of a K–12 and adult ESL enrollment survey—1991. *TESOL Matters, 1*(5), 4.

Paine, L. (1989). *Orientation towards diversity: What do prospective teachers bring?* (Research Report 89–9). East Lansing, MI: National Center for Research on Teacher Education.

Popkewitz, T. S. (1991). *A political sociology of educational reform.* New York: Teachers College Press.

Sears, J. (1992). Educators, homosexuality, and homosexual students: Are personal feelings related to professional beliefs? In K. M. Harbeck (Ed.), *Coming out of the closet: Gay and lesbian students, teachers, and curricula* (pp. 29–79). New York: The Haworth Press.

Sleeter, C. E., & Grant, C. A. (1987). An analysis of multicultural education in the United States. *Harvard Educational Review, 57*(4), 421–444.

Smith, B. O. (1969). *Teachers for the real world.* Washington, DC: American Association of Colleges for Teacher Education.

Tabachnick, B. R., Zeichner, K. M., Densmore, K., & Hudak, G. (1983, April). *The development of teacher perspectives.* Paper presented at the annual meeting of the American Educational Research Association, Montreal, Quebec, Canada.

Winitsky, N., Stoddart, T., & O'Keefe, P. (1991). Great expectations: Emergent professional development schools. *Journal of Teacher Education, 43*(1), 3–18.

Zeichner, K. M. (1992). *Educating teachers for cultural diversity.* East Lansing, MI: National Center for Research on Teacher Education.

Zeichner, K. M., & Tabachnick, B. R. (1985). The development of teacher perspectives: Social strategies and institutional control in the socialization of beginning teachers. *Journal of Education for Teaching, 11*(1), 1–25.

Zimpher, N. (1989). The RATE Project: A profile of teacher education students. *Journal of Teacher Education, 40*(6), 27–30.

CHAPTER 7

Educating Teachers for Cultural Diversity

Ken Zeichner

This chapter addresses various dimensions of one of the major policy issues in U.S. teacher education for the foreseeable future—the need to help all teachers acquire the attitudes, knowledge, skills, and dispositions necessary to work effectively with a diverse student population.[1] In the coming years, these students will be increasingly different in background from one another and from their teachers, and poor. The demographic composition of the teaching corps is unlikely to change significantly, even under the most optimistic scenario for the success of current efforts to recruit more teachers of color. As Banks (1991) argues, even if we are successful in increasing the percentage of teachers of color in the year 2,000 from 5% to the projected 15%, 85% of the nation's teachers will still be white and mostly monolingual. In many areas of the country, since most of the students these new teachers will be asked to teach will have backgrounds and life experiences very different from their own, teaching will require a great deal of intercultural communication. Even when teachers and students share a significant part of their cultural background however, one cannot assume that teachers can easily translate cultural knowledge into culturally relevant pedagogy (Montecinos, 1995). The task is one of preparing all teachers to teach a culturally diverse student body.

Although an adequate definition of diversity must be broad and inclusive, my use of the terms *diversity* and *diverse learners* in this chapter focuses primarily on differences related to social class, ethnicity, race, and language.[2] At the outset, I would like to express my agreement with Grant and Secada's (1990) and Ladson-Billings's (1991a) conclusion about the marginal status of the issue of preparing teachers for diversity in the mainstream teacher education literature. Despite a substantial literature that addresses the growing disparity between the characteristics of our teaching force and those of the students in our public schools, the problems associated with recruiting more teachers of color, and the problems of inequity in schools and society, there has been very little attention in the current literature of teacher education reform to issues of educational and social inequity and to ideas about how to prepare teachers to more effectively teach an increasingly diverse student population (Liston & Zeichner, 1991).

Many of the documents I reviewed were part of the unpublished educational literature or in less accessible journals, or were obtained through personal contacts rather than literature searches. The fact that much of the literature on preparing teachers for diversity is not readily available to the general teacher education community confirms the low status of this issue in the "official" agenda for teacher education reform. It also confirms the way in which the voices of many researchers of color have been marginalized in educational scholarship (Gordon, 1992). With the exception of the Holmes Group's (1990) *Tomorrow's Schools*, the most widely publicized of the "reports" on teacher education and proposals for reform (Carnegie Forum on Education and the Economy, 1986; Goodlad, 1990; Holmes Group, 1986) give only surface attention, at best, to issues related to educational equity and teacher education when it comes to detailing proposals for improving teacher education programs (Gordon, 1988; Grant & Gillette, 1987; Zeichner, 1990a).

Despite its marginal position in the literature, the problem of preparing teachers to teach a diverse student body is not a new concern in U.S. teacher education. For example, in 1969 the widely publicized task force report of the National Institute for Advanced Study in Teaching Disadvantaged Youth (Smith, 1969) clearly identified the failure of teacher education programs to prepare teachers to effectively teach what at that time were referred to as "culturally disadvantaged" students (also see Eddy, 1969). In concluding that most teacher education programs prepared education students to teach children much like themselves, instead of children of any social origin, this report called for a major overhaul of teacher education programs in terms of their approach to issues of diversity and equity.

> Racial, class, and ethnic bias can be found in every aspect of current teacher preparation programs. The selection processes militate against the poor and minority. The program content reflects current prejudices; the methods of instruction coincide with learning styles of the dominant group. Subtle inequalities are reinforced in institutions of higher learning. Unless there is scrupulous self-appraisal, unless every aspect of teacher training is carefully reviewed, the changes initiated in teacher preparation as a result of the current crisis will be, like so many changes which have gone before, merely differences which make no difference. (pp. 2–3)

The situation has not changed very much in the years since Smith delivered this condemnation of teacher education. There is abundant evidence, for example, that "culturally encapsulated" cohorts of prospective teachers continue to be prepared by programs in our colleges and universities for mythical culturally homogeneous school settings (Hodge, 1990; Trent, 1990). While most teacher education programs formally acknowledge the significance of the pluralistic preparation of teachers (at least enough to satisfy accreditation bodies, such as National Council for Accreditation of Teacher Education [NCATE], that have multicultural standards), in practice, most programs embody a monocultural approach (Goodlad, 1990).

For example, according to Gollnick (1992a), of the first 59 institutions that sought national accreditation for their teacher education programs under the new NCATE standards, only 8 (13.6%) were in compliance with the minimum multicultural requirements for teacher education programs. There is also clear evidence that with the exception of prospective teachers from historically black institutions (Reed & Simon, 1991), teacher education students generally try to avoid teaching in urban schools and other schools serving the poor (Haberman, 1987, 1991a; Wahab-Zaher, 1989), where the need is greatest and the work most demanding.

If teacher education programs were successful in educating teachers for diversity, there might not be such a massive reluctance by today's beginning teachers to work in urban schools and in other schools serving the poor and ethnic- and language-minority students (American Association of Colleges for Teacher Education [AACTE], 1990; Howey, 1992). Just educating teachers who are willing to teach in these schools, however, only begins to address the problem of preparing teachers who will successfully educate the students who attend these schools. Educating teachers for diversity must obviously also include attention to the quality of instruction that will be offered by these teachers. More of the same kind of teaching that has largely failed to provide even a minimally adequate education to large numbers of poor white and ethnic- and language-minority students does not improve the situation one bit.

THE GROWING DISPARITY: DEMOGRAPHIC CHANGES

Probably the area that has received the most attention in the literature related to educating teachers for diversity is the increasing gap between the backgrounds of teachers and their students.

The Students

There is no doubt that the student population in our public schools has become increasingly diverse and that it will continue to do so for the foreseeable future. It is predicted that about 40% of the nation's school-age youth will be students of color by the year 2020 (Pallas, Natriello, & McDill, 1989). Already, students of color comprise about 30% of our public school students, and are the majority in 25 of the nation's 50 largest school districts (Banks, 1991) and in some states, like New Mexico, Texas, and California (Quality Education for Minorities Project, 1990). In the 20 largest school districts, students of color comprise over 70% of the total school enrollment (Center for Education Statistics, 1987).

These students of color are more likely to be poor, hungry, and in poor health and to drop out of school than their white counterparts (Children's Defense Fund, 1991). The failure of schooling to enable all children to receive a high-quality education regardless of race or ethnocultural background represents a major crisis in U.S. education and is clearly in conflict with the purposes of education in a democratic society.

This crisis of inequality is not limited to our large urban centers. Even in places as middle-class and white as Madison, Wisconsin, for example, the inequality can be seen in such indices as the differential levels of achievement of white and African-American students in the public school system (Ptak, 1988). These problems can also be seen outside of urban areas where poverty and inequality hamper many rural students (Ornstein & Levine, 1989). During the last decade, the economic situation in rural areas has worsened dramatically (O'Hare, 1988). Since 1978, for example, poverty in rural areas has grown at twice the rate as in urban areas (Rosewater, 1989). Throughout the public school systems of the United States, the failure to educate poor and ethnic- and language-minority students is clearly evident in such measures as high school graduation and dropout rates, achievement test scores, school attendance and suspension rates, and classification patterns for special education and gifted and talented programs (e.g., Bastian, Fruchter, Gittel, Greer, & Haskings, 1985; Committee on Policy for Racial Justice, 1989; Quality Education for Minorities Project, 1990).

The Prospective Teachers

The composition of the teacher education student group is in stark contrast to the demographics of public school pupils. Several recent studies have clearly shown that teacher education students are overwhelmingly white, female, monolingual, and from a rural (small town) or suburban community, and that they come to their teacher education programs with very limited interracial and intercultural experience (AACTE, 1987, 1989; Irvine, 1989; LaFontaine, 1988), even in states like California with a lot of cultural diversity (Ahlquist, 1991). Teacher education students also feel uncomfortable about personal contact with ethnic- and language-minority parents (Larke, 1990a).

According to the recent AACTE (1989) data on teacher education students across the United States, few teacher candidates come from urban areas of any size, and only 15% would like to teach in urban areas. Zimpher (1989) concludes her analysis of these data with the observation that there appears to be a general affinity among teacher education students to teach students who are like themselves in communities that are familiar to them.

Recent research has also shown that many teacher education students come to their preparation programs viewing student diversity as a problem rather than as a resource; that their conceptions of diversity are highly individualistic (e.g., focusing on personality factors like motivation and ignoring contextual factors like ethnicity); and that their ability to talk about student differences in thoughtful and comprehensive ways is very limited (Paine, 1989). These students generally have very little knowledge about different ethnic groups in the United States, their cultures, their histories, their participation in and contributions to life in the United States (Wahab-Zaher, 1989; Wayson, 1988) and often have negative attitudes about cultural groups other than their own (Law & Lane, 1987). Goodlad (1990) has also found that most teacher education students are not even convinced that all students are capable of learning.

> The idea of moral imperatives for teachers was virtually foreign in concept and strange in language for most of the future teachers we interviewed. Many were less than convinced that all students can learn; they voiced the view that they should be kind and considerate to all, but they accepted as fact the theory that some simply cannot learn. (p. 264)

While it is possible for these and similar factors to be remedied by preservice teacher education programs, the likelihood is that they are not adequately addressed by programs as they are currently organized. Although research on teacher learning has demonstrated that teacher education programs, under certain conditions, are able to have an impact on certain aspects of teacher development (e.g., Grossman & Richert, 1988), the empirical evidence overwhelmingly supports a view of preservice teacher education as a weak intervention (Kennedy, 1991; Zeichner & Gore, 1990).

The Teacher Educators

Another dimension that must be considered in an analysis of demographic trends in teaching and teacher education is teacher educators in college and universities. Here we find a situation of cultural insularity much like that for prospective teachers with regard to ethnicity, but very unlike them with regard to gender. Recent studies of preservice teacher education across the United States have shown that the gender distribution among education faculty and students mirrors the larger patriarchal distribution in schools among teachers and administrators. Ducharme and Agne (1989) conclude that the education professorate is approximately 65% male, and 35% female. When Ducharme and Agne (1989) examined the racial dimensions of the teacher educator group, the problem was more severe:

Minorities are much less represented in the education professorate than are women. In the RATE study, 2.9% of the full professors are minority; 6.4% at the associate level; and 9.9% at the assistant professor level. The representation of minorities appears to be growing, but the growth may be short lived inasmuch as these institutions showed a total of only 8% minority in doctoral programs. (p. 75)

The lack of professors and students of color in teacher education programs makes the task of educating teachers for diversity especially difficult to achieve, it is widely agreed, because of the importance of a culturally diverse learning community to the education of teachers for diversity.

If we are going to promote an appreciation for diversity and equity in the organization and content of our programs, it must be simultaneously reflected in the make-up of our programs, both among students and faculty. Prospective teachers will be better prepared to help students appreciate cultural diversity, if they have learned through experience to appreciate it as a reality and not an academic exercise—a reality they experience through interactions with a diverse faculty and student body. (Hixson, 1991, p. 18)

Also, the reluctance of teacher education program graduates to seek employment in urban school districts is not surprising when one considers that less than 5% of the 45,000 or so education faculty in the United States have taught for even a year in the classrooms of one of our large urban school districts (Haberman, 1987). It is also reasonable to suspect, given the socialization patterns of education faculty (Lanier & Little, 1986), that most of the education faculty who must be counted on to improve the preparation of teachers for diversity are as lacking in interracial and intercultural experience as their students. Thus, there is a real question as to whether the expertise that is needed to address the preparation of teachers for diversity is currently found within the faculty who staff our teacher education programs. Staff development for teacher education faculty will undoubtedly be an important component of whatever strategies are taken to address the problem of diversity in teacher education.[3]

HOW TEACHERS NEED TO CHANGE

Before considering different approaches to the problem of preparing teachers for cross-cultural teaching, I want to spend some time outlining, in brief, the kind of teaching toward which these efforts are aimed. A relatively large literature has accumulated in the last decade in which statements have been made about the characteristics of successful teaching for ethnic- and language-minority students. Some of this literature has made statements intended to apply to the teaching of minority students in general (Cummins, 1986; National Center for

Research on Teacher Education [NCRTE], 1989), while others have outlined elements of good pedagogy for a particular segment of this population, such as language-minority students (Garcia, 1990; Grant, 1991; Moll, 1988; Tikunoff & Ward, 1991; Trueba, 1989b), or for particular ethnic groups such as Latino or African-American students (e.g., Hollins & Spencer, 1990; Ladson-Billings, 1990, 1991c; Lucas, Henze, and Donato, 1990).

It has also been very common within this literature for scholars to stress the tremendous variation within certain of the general ethnic group categories such as Hispanic American and Asian American, and to discuss what is needed to teach specific groups within a general ethnic classification. An example of this would be statements about the teaching of Chicanos, Puerto Ricans, and Cuban Americans within the category of Hispanic American or about the teaching of Hmong students and Chinese Americans within the category of Asian American (Quality Education for Minorities Project, 1990; Trueba, Jacobs, and Kirton, 1990; Valencia, 1991). Even within these more specific categories (e.g., Puerto Rican) there is still tremendous variation according to geographical location, social class, gender, sexual orientation, language proficiencies, length of time in the United States, and so forth. Scholars who discuss the successful teaching of specific groups of ethnic- and/or language-minority students are often very critical of those who lump together the needs of different groups of students and/or treat specific ethnic groups as monolithic entities possessing discernible uniform traits (Garcia, 1974; Gibson, 1984).

> When we get to the place where we assign characteristics to groups, saying black kids are tactile-kinetic learners and white kids are abstract analytical learners, then we're engaging in the worst sort of stereotyping . . . what we should not lose sight of is that variation within cultural groups is often greater than variation between groups. (Murrell, 1990, p. 50)

Despite the importance of these observations about the different needs of specific ethnic- and language-minority groups and the diversity within groups, the general statements in the literature about successful teachers and teaching for different ethnic- and language-minority students are remarkably similar. With a few exceptions, there appears to be a common set of dispositions, knowledges, and skills that are needed to teach ethnic- and language-minority students, regardless of the particular circumstances of specific groups of students. Teachers will apply these knowledges and skills in different ways, of course. I am not suggesting a uniform pedagogy with no room for adaptation to different contexts. One of these capabilities, as will be discussed shortly, seems to be the desire and ability of the teacher to learn about the special circumstances of their own students and communities, and the ability to take this knowledge into account in their teaching (Irvine, 1989).

Throughout the recent history of teacher education in the United States, the position has been taken by some that no special kind of teaching is needed for particular groups of students, such as ethnic- and language-minority students. It has been argued that good teaching in one context is good teaching in another, and that the same knowledge, skills, and dispositions will enable a teacher to be successful in all classrooms, and for schools to be successful with all students (e.g., Gentile, 1988). Very little is said in the teaching and school-effectiveness literature (e.g., Good, 1990) about how the particular social-class, ethnic, and language backgrounds of the students should influence instruction.

Much of the research literature on school and teaching effectiveness is culture-blind (Murrell, 1990). Even these generic models of effective instruction, however, can contribute much to our understanding of effective instruction for ethnic- and language-minority students. One such contribution is the finding that teachers who have a sense of efficacy (i.e., believe that they are capable of making a difference in their students' learning) are more likely to have academically successful students (Brophy & Good, 1986). But it is not possible, in the view of some scholars, to create a model of the good teacher without taking issues of culture and context into account (e.g., Cole & Griffin, 1987; Delpit, 1988). In fact, culture and context seem to be the key elements in contemporary analyses of the kind of teaching that promotes the success of ethnic- and language-minority students. In the sections below, I review several of the most important aspects of successful teaching for poor students of color as described in the literature.

High Expectations

The first common element is the belief by teachers that all students can succeed, and the communication of this belief to students (e.g., Delpit, 1988; Lucas et al., 1990; Quality Education for Minorities Project, 1990). Equally important is the personal commitment by teachers to work toward achieving success for all students, particularly those poor students of color who have often not succeeded in school (Hodge, 1990). This may seem commonsensical, but as was pointed out earlier, many teacher education students continue to cling to the belief that some students just cannot learn, whatever the school context (Goodlad, 1990).

The literature is clear about the importance of creating a classroom context in which all students feel valued and capable of academic success (Cummins, 1986; Olsen & Mullen, 1990). In her studies of successful teachers of African-American students, Ladson-Billings (1990) describes some of the ways in which teachers' beliefs about the ability of all of their students to succeed were communicated to students.

> As I talked with and observed all of the teachers in the study, I was astounded at their constant faith in their students. Even when they scolded the students, the teachers would remark "You're too smart to be doing that," or "You cannot convince me that you're not worth the effort." (p. 23)

Part of what is involved here, according to Ladson-Billings (1994), is that a personal bond is created between teacher and pupils. The teacher ceases seeing his or her students as "the Other" and addresses students' psychological and social development along with their academic development (Comer, 1988). Expectations are high for students' success, but they are not expressed in a manner that undercuts the care and concern that are crucial to the development of a student's positive self-image and sense of efficacy. If teachers treated the fates of their students as they treat those of their own children, according to Grumet (1988), we would come closer to realizing the purposes of education in a democratic society. Few of us would "excuse our own children from their futures" in the way that we sometimes do other people's children:

> Ethics and the common culture provide the procedural form and cultural content for our current concepts of schooling. And if ethics and the common culture could gather together the concern and attention that we devote to our own children and extend this nurture to other people's children, then we might indeed find in the school the model for a just society that Dewey envisioned. (p. 164)

Another way in which faith in the ability of students to succeed is communicated is by providing students with academically demanding work instead of the watered-down and mechanical curriculum that is so often the norm for many ethnic- and language-minority students (e.g., Anyon, 1980; Levin, 1987; McNeil, 1986; Oakes, 1986). Moll (1988) describes the way in which teachers' expectations ought to shift, in his analysis of successful teaching for Latino students:

> In contrast to the assumption that working class children cannot handle an academically rigorous curriculum, or in the case of limited-English proficient students, that their lack of English fluency justifies an emphasis on low level skills, the guiding assumption in the classrooms analyzed seemed to be the opposite: that students are as smart as allowed by the curriculum. The teachers assumed that the children were competent and capable and that it was teachers' responsibility to provide the students with a challenging, innovative, and intellectually rigorous curriculum. (p. 467)

Scaffolding

It is not enough, however, merely to make the curriculum more rigorous. The lack of respect for their cultural traditions and languages, so long the norm in our public schools, will continue to ensure that many ethnic- and language-minority students do not achieve academic success. The literature is clear about the need for some type of scaffolding or bridging between the cultures of the school and home. The point here is to allow cultural elements that are relevant to the students to enter the classroom.[4]

In some cases, the intent seems to be to use the scaffolds to help students eventually give up the culture of the home for the dominant culture of the school. Cummins (1986) refers to this as the "subtractive approach." Fordham's (1988) analysis of the phenomenon of "racelessness" among African-American high school students is an example of this situation.[5]

In other cases, the intent seems to be to use the scaffolds to help students learn the culture of the school while maintaining identification and pride in the home culture. Cummins (1986) refers to this as the "additive approach" and Ferdman (1990) as the "pluralist approach." Ladson-Billings's (1990, 1991c, 1994) discussion of "culturally relevant teaching" in which students' culture is utilized as a way to both maintain student culture and to learn and overcome the negative effects of the dominant culture is an example of this approach to building bridges between home and school. Ladson-Billings (1990) argues that the ability to foster academic excellence *and* the maintenance of cultural integrity represent pedagogical excellence, nothing less. The maintenance of ethnocultural identity seems to be critical to the academic success of ethnic- and language-minority students in most cases.

In scaffolding, supports are constructed for students that enable them to move through related experiences from the home toward the demands of the school (Mehan & Trujillo, 1989). Many different ways of providing these supports and of providing greater "cultural synchronization" (Irvine, 1989) between the home and the school are discussed in the literature. These include the use of particular teaching strategies, such as sheltered bilingual education (Watson, Northcutt, & Rydell, 1989) and assisted teaching (Tharp & Gallimore, 1988), and the reorganization of lesson formats, standards for behavior, curriculum materials, and assessment practices to make them more inclusive and sensitive to linguistic and cultural variations (e.g., Cole & Griffin, 1987; Cummins, 1986; Olsen & Mullen, 1990).[6] Here it is argued that the curriculum should be inclusive of a wider variety of traditions and connected to students' own experiences, and that instruction should build on students' experiences to expand their knowledge and capabilities (Tabachnick, 1991).

There are two critical elements involved in the principle of cultural inclusion. First, there is the incorporation of the languages and cultures of the learners into the academic and social context of schooling in ways that facilitate and support academic learning and cultural identity (Hollins & Spencer, 1990). Here we have the creation of classroom settings that permit students to apply language and task completion skills already in their repertoires (Cole & Griffin, 1987).

Second, there is the explicit teaching of the codes and customs of the school (the culture of the classroom) so that students will be able to fully participate in the mainstream (Knapp & Turnbull, 1991). As Delpit (1988) puts it, students are helped to establish their own voices, but are coached so that those voices produce notes that will be heard clearly in the larger society.

Singer (1988) points out that this dual goal of maintaining ethnocultural identity and providing access to the codes of power requires that the teacher use a combination of culturally congruent and consciously incongruent teaching and curriculum strategies. Although total cultural congruence in the teacher's approach is not possible because of the multiple cultural identities present in every classroom (Bloch & Tabachnick, 1991), it is possible to incorporate practices into a classroom that are sensitive to the cultural and/or linguistic variations in that particular classroom and that result in all students in that classroom feeling that their own particular cultural identity is respected by the teacher (Nieto, 1992).

Teacher Knowledge

In order for teachers to be able to implement the principle of cultural inclusion in their classrooms, they need general sociocultural knowledge about child and adolescent development, about second-language acquisition, and about the ways that socioeconomic circumstances, language, and culture shape school performance and educational achievement (Cazden & Mehan, 1990; Comer, 1988; Hodge, 1990; Lee, 1989; Nieto, 1986). They must also have specific knowledge about the languages, cultures, and circumstances of the particular students in their classrooms. In addition, as Trueba (1989a) and Montero-Sieburth (1989) point out, teachers must be able to utilize this knowledge in the organization of the curriculum and instruction to stimulate student learning. It is clearly possible for teachers to have the knowledge, but not know how to employ it pedagogically (Diez & Murrell, 1992). Finally, according to some writers (e.g., Banks, 1991; Hollins, 1990), teachers need a clear sense of their own ethnic and cultural identities in order to be able to understand those of their students and their families.

There is a danger involved in the accumulation of knowledge about specific cultures that is commented on frequently in the literature: that it can actually increase the chances that teachers will act in inappropriate ways. Mehan and Trujillo (1989) summarize one aspect of the problem:

> Because it is impossible for beginning teachers to acquire a sufficient ethnological knowledge base of the language groups he or she will encounter, the knowledge they do acquire tends to be stereotypic. It can also be dangerous because these stereotypic notions often lead to a cultural deprivation view. (p. 2)

This potential problem is related to the fact that despite the importance of teachers' understanding of general aspects of the cultures and languages of their students (Grant, 1991), there is no such thing as a typical Latino or African-American student, or a typical student from any specific ethnocultural background. As Villegas's (1991) analysis of the literature on culturally responsive pedagogy emphasizes, teaching practices found to be successful in one community may not be effective in other communities, even when the communities are similar in ethnic composition. Successful teaching for ethnic- and language-minority students must be sensitive to the differences in particular students' backgrounds and experiences and must affirm respect for individual as well as group characteristics. Lucas and colleagues' (1990) descriptions of high schools that were highly successful with Latino students clearly underlines this point:

> While faculty and staff were sensitive to the importance of students' languages and cultures, they did not treat students simply as members of an undifferentiated ethnic group. They recognized students' individual strengths, interests, problems, and concerns rather than characterizing them by reference to stereotypes. (p. 325)

What teachers must be capable of, according to some, is gaining information from their own students and the local community, and learning how to transform it for pedagogical use (Cazden & Mehan, 1990). The disposition and skill to conduct research on their own students and their students' families and communities is necessary because in the final analysis, it is each student's everyday life experiences, which are influenced in unique ways by factors such as social class, ethnicity, language, cuture, gender, and so forth, that influence the academic and social development of students (Huber, 1992; Laosa, 1977).

Heath's (1983) work in Appalachia is a widely cited example of teacher research in this tradition. In this seminal study, when teachers began to more closely monitor their own practices and to understand the differences in the way in which language was used in their classrooms and in the children's homes, they began to overcome some of the gaps in communication that had previously served as obstacles to the achievement of working-class black students in a newly integrated school.

Teachers must be knowledgeable about a variety of strategies like the ones employed by Heath (1983). These strategies include, according to Villegas (1991),

> making home visits, conferring with community members, talking with parents, consulting with minority teachers, and observing children in and out of school to discern patterns of behavior that may be related to their cultural background. (pp. 36–37)

Teaching Strategies

When we consider the specific instructional methods that are thought to be successful with ethnic- and language-minority students, the consensus seems to be that a focus on meaning-making and content is the key. This is opposed to the common focus on decontextualized skills often experienced by ethnic- and language-minority students (Moll, 1988). Successful teachers of these students create opportunities for students to learn to use, try, and manipulate language, symbols, and information in the service of making sense or creating meaning. It is the sense-making and knowledge construction by students that is central.

Cummins (1986) contrasts two general orientations to teaching, the transmission model and the reciprocal interaction model. In the transmission model, which Cummins argues is associated with the disempowerment of minority students,

> the teacher initiates and controls the interaction, constantly orienting it towards the achievement of instructional objectives. . . . The curriculum . . . emphasizes correct recall of content taught by means of highly structured drills and workbook exercises. (p. 28)

In the reciprocal interaction model, an orientation Cummins (1986) thinks is associated with the empowerment of minority students and their academic success, there is a genuine dialogue between teachers and students; teachers guide and facilitate rather than control student learning; and student-student interaction and a collaborative learning context are encouraged:

> A central tenet of the reciprocal interaction model is that talking and writing are a means to learning. . . . This model emphasizes the development of higher level cognitive skills rather than just factual recall, and meaningful language use by students rather than the correction of surface forms. (p. 28)

The conclusion that the reciprocal interaction model is more closely related to the academic success of ethnic and minority students than the more common transmission model does not mean that only a particular set of teaching methods or curricular programs is appropriate for classroom use. Although there have been many attempts in the literature to identify such practices and curricular materials (e.g., Natriello, McDill, & Pallas, 1990; Slavin & Madden, 1989), important questions have been raised about the efficacy of some allegedly progressive reciprocal practices (e.g., Delpit, 1986). Reyes (1992) argues, for example, that currently popular forms of "process instruction" (an inclusive term that refers to whole-language, the writing process, and literature-based instruction) is not always successful with linguistically different students unless culturally and linguistically supportive adaptations are made for these students.

> Teachers must rise above the euphoria over whole language and writing process and recognize that these programs are not perfect or equally successful for all. They are successful only to the extent that teachers understand the theories, assume the role of mediators—not merely facilitators—and create culturally and linguistically sensitive learning environments for all learners. (p. 440)

What is agreed on in the literature, despite some ambiguity with regard to particular practices and programs, is that teachers need a wide variety of teaching strategies and practices in order to be able to respond to the varied needs of their students (e.g., Anderson, 1987; Nieto, 1992). There is agreement about the need for teachers to have a deep understanding of the subjects they teach so that they will be able to "create the multiple representations necessary to address the diversity of prior experiences and understandings present in their classrooms" (McDiarmid, 1989, p. 92).

There is also consensus in the literature about a number of other things that teachers need to know or to be able to do to successfully teach ethnic- and language-minority students. These include the ability to develop an inclusive multicultural curriculum that incorporates the contributions of different social groups (Tabachnick, 1991), and the ability to create a collaborative classroom environment utilizing such practices as cooperative grouping, peer tutoring, and mixed ability grouping (Hixson, 1991; Quality Education for Minorities Project, 1990). There is almost universal condemnation in the literature of the practices of ability grouping in the elementary school and tracking in the secondary school and a strong feeling by many that teachers must have knowledge of the ways that schools structure inequality through such practices (Hodge, 1990).

Assessment and Parent Involvement

Two other areas that receive a lot of attention in the literature are assessment and parent involvement. It is argued that teachers need a good understanding of the school community and of how to involve parents and other community members in authentic ways in the school program (Ada, 1986; Grant, 1991). Parents and other community members should be encouraged to participate in students' education and be given a significant role in determining what an appropriate education is for students in particular contexts (Delgado-Gaitan, 1991; Delpit, 1988; Zeichner, 1991a). According to Comer (1988), the sharing of information and power within a school by adults, across racial, class, and cultural lines, makes it more probable that students will be able to cross these lines as well and perform well on both sides. Harrison (1993) argues, however, that for these interactions to do any good, they must be structured in culturally appropriate ways so that a basic trust can develop between school staff and community members. She thinks that this trust between school and community is essential to the success of children in school and that genuine parent involvement is much more critical to school success than particular instructional approaches:

> The difference between success and failure may hinge on whether or not parents have the power to make choices about appropriate education for their children, not on specific instructional techniques. (p. 162)

Assessment is thought to be one of the major obstacles to the school success of ethnic- and language-minority students (First, Kellogg, Willshire-Carrera, Lewis, & Almeida, 1988). Cummins (1986) argues that teachers must become advocates for minority students with regard to assessment, rather than legitimizing the location of the problem in students. The literature clearly encourages teachers to learn about curricular-based assessment practices that are used to understand students' performance in a variety of contexts, such as student portfolios, checklists and inventories, and notes from teachers' observations (e.g., Moll, 1988; National Coalition of Advocates for Students [NCAS], 1991; Valencia, 1991).

Finally, some have been very critical of the home-school incompatibility theory and the solution of cultural inclusion that has figured so prominently in the literature in the areas of curriculum, instruction, and assessment. Here it is argued that it is too simplistic to claim that cultural dissonance between the school and the home is responsible for the academic failure of ethnic- and language-minority students because this concept leaves unexamined the social, economic, and political inequalities underlying the problems within schools while claiming to offer fundamental solutions to them (Villegas, 1988). From this perspective, effective teachers of ethnic- and language-minority students, in addition to their activities within the school, have to be involved in the broader political struggles for achieving a more just and humane society. They must be involved in helping to establish the societal preconditions for the achievement of broad-scale school and societal reforms.

For as Weiner (1989) points out, while teacher education programs can educate teachers to teach diverse students with respect, creativity, and skill within their classrooms, they cannot prepare individual teachers to substitute for the political and social movements that are needed to alter the systemic deficiencies of our society and its school systems. Along these lines, McCarthy (1990) criticizes what he sees as an unwarranted optimism on the part of many about the impact of multicultural education alone on the social and economic futures of minority students. He argues that the objective of building bridges between the home and the school privileges individual mobility over systemic change.

In summary, while these criticisms do not challenge the wisdom of the strategy of building bridges between home and school, or the strategy of culturally relevant instruction within the classroom, they do question the adequacy of educational reforms alone for dealing with the economic, social, and political dimensions of the problems of poor students of color. These critics of home-school compatibility theories assert that teachers need information about the dynamics of privilege and economic oppression in the United States and that the development of teachers' social consciousness and their moral commitment to work toward the elimination of societal inequalities outside the school as well as within is a critical aspect of educating teachers for an educational system that realizes the purposes of education in a democratic society (Francis-Okongwu & Pflaum, 1993; Zeichner 1991b). Figure 7.1 provides a summary of what teachers should be like, know, and do in order to teach all students in our culturally diverse society.

ALTERNATIVE APPROACHES TO
TEACHER EDUCATION FOR DIVERSITY

Several different strategies have been employed in teacher education programs in an attempt to better prepare teachers to teach poor students of color and of limited English proficiency. There are two ways in which these strategies have been used by teacher educators. One is for "teacher education for diversity" to be integrated throughout the various professional courses and field experiences in a teacher education program. In this infusion approach (Burstein, Vaughn, Wilcoxen, & Brewer, 1992), entire programs focus primarily on preparing teachers to work with ethnic- and language-minority students. Programs either focus on preparing teachers to educate a variety of different groups of students of color, such as are found in most urban school districts (e.g., McCormick, 1991), or on the preparation of teachers to educate specific groups of students, such as Native American students, African-American students, and so forth (e.g., Tippeconnic, 1983).

In addition to professional education course work, it is also possible to address the issue of cultural diversity in the various arts and sciences courses taken by students prior to certification. This is especially important, as Hixson (1992) points out, in states where professional education course work is minimal. One example of this broader university-wide approach to the issue of cultural diversity is the requirement recently implemented at several major universities that all undergraduate students be required to complete a certain minimum number of credits in ethnic studies courses prior to their graduation.

FIGURE 7.1. Key elements of effective teaching in a culturally diverse society.

- Teachers have a clear sense of their own ethnic and cultural identities.

- High expectations for the success of all students (and a belief that all students can succeed) are communicated to students.

- Teachers are personally committed to achieving equity for all students and believe that they are capable of making a difference in their students' learning.

- Teachers have developed a personal bond with their students and cease seeing their students as "the other."

- Students are provided with an academically challenging curriculum that includes attention to the development of higher level cognitive skills.

- Instruction focuses on the creation of meaning about content by students in an interactive and collaborative learning environment.

- Learning tasks are often seen as meaningful by students.

- The curriculum is inclusive of the contributions and perspectives of the different ethnocultural groups that make up the society.

- Scaffolding is provided by teachers that links the academically challenging and inclusive curriculum to the cultural resources that students bring to school.

- Teachers explicitly teach students the culture of the school and seek to maintain students' sense of ethnocultural pride and identity.

- Parents and community members are encouraged to become involved in students' education and are given a significant voice in making important school decisions in relation to program, i.e., sources and staffing.

- Teachers are involved in political struggles outside of the classroom aimed at achieving a more just and humane society.

Another way for teacher education for diversity to be dealt with by teacher educators is as a subtopic or an add-on to a regular teacher education program in one or a few courses or field experiences, where the other courses remain untouched by issues of diversity. This is the segregated approach. Probably the most common way in which the segregated approach is implemented is with the addition of a course on multicultural education or ethnic studies to a program (e.g., Bennett, 1988).

Despite a clear preference for the integrated approach by scholars who have assessed the work of teacher education programs (Gay, 1986), the segregated approach is clearly dominant in U.S. teacher education programs (Grant &

Sleeter, 1985). There are very few teacher education programs of a permanent nature that have integrated attention to diversity throughout the curriculum. It is also very common for any course work related to cultural diversity, beyond basic survey courses, to be optional versus compulsory (Gay, 1986).

There is good reason for the preference for an integrated approach to issues of cultural diversity. Research studies have clearly demonstrated the very limited long-term impact of the segregated approach on the attitudes, beliefs, and teaching practices of teacher education students (e.g., Bennett, 1988; Grant & Koskella, 1986; Haberman & Post, 1992; McDiarmid, 1990). Sleeter (1988) concluded from her analysis of course work in multicultural education in Wisconsin teacher education institutions that

> including a relatively small amount of multicultural education training in students' preservice programs does not have much impact on what they do. It may give them a greater repertoire of teaching strategies to use with culturally diverse students, and it may alert them to the importance of maintaining high expectations. For significant reform of teaching to occur however, this intervention alone is insufficient. (p. 29)

Given the small number of programs that represent an integrated approach, I will focus here on the specific instructional strategies discussed in the literature by teacher educators, independent of how they have been employed within the context of particular teacher education programs. These strategies served as a set of orientating categories for case studies of several exemplary programs that were conducted by the National Center for Research on Teacher Learning (NCRTL) between 1990 and 1995 (e.g., Zeichner & Melnick, 1995).

Countering Low Expectations

There are several ways in which teacher educators attempt to deal with the problem of low expectations for ethnic- and language-minority students that Goodlad (1990) found to be widespread among teacher education students across the United States. One way in which this is done is by exposing students, through either readings or direct contact, to examples of successful teaching for ethnic- and language-minority students. An example of this is PROTEACH at the University of Florida, where students are required to read specific books and articles describing the successful teaching of such students (Ross, Johnson, & Smith, 1991). The kinds of readings that would be used to demonstrate to students that it is possible for schools to succeed with pupils who most often are failed by our current system would include Lucas and colleagues' (1990) rich descriptions of several California high schools serving Latino students, Ladson-Billings's (1990, 1994) studies of successful teachers of African-American students, Moll's

(1988) studies of successful teaching of Latino students, and Paley's (1989) account of the complexities of interracial teaching, which includes a vivid demonstration of the inadequacies of a "culture-blind" approach to teaching.

This attention to cases of success is often supplemented by helping prospective teachers examine the ways in which schools help structure inequality through various practices in curriculum, instruction, grouping, and assessment. There are many powerfully documented cases of failures that can be instructive for students (e.g., Anyon, 1980; McNeil, 1986; Rist, 1970). For example, students could read and discuss particular cases in which the principles of culturally relevant teaching are violated. Fine's (1987) study of an urban high school vividly documents the ways in which students of color were silenced by school practices that violated the principle of cultural inclusion:

> The intellectual, social, and emotional substance which constitutes minority students' lives was routinely treated as irrelevant to be displaced and silenced. . . . At the level of the curriculum, texts, and conversation in classrooms, school talk and knowledge were radically severed from the daily realities of adolescents' lives and more systematically allied with the lives of teachers. (pp. 163–164)

Another way in which the problem of low expectations has been addressed is by the use of the selection process to screen prospective teachers on the basis of cultural sensitivity and commitment to the education of all students. Haberman's (1987) work at the University of Wisconsin–Milwaukee on the development of an admissions interview to screen candidates for urban teaching is illustrative of this approach. This interview is now being used by several large urban school districts (e.g., Houston) to screen teachers for alternative certification programs.

Yet another way in which teacher educators have proposed to counter the low expectations of many teacher education students for poor students of color and to give teachers a framework for organizing classroom learning environments is to give serious attention in teacher preparation programs to research on the relationships among language, culture, and learning. This research, which has accumulated over the last decade, has convincingly demonstrated the superiority of a situational view of intelligence and competence, which sees behavior as a function of the context of which it is a part (Cazden & Mehan, 1990; Mehan & Trujillo, 1989). This research also provides us with numerous examples of how learning environments are created in schools that facilitate the success of students of color (e.g., Heath, 1983; Tharp & Gallimore, 1988; Trueba, 1989b). Comer's (1988) call for grounding the preparation of teachers in knowledge of human development is one aspect of this general strategy. An example of this approach is found at the State University of New York (SUNY) at Binghamton; teacher education students both read and conduct their own ethnographies, which address the relationships among language, culture, and learning (Teitelbaum & Britzman, 1991). Bowers and Flinders (1990) argue that there are two things that teachers realize after being exposed to this sociocultural knowledge base:

> The first has to do with the need to view students' behavior, in part, as the expression of patterns learned through membership within their primary culture. The second has to do with the belief that teachers' professional judgment should include a knowledge of how their own cultural patterns may both obstruct students' ability to learn and influence their own judgments about students' performance. (p. 72)

Creating a Cultural Autobiography

One of the processes with which teacher education for diversity often begins is helping teacher education students to better understand their own cultural experience, and develop more clarified ethnic and cultural identities. There is a consensus in the literature that the development of one's own cultural identity is a necessary precursor to cross-cultural understanding (e.g., Banks, 1991; Nieto, 1992; Quintanar-Sarellana, 1991). Examples of this approach to helping mainstream teacher education students locate themselves within our culturally diverse society include the work of King and Ladson-Billings (1990) at Santa Clara University, the work of Hollins (1990) at the University of California-Hayward, and the work of Gomez and Tabachnick (1991) at the University of Wisconsin–Madison. All of these examples involve an autobiographical component in which students learn to recognize and appreciate their own cultural heritage as distinctive and worthwhile.

> Part of the teacher education curriculum should be aimed at resocializing preservice teachers in ways that help them view themselves within a culturally diverse society. This could entail restructuring self-perceptions and world views. Part of designing appropriate experiences for preservice teachers is making meaningful connections between the students' personal/family history and the social context of life as experienced by different groups within a culturally diverse society. (Hollins, 1990, pp. 202–203)

Attitude Change

A next step according to some teacher educators is to learn more about and then to reexamine the attitudes and values students hold toward ethnic groups other than their own. As Banks (1991) argues:

Helping students understand their own cultural experience and to develop more clarified cultural and ethnic identifications is only the first step in helping them to better understand and relate to other ethnic and racial groups. They also need experiences that will enable them to learn about the values and attitudes they hold toward other ethnic and cultural groups, to clarify and analyze those values, to reflect upon the consequences of their values and attitudes, to consider alternative attitudes and values, and to personally confront some of their latent values and attitudes toward other races. (p. 141)

Some teacher educators who have written about their efforts to help their students reexamine their attitudes and beliefs about various ethnic groups have stressed the importance of both the intellectual challenge and the social support that come from a group of students to the process of attitude change (e.g., Gomez & Tabachnick, 1991; King & Ladson-Billings, 1990). The existence of a cohesive cohort group in which students stay in close contact with each other over a period of time is often cited as a critical element (e.g., Grant, Zeichner, & Gillette, 1988). Even with the existence of collaborative learning environments, however, the process of helping students confront their negative attitudes about other ethnic and language groups is often very difficult (Ahlquist, 1991).

Banks (1991) uses case studies (some of which are written by students) in his ethnic studies course at the University of Washington to help his students examine their attitudes and values regarding other groups. Kleinfeld (1992) also offers an example of cases used in a teacher education program to promote intercultural understanding. Shulman and Mesa-Bains's (1992) edited collection of cases and commentaries is another excellent source in this area.

Gomez (1991) helps her language arts students at the University of Wisconsin–Madison reexamine their attitudes toward people of color by having them read various accounts of what it is like for many minorities to live and be educated in the United States. Gomez asks her teacher education students to read such works as Richard Rodriguez's (1982) autobiographical account of his schooling, *Hunger of Memory*, and Taylor and Dorsey-Gaines's (1988) stories of the lives of poor urban African-American families, *Growing Up Literate*. Through these and other class assignments that are implemented in a concurrent practicum experience, students are helped to become more sensitive to the cultures and lives of their own pupils and to learn effective strategies for teaching literacy skills to all of the diverse learners in their classrooms.

Field Experiences

Often teacher educators put education students in direct contact with children and/or adults with ethnic and/or racial backgrounds different from their own. These experiences include relatively brief community field experiences outside of school settings with poor children and adults of color that are connected to course work and coupled with guided reflective analysis of the experiences (Beyer, 1991; Fuller & Ahler, 1987; Haberman & Post, 1992; Ladson-Billings, 1991b). These community field experiences are often used as a basis for helping prospective teachers learn how to interact in authentic ways with parents and other adults from different ethnocultural backgrounds.[7] Carry-over of the learnings gained from these extrascholastic experiences to work in classrooms has not been demonstrated.

One example of a community field experience is the human service project option in the required school and society course at Knox College. The purpose of this option, according to Beyer (1991), is to enable prospective teachers, many of whom have led lives that have kept them distant from poverty, to come to grips with social inequality in a direct way. In addition to reading about poverty in the school and society course, students who elect this option work in various social service agencies or in a more informal setting such as a home.

Other direct experiences often include the required completion of a minimum number of practicum and student teaching experiences in schools serving ethnic- and language-minority students (Bowen & Salsman, 1979; Ross et al., 1991),[8] and intensive cultural immersion experiences in which students live and teach in a minority community and often do extensive community service work (e.g., Mahan, 1982). This latter approach of cultural immersion was characteristic of the National Teacher Corps program, which existed from 1965 to 1980 (Smith, 1980). With this strategy, community people without professional education backgrounds are often hired as part-time consultants, in part to compensate for the lack of diversity typical of teacher education faculties (Rivlin & Sciara, 1974).

Another possibility that combines elements of the previous strategies into one program component is to require practicum and student teaching experiences in schools serving students of color that include a community component as part of the clinical experience. Hillard (1974) argues that practicum and student teaching courses will do a better job of preparing teachers to be competent in cross-cultural settings if they extend beyond the school into the diverse communities served by particular schools. Linking a community field experience to a course where students are serving in the role of student teacher may help students develop competencies in understanding and dealing with the community served by their schools, in ways that go beyond what can be gained from a community field experience standing alone in the teacher education curriculum (Mungo, 1982). For example, Noordhoff and Kleinfeld (1993) encourage student teachers in the Teachers for Alaska (TFA) Program

> to put themselves in roles outside of the classroom (e.g., community basketball, skin sewing or beading groups, church attendance) and to spend time in places

such as the store or post office where people are likely to congregate or share news. We advise our students to seek out the expertise of teacher's aides who live in the community and to make home visits. (p. 19)

The purpose of these visits in the Teachers for Alaska Program is to help student teachers learn how to tailor their instruction to the particular cultural context in which they are working rather than merely sensitizing them to different cultural realities. How student teachers use the information they gain about their students and the students' communities is of central concern.

Often these field experiences in schools serving ethnic- and language-minority students are coupled with seminars that provide structured and guided reflection about teaching in these schools. Gomez and Tabachnick (1992), operating out of the tradition of narrative inquiry, have their students at the University of Wisconsin–Madison tell stories about their teaching in their weekly seminars. Gomez and Tabachnick (1991, 1992) present convincing evidence that telling stories about teaching in a collaborative context that is intellectually challenging and socially supportive helps student teachers reexamine the "scripts" that guide their teaching. The literature on clinical teacher education and on teacher development clearly supports the view that this kind of guided reflection about teaching during practicums and student teaching is critical to determining the educational value of the experience, and that teaching experience without such guided reflection is often miseducative (see Baty, 1972; Zeichner, 1990b). The necessity of direct intercultural experience however, is universally supported.

If teachers are to work successfully with students from cultures different from their own, it is imperative that the training program provide for more than intellectualization about cross cultural issues. Teacher growth in this area is possible only to the extent that the teacher's own behavior in a cross cultural setting is the subject of examination and experimentation. (Hillard, 1974, pp. 49–50)

Furthermore, the extension of these direct intercultural experiences outside of the school into culturally diverse communities, and the making of friends from other cultural backgrounds, seems to be a common characteristic of teacher education programs with a successful track record of educating teachers for cultural diversity (Zeichner & Melnick, 1995).

Cultural Knowledge

Another strategy that is used by teacher educators in teacher education for diversity is to attempt to overcome the lack of knowledge by teacher education students about the histories of different ethnic groups and their participation in and contributions to life in the United States. Ellwood (1990) argues that an ethnic studies component in a teacher education program can potentially do a lot to prevent mistakes that are rooted in cultural ignorance:

> If student teachers studied linguistics long enough to understand that say, an African-American dialect is as rule bound and linguistically sophisticated as the dialect which has gained prominence as "standard American English," they may be less inclined to judge their students as unintelligent simply because they speak a different dialect. If they also studied Afro-American history and literature, gaining an appreciation for the immense love of language running through African-American culture, they might be able to recognize in their own Black students, skills and linguistic strengths that could be built upon in the classroom. Similarly, if we gained an appreciation for the tenacious struggles minority people have waged historically in this country around education, it might be a little bit harder to jump to the immensely unlikely conclusion that "those parents" do not care about the education of their children. (p. 3)

Ladson-Billings's (1991b) work at Santa Clara University shows that the approach of exposing students to aspects of our history that they have not been exposed to in their schooling appears to cause many students to question their own education and why they were not given access to certain points of view.[9] For example, two of Ladson-Billings's former students remarked in their journals after viewing *Eyes on the Prize* (an award-winning civil rights documentary):

> This [video] made me so angry because of how little I know about the Civil Rights movement. I'm 21 years old and almost all of this is completely new to me. [White female, liberal studies major] (p. 13)

> I had no idea of the riots and marches and violence that went on for civil rights. Why wasn't I taught this? [White male communications major] (p. 13)

Another part of this strategy is to provide students with information about some of the unique characteristics and learning styles of students from different ethnic groups (Gilbert & Gay, 1985; Huber & Pewewardy, 1990). Because these are general characteristics, however, which are not limited to specific cultural groups or necessarily applicable to individual learners in specific classrooms, a necessary supplement to the information about general group characteristics is teaching teacher education students how to learn about and then incorporate into their instruction information about their own students, their families, and communities.

McDiarmid and Price (1990) describe how group-level information alone (what is often referred to in the literature as the ethnic-studies approach) is likely to affect teacher education students:

The presentation of information on ethnic and religious groups may actually encourage prospective teachers to generalize and, eventually to prejudge pupils in
their classrooms. More commonly, teacher education students may become un-
sure how to think about culturally different children. On the one hand, they are
taught to be suspicious of any generalization about a group of people, on the other,
they encounter materials and presentations that, in fact make generalizations about
normative values, attitudes, and behaviors among different groups. (p. 15)

One example of a teacher education program that attempts to teach prospective teachers to do research about their own students, their families, and
communities in the tradition of Heath's (1983) seminal work in Appalachia is
the Teachers for Alaska program at the University of Alaska (Noordhoff &
Kleinfeld, 1993). This program supplements general information about particular groups of Native Alaskans with a focus on developing prospective teachers'
dispositions to find out about the context, helping teachers learn experientially
about their particular students and their communities, and then helping them
learn how to use their information in their teaching to tailor their instruction to
particular cultural contexts. One way in which TFA faculty help prospective teachers learn how to tailor instruction to particular contexts is by providing them
with examples of such adaptations that have been preserved in case studies
written by local teachers.

There is much discussion in the literature about how to take knowledge
about particular ethnic groups or contexts and make use of it in developing
multicultural curriculum materials and culturally relevant instructional strategies and classroom organizational structures. Much of this work focuses on the
integration of a multicultural perspective into all that a teacher does in a classroom (e.g., Bennett, 1990; Sleeter & Grant, 1988; Tiedt & Tiedt, 1990). With
regard to curriculum, the emphasis is often on two things: (1) skill in analyzing
existing curriculum materials for ethnocentric bias and adapting them to correct biases and (2) skill in developing inclusive curriculum materials, often taking
advantage of knowledge about the local community.

Instructional Strategies

With regard to instruction, students are often taught various instructional strategies that are sensitive to cultural and linguistic differences and that enable them
to build on the knowledge and experiences (the cultural resources) that students bring with them to school. One example of a culturally congruent instructional strategy is the Vygotskian-based method of "assisted teaching" (Tharp &
Gallimore, 1988). Prospective teachers are also taught about a variety of
curriculum-based and culturally sensitive methods of assessing students' work
and about the ways in which many conventional assessment methods discrimi-
nate against ethnic- and language-minority students.

In summary, the major strategies that are discussed in the literature for educating teachers for diversity are included in Figure 7.2. While there are more detailed presentations available in the literature both about the specific knowledge, skills, and dispositions that teachers must have in order to successfully teach ethnic- and language-minority students (e.g., Garcia, 1990; Hunter, 1974) and about the elements of a culturally responsive teacher education curriculum (Irvine, 1989), the strategies outlined here capture the essence of teacher education for diversity as it is portrayed in the literature.

DIFFERENT VIEWS OF TEACHER LEARNING

The different strategies of teacher education for diversity that are described in the literature reflect different views about how teachers learn to teach. First, different strategies can be distinguished according to the degree to which they emphasize factors of selection or socialization. Strategies that emphasize socialization can be further distinguished according to the degree to which they attempt to influence prospective teachers by facilitating changes in the fundamental values, attitudes, dispositions, and belief systems of students.

One point of view, exemplified by the work of Haberman (1987, 1991a, 1991b), does not place much faith in the power of conventional preservice teacher education programs to prepare white, monolingual teacher education students to teach diverse learners, and places the emphasis on selection mechanisms rather than on socialization strategies. Haberman (1991a, 1991b) argues that most typical majority teacher education students are developmentally not capable of dealing with the complexities associated with intercultural teaching and that teacher education programs are not capable of producing in these students the kind of fundamental changes in values, attitudes, and dispositions that are needed for the successful teaching of ethnic- and linguistic-minority pupils.

Some empirical data exist that support Haberman's position and show how various strategies of teacher education for diversity often legitimate and strengthen the very attitudes, values, and dispositions they were designed to correct. Haberman and Post's (1992) analysis of a human relations experience offered to students at the University of Wisconsin–Milwaukee and Ginsburg's (1988) analysis of the impact of multicultural course content at the University of Houston are examples of studies that do not leave one optimistic about the potential for conventional preservice teacher education programs to facilitate fundamental change in students.[10] For example, Haberman (1991a) concludes about the failure of the human relations experience to change students' values related to cultural awareness:

FIGURE 7.2. Key instructional strategies of "teacher education for diversity."

- Admissions procedures screen students on the basis of cultural sensitivity and a commitment to the education of all students, especially poor students of color who frequently do not experience success in school.

- Students are helped to develop a clearer sense of their own ethnic and cultural identities.

- Students are helped to examine their attitudes toward other ethnocultural groups.

- Students are taught about the dynamics of prejudice and racism and about how to deal with them in the classroom.

- Students are taught about the dynamics of privilege and economic oppression and about school practices that contribute to the reproduction of societal inequalities.

- The teacher education curriculum addresses the histories and contributions of various ethnocultural groups.

- Students are given information about the characteristics and learning styles of various groups <u>and</u> individuals and are taught about the limitations of this information.

- The teacher education curriculum gives much attention to sociocultural research knowledge about the relationships among language, culture, and learning. Students are taught various procedures by which they can gain information about the communities represented in their classrooms.

- Students are taught how to assess the relationships between the methods they use in the classroom and the preferred learning and interaction styles in their students' homes and communities.

- Students are taught how to use various instructional strategies and assessment procedures sensitive to cultural and linguistic variations and how to adapt classroom instruction and assessment to accommodate the cultural resources that their students bring to school.

- Students are exposed to examples of the successful teaching of ethnic- and language-minority students.

- Students complete community field experiences with adults and/or children of another ethnocultural group with guided reflections.

- Students complete practicum and/or student teaching experiences in schools serving ethnic- and language-minority students.

- Students live and teach in a minority community (immersion).

- Instruction is embedded in a group setting that provides both intellectual challenge and social support.

Indeed, many of our students became more insensitive and hardened in their positions by attributing more negative values to school children, their parents, and their neighborhoods. After 120 hours of direct experience in schools serving a multicultural population, these preservice students became better at supporting their original predispositions. . . . Rather than the cure-all assumed by teacher educators, direct experience in these culturally diverse situations merely served to enhance and strengthen the social values with which our students began. (p. 29)[11]

Others, while sharing Haberman's belief about the importance of changes in the basic values and dispositions of students, have offered many different ideas about how to bring these changes about. Efforts to help students develop a clearer sense of their own cultural identities and to reexamine their attitudes toward and beliefs about different ethnocultural groups aim at the same kind of fundamental changes in students. So too do many of the community field experiences and immersion experiences described in the literature. Some evidence exists that is in conflict with the research cited earlier about the impotency of teacher education experiences. Teacher educators such as Beyer (1991), Burstein and Cabello (1989), Gomez and Tabachnick (1991), Ladson-Billings (1991b), and Larke (1990b) have presented stories and journal writings of their students that demonstrate the powerful impact of some of these experiences. For example, one of Ladson-Billings's (1991b) students commented about her community field experience volunteering in a soup kitchen and shelter for the homeless two hours per week:

This experience affected me in a very powerful way. Being a part of this atmosphere, brief as it was, taught me a few things about our society. It showed me a completely new perspective on life that I had never before been exposed to. I learned quite a bit about the differences and similarities between my life and their lives. . . . Talking to Elvin [a boy in the shelter] showed me how very similar he is to me. It was apparent to me that his life could have taken a very different path, and that likewise, that my life could have taken a very different path. This realization was very sobering to me and it taught me to empathize with his situation. On the other hand, the world of Julian Street is so very different from my world on campus. I noticed how easy it is to become narrow minded when my perspectives are constantly being influenced by the same atmosphere. (pp. 15–16)

Beyer (1991) presents some of the journal writings of one of his students, who discusses the impact of viewing the documentary film *The Women of Summer*, about the reunion of a group of women from Bryn Mawr College's summer school for women workers, in an educational foundations class:

Saw Women of Summer and I couldn't believe it. The entire time I was in complete awe. . . . These women did things because they felt it, not because it was the proper or socially acceptable thing to do . . . I sat through the movie with my textbooks and notepads, wearing nice clothes and feeling relatively secure in my life. All the time I'm wondering what does this all mean? Everything I have and all my material possessions don't add up to much when compared to the action that these women took. (p. 124)

Finally, Hollins (1990) shares a journal entry by one of her students in her educational foundations course at California State University–Hayward about the impact of class activities that were designed to help students develop a greater sense of their own ethnocultural identities:

I got a renewed sense of my identity and I focused on the idea that I too belong to an ethnic group. With this realization came a renewed sense of pride in my ethnic origins. I have begun to understand the pride that the other ethnic groups feel and the damage that our society causes by stigmatizing people who are different. (pp. 206–207)

Whether these and other similar changes in the perspectives of students are associated with long-lasting impact on students' world views, values, and dispositions is still an open question. Very little evidence exists in the literature that the changes documented by teacher educators are long-lasting (Bennett, 1988) or that they influence the way in which prospective teachers actually teach (Grant & Koskella, 1986). Generally we know very little about the development of teacher education students' cognitions, beliefs, and skills with respect to the teaching of diverse learners (Grant & Secada, 1990; Sleeter, 1985), including how particular teacher education strategies influence teacher learning.

We do know, however, that direct intercultural experience is important to the teaching of diverse students, and that carefully structured guided reflection about these experiences is important to making these experiences ones that result in shifts in the attitudes, beliefs, dispositions, and theories that govern teachers' practices. The literature clearly gives us clues about the way in which case studies of teacher education for diversity should be constructed.

CONCLUSION

This chapter has attempted to describe the emerging consensus in the litera- ture (as well as some of the debates) with regard to teaching across cultures in elementary and secondary school classrooms, and the variety of organizational structures and teaching strategies used in U.S. teacher education programs to prepare teachers for cultural diversity. It has focused on the preparation of white, monolingual student teachers to teach poor students of color who have not tra- ditionally succeeded in school. There is a sense, however, in which all teaching is intercultural regardless of the specific context in which it occurs. Because of the multiple microcultural identities of all students, regardless of their back-grounds, along the lines of gender, race, social class, language, religion, excep-tionalities, and so forth; all human experience is intercultural and all individuals are intercultural beings (Gollnick, 1992b). And because all human experience is intercultural, *individuals* within any given group will be affected somewhat differently by particular teacher actions. There is often as much variation within cultural groups as there is between groups.

Accordingly, this chapter has stressed the dangers of labeling students ac-cording to any single subcultural group membership and has emphasized the importance of teachers' learning how to study both the cultures of their own classrooms and the home and community cultures that their students bring to school with them.

Although various aspects of culturally responsive teaching (e.g., high ex-pectations, scaffolding), are discussed throughout the chapter as the most likely ways to promote school success for poor students of color, some of the limita-tions as well as some of the complexities of this cultural compatibility theory are also addressed. For example, as Villegas (1988) has pointed out, greater cultural compatibility in the classroom by itself does not begin to address the social, economic, and political inequalities underlying many school problems. And, as Bloch and Tabachnick (1991) point out, most examples in the litera-ture of successful efforts of cultural inclusion or culturally compatible teaching have occurred in relatively homogeneous environments where students share many characteristics. What cultural compatibility means in more multicultural contexts in which students share fewer characteristics with each other is not as clear. As Bloch and Tabachnick (1991) argue, when more than one ethnocultural group is involved in a classroom, adjustments made by the teacher for one group may not be important or successful for another group or for all of the different subgroups within each group.

Another important issue related to teacher education for diversity is the question of teacher development over time. Although I have mapped out two frameworks representing the range of existing positions on what and how teach-ers should be taught to teach across cultures, there is very little discussion in the literature of how this learning should be related to a teacher's career. The implication is that prospective teachers need to learn how to be and do all of the things that are discussed in this report by the time that they begin their first year of teaching. Given what we know about what student teachers bring to teacher education (e.g., the lack of interracial experience), and about the com-plexity of the process of teachers' learning to teach across cultures, this is prob-ably an unrealistic expectation (Villegas, 1993). Much more work needs to be done to look at the process of teacher education for diversity developmentally. Learning to be the kind of teacher described in this chapter is probably a career-long process. Identifying which things should be addressed within preservice teacher education and which things either can or must wait until later in a teacher's career is an important task.

Also, despite the agreement by many researchers about certain aspects of what teachers need to know, be like, and be able to do to successfully teach cross-culturally, there is still a lot of uncertainty about both the elements of successful teaching across cultures and how to prepare teachers for cultural diversity. Given this uncertainty, and the probable long-term nature of the process of teacher learning associated with learning to teach across cultures, one of the most important things we can do as teacher educators, as Zimpher and Ashburn (1992) argue, is to use an approach that enables teachers to talk and think together about the various kinds of problems they encounter related to cultural diversity and how they are addressing them. While the concepts of reflective teaching and teachers as researchers implied by this suggestion by themselves do not necessarily help us do a better job of addressing the needs of all students in our diverse society, they can be construed in ways that directly connect the deliberations of teachers to the ongoing struggle for a more humane and decent society (Zeichner, 1993).

Finally, as has been pointed out in this chapter, most of our existing knowledge about teacher education for diversity comes from very brief and often vague self-reports about the use of particular teacher education strategies and program structures. There are few detailed descriptions available that illuminate the lived reality of these efforts and their consequences over the long term for the prospective teachers who participate in them. A much closer look at the reality and the long-term consequences of these various approaches to teacher education for diversity is now needed. We must learn more about the particular kinds of field experiences and courses that facilitate the personal and professional transformations that student teachers must undergo to become successful teachers in cross-cultural situations.

NOTES

1. I would like to thank the following people for their comments and criticisms of an earlier draft of this chapter: Mimi Bloch, Ann DeVaney, Mary Dillworth, Mary Gomez, Carl Grant, Karen Hoeft, Mary Kennedy, Gloria Ladson-Billings, Bill McDiarmid, Susan Melnick, Lynn Paine, Bob Tabachnick, Bill Tate, Henry Trueba, and Ana Maria Villegas.

2. While gender clearly interacts with these factors in influencing the character of the classroom environment and the quality of student learning (e.g., see Fordham's [1988] discussion of gender differences in the socialization of academically successful African-American high school students), an analysis of the specific ways in which gender intersects with teaching and teacher education is beyond the scope of this chapter. For an excellent discussion of some of the important issues related to gender and teacher education see Maher & Rathbone (1986).

3. See Zeichner & Hoeft (in press) for a discussion of various staff-development initiatives and institutional arrangements that have been used to enhance the capacity of teacher education institutions and their faculty to prepare teachers for diversity.

4. See Bloch & Tabachnick (in press) for a discussion of the complexities associated with this concept of cultural relevance in instruction.

5. Fordham's (1988) work demonstrates that some highly academically successful African-American high school students give up their cultural identities in order to achieve academic success. Although this phenomena of "racelessness" undoubtedly occurs in other cases as well, it is more common to see cases of success for ethnic- and language-minority students in which a strong effort has been made to instill pride in students about their ethnocultural backgrounds. Lucas, Henze, and Donato's (1990) rich descriptions of high schools that were successful in facilitating academic achievement for Latino students is an example of how the maintenance of cultural identity is important to academic success. See Ferdman's (1990) discussion of how literacy instruction ought to support students' cultural identities for one explanation of why this may be so.

6. One of the most frequently cited examples of the adjustment of instructional patterns to take account of culturally conditioned learning styles is the Kamehameha Early Education Program in Hawaii (Tharp & Gallimore, 1988). In one aspect of this program, when reading instruction was changed to permit students to collaborate in discussing and interpreting texts, dramatic improvements in reading achievement were found (Au & Jordan, 1981). Other examples include the use of community-related themes in classroom writing projects (Moll & Diaz, 1987); and the use of interaction patterns commonly found in African-American churches (choral and responsive reading) in African-American classrooms (Hollins, 1982).

7. Sometimes, as in the case of Wisconsin, state standards for teacher education require students to complete community field experiences as part of required human relations training. The Wisconsin human relations requirement (PI4.11) mandates that teacher education programs include certain topics in their courses (e.g., study of the history, culture, customs, social institutions, values, life-styles, and contributions of specific ethnic groups) and direct involvement with both adult and pupil members of ethnic groups different from that of a prospective teacher (Wisconsin Department of Public Instruction, 1988).

8. California requires, for example, that all teacher education students experience a variety of culturally different classrooms and schools prior to certification (California Commission on Teacher Credentialing, 1988). Scholars such as Ford (1992) stress that placements in culturally diverse schools should be in situations where teachers are succeeding with ethnic- and language-minority students, a reality that is often not provided for by requirements such as the one in California.

9. Also see Adler's (1991) discussion of the use of literature to help correct teacher education students' distorted perspectives on the history of various ethnic groups. In the Urban Education Program of the Associated Colleges of the Midwest (e.g., Zeichner & Melnick, 1995), Marilyn Turkovich has developed and teaches a course, Dimensions of Multicultural Education and Global Awareness, which, among other things, exposes prospective teachers to U.S. and world history from the perspectives of oppressed groups.

10. Also see Fish's (1981) evaluation of the impact of a human relations field experience component in Wisconsin in which prospective teachers' attitudes toward blacks significantly worsened after the completion of the field experience.

11. See Ahlquist's (1991) very thoughtful analysis of power relations and student resistance in her multicultural foundations class at San Jose State University. This paper underscores the difficulties associated with the preparation of culturally sensitive teachers in conventional preservice teacher education programs.

REFERENCES

Ada, A. F. (1986). Creative education for bilingual teachers. *Harvard Educational Review, 56*(4), 386–393.

Adler, S. (1991). Forming a critical pedagogy in the social studies methods class: The use of imaginative literature. In B. R. Tabachnick & K. Zeichner (Eds.), *Issues and practices in inquiry-oriented teacher education* (pp. 77–90). Bristol, PA: Falmer Press.

Ahlquist, R. (1991). Position and imposition: Power relations in a multicultural foundations class. *Journal of Negro Education, 60*(2), 158–169.

American Association of Colleges for Teacher Education. (1987). *Teaching teachers: Facts and figures.* Washington, DC: Author.

American Asssociation of Colleges for Teacher Education. (1989). *Teaching teachers: Facts and figures.* Washington, DC: Author.

American Association of Colleges for Teacher Education. (1990). *AACTE/Metropolitan Life survey of teacher education students.* Washington, DC: Author.

Anderson, A. (1987). Cultural patterns affecting teacher and student expectations. In R. Dash (Ed.), *Round table report: The challenge—preparing teachers for diverse student populations.* Northridge, CA: Southern Service Center Far West Laboratory for Educational Research & Development.

Anyon, J. (1980). Social class and the hidden curriculum of work. *Journal of Education, 162,* 67–92.

Au, K., & Jordan, C. (1981). Teaching reading to Hawaiian children: Finding a culturally appropriate solution. In H. Trueba, G. P. Guthrie, & K. H. Au (Eds.), *Culture & the bilingual classroom.* Rowley, MA: Newbury House.

Banks, J. (1991). Teaching multicultural literacy to teachers. *Teaching Education, 4*(1), 135–144.

Bastian, A., Fruchter, N., Gittel, M., Greer, C., & Haskings, K. (1985). *Choosing equality: The case for democratic schooling.* Philadelphia, PA: Temple University Press.

Baty, R. (1972). *Reeducating teachers for cultural awareness.* New York: Praeger.

Bennett, C. (1988, April). *The effects of a multicultural education course on preservice teachers—attitudes, knowledge & behavior.* Paper presented at the annual meeting of the American Educational Research Association, New Orleans, LA.

Bennett, C. (1990). *Comprehensive multicultural education: Theory & practice.* Boston: Allyn & Bacon.

Beyer, L. (1991). Teacher education, reflective inquiry and moral action. In B. R.

Tabachnick & K. Zeichner (Eds.), *Issues and practices in inquiry-oriented teacher education* (pp. 113–129). Bristol, PA: Falmer Press.

Bloch, M., & Tabachnick, B. R. (1991, April). *Learning out of school: Critical perspectives on the theory of cultural compatibility*. Paper presented at the annual meeting of the American Educational Research Association, Chicago, IL.

Bloch, M., & Tabachnick, B. R. (in press). Rhetoric or reality: Improving parent involvement in school reform. In N. P. Greenman & K. Borman (Eds.), *Changing schools: Recapturing our past or inventing the future*. Albany: SUNY Press.

Bowen, E., & Salsman, F. (1979). Integrating multiculturalism into a teacher training program. *Journal of Negro Education, 48*(3), 390–395.

Bowers, C. A., & Flinders, D. (1990). *Responsive teaching: An ecological approach to classroom patterns of language, culture, and thought*. New York: Teachers College Press.

Brophy, J., & Good, T. (1986). Teacher behavior and student achievement. In M. Wittrock (Ed.), *Handbook of research on teaching* (3rd ed., pp. 328–375). New York: Macmillan.

Burstein, N., & Cabello, B. (1989). Preparing teachers to work with culturally diverse students: A teacher education model. *Journal of Teacher Education, 40*(5), 9–16.

Burstein, N., Vaughn, K., Wilcoxen, A., & Brewer, V. (1992). Infusing multicultural perspectives across the curriculum. In C. Grant (Ed.), *Toward education that is multicultural: Proceedings of the first annual meeting of the National Association for Multicultural Education* (pp. 161–179). New York: Silver Burdett.

California Commission on Teacher Credentialing. (1988). *Adopted standards of program evaluation and effectiveness*. Sacramento, CA: Author.

Carnegie Forum on Education and the Economy. (1986). *A nation prepared: Teachers for the 21st century*. New York: Carnegie Corporation.

Cazden, C., & Mehan, H. (1990). Principles from sociology and anthropology: Context, code, classroom, and culture. In M. Reynolds (Ed.), *Knowledge base for the beginning teacher* (pp. 47–57). Washington, DC: American Association of Colleges for Teacher Education.

Center for Education Statistics. (1987). *The condition of education*. Washington, DC: U.S. Government Printing Office.

Children's Defense Fund. (1991). *The state of America's children*. Washington, DC: Author.

Cole, M., & Griffin, P. (1987). *Contextual factors in education*. Madison: Wisconsin Center for Education Research.

Comer, J. (1988). Educating poor minority children. *Scientific American, 259*(5), 42–48.

Committee on Policy for Racial Justice. (1989). *Visions of a better way: A black appraisal of public schooling*. Washington, DC: Joint Center for Political Studies Press.

Cummins, J. (1986). Empowering minority students: A framework for intervention. *Harvard Educational Review, 56*(1), 18–36.

Delgado-Gaitan, C. (1991). Involving parents in the schools: A process of empowerment. *American Journal of Education, 100*(1), 20–46.

Delpit, L. (1986). Skills and other dilemmas of a progressive black educator. *Harvard Educational Review, 56*(4), 379–385.

Delpit, L. (1988). The silenced dialogue: Power and pedagogy in educating other people's children. *Harvard Educational Review, 58*(3), 280–298.

Diez, M., & Murrell, P. (1992). *Assessing abilities of expert teaching practices in diverse classrooms.* Unpublished manuscript. Alverno College, Milwaukee, WI.

Ducharme, E., & Agne, R. (1989). Professors of education: Uneasy residents of academe. In R. Wisniewski & E. Duchorne (Eds.), *The professors of teaching* (pp. 67–86). Albany: State University of New York Press.

Eddy, E. (1969). *Becoming a teacher: The passage to professional status.* New York: Teachers College Press.

Ellwood, C. (1990). The moral imperative of ethnic studies in urban teacher education programs. In M. Diez (Ed.), *Proceedings of the fourth national forum of the Association of Independent Liberal Arts Colleges for Teacher Education* (pp. 1–6). Milwaukee: Alverno College.

Ferdman, B. (1990). Literacy and cultural identity. *Harvard Educational Review, 60*(2), 181–204.

Fine, M. (1987). Silencing in public schools. *Language Arts, 64*(2), 157–174.

First, J., Kellogg, J. B., Willshire-Carrera, J., Lewis, A., & Almeida, C. A. (1988). *New voices: Immigrant students in U.S. public schools.* Boston: National Coalition of Advocates for Students.

Fish, J. (1981). *The psychological impact of field work experiences and cognitive dissonance upon attitude change in a human relations program.* Unpublished doctoral dissertation, University of Wisconsin-Madison.

Ford, B. (1992). Developing teachers with a multicultural perspective. In C. Grant (Ed.), *Toward education that is multicultural: Proceedings from the first annual meeting of the National Association for Multicultural Education.* New York: Silver Burdett.

Fordham, S. (1988). Racelessness as a factor in black students' school success: Pragmatic strategy or pyrrhic victory? *Harvard Educational Review, 58*(1), 54–84.

Francis-Okongwu, A., & Pflaum, S. (1993). Diversity in education: Implications for teacher preparation. In F. Pignatelli & S. Pflaum (Eds.), *Celebrating diverse voices: Progressive education and equity* (pp. 112–132). Newbury Park, CA: Corwin.

Fuller, M., & Ahler, J. (1987). Multicultural education and the monocultural student: A case study. *Action in Teacher Education, 9*(3), 33–40.

Garcia, E. (1974). Chicano cultural diversity: Implications for competency-based teacher education. In W. A. Hunter (Ed.), *Multicultural education through competency-based teacher education.* Washington, DC: American Association of Colleges for Teacher Education.

Garcia, E. (1990). Educating teachers for language minority students. In W. R. Houston (Ed.), *Handbook of research on teacher education* (pp. 712–729). New York: Macmillan.

Gay, G. (1986). Multicultural teacher education. In J. Banks & J. Lynch (Eds.), *Multicultural education in Western societies* (pp. 154–177). New York: Praeger.

Gentile, J. R. (1988). *Instructional improvement: Summary and analysis of Madeline Hunter's essential elements of instruction & supervision.* Oxford, OH: National Staff Development Council.

Gibson, M. (1984). Approaches to multicultural education in the United States: Some concepts and assumptions. *Anthropology and Education Quarterly, 15,* 94–119.

Gilbert, S., & Gay, G. (1985). Improving the success in school of poor black children. *Phi Delta Kappan, 67*(2), 133–137.

Ginsburg, M. (1988). *Contradictions in teacher education and society.* London: Falmer Press.

Gollnick, D. (1992a). Multicultural education: Policies and practices in teacher education. In C. Grant (Ed.), *Research & multicultural education* (pp. 218–239). London: Falmer Press.

Gollnick, D. (1992b). Race, class, & gender in teacher education. In M. Dillworth (Ed.), *Diversity in teacher education* (pp. 63–78). San Francisco: Jossey-Bass.

Gomez, M. (1991). Teaching a language of opportunity in a language arts methods class: Teaching for David, Albert & Darlene. In B. R. Tabachnick & K. Zeichner (Eds.), *Issues and practices in inquiry-oriented teacher education* (pp. 91–112). Bristol, PA: Falmer Press.

Gomez, M., & Tabachnick, B. R. (1991, April). *Preparing preservice teachers to teach diverse learners.* Paper presented at the annual meeting of the American Educational Research Association, Chicago, IL.

Gomez, M., & Tabachnick, B. R. (1992). Telling teaching stories. *Teaching Education, 4*(2), 129–138.

Good, T. (1990). Building the knowledge base of teaching. In D. Dill (Ed.), *What teachers need to know* (pp. 17–75). San Francisco: Jossey-Bass.

Goodlad, J. (1990). *Teachers for our nation's schools.* San Francisco: Jossey-Bass.

Gordon, B. (1988). Implicit assumptions of the Holmes & Carnegie reports: A view from an African-American perspective. *Journal of Negro Education, 57*(2), 141–158.

Gordon, B. (1992). The marginalized discourse of minority intellectual thought in traditional writings on teaching. In C. Grant (Ed.), *Research and multicultural education* (pp. 19–31). London: Falmer Press.

Grant, C. (1991). *Educational research and teacher training for successfully teaching limited English proficient students.* Paper presented at the Second National Research Symposium on Limited English Proficient Student Issues, Washington, DC.

Grant, C., & Gillette, M. (1987). The Holmes report and minorities in education. *Social Education, 51,* 517–521.

Grant, C., & Koskella, R. (1986). Education that is multicultural and the relationship between preservice campus learning and field experiences. *Journal of Educational Research, 79,* 197–203.

Grant, C., & Secada, W. (1990). Preparing teachers for diversity. In W. R. Houston (Ed.), *Handbook of research on teacher education* (pp. 403–422). New York: Macmillan.

Grant, C., & Sleeter, C. (1985). The literature on multicultural education: Review and analysis. *Educational Review, 37,* 97–118.

Grant, C., Zeichner, K., & Gillette, M. (1988). *Preparing teachers to work effectively with diverse students in multicultural settings: Final report.* Washington, DC: U.S. Department of Education.

Grossman, P., & Richert, A. (1988). Unacknowledged knowledge growth: A reexamination of the effects of teacher education. *Teaching & Teacher Education, 4,* 53–62.

Grumet, M. (1988). *Bitter milk: Women and teaching.* Amherst: University of Massachusetts Press.

Haberman, M. (1987). *Recruiting and selecting teachers for urban schools.* New York: ERIC Clearing House on Urban Education, Institute for Urban & Minority Education.

Haberman, M. (1991a). Can culture awareness be taught in teacher education programs? *Teaching Education, 4*(1), 25–31.

Haberman, M. (1991b). The rationale for training adults as teachers. In C. Sleeter (Ed.), *Empowerment through multicultural education.* Albany, NY: State University of New York Press.

Haberman, M., & Post, L. (1992). Does having a human relations experience affect preservice students perceptions of low-income minority children? *Midwestern Educational Researcher, 5*(2), 29–31.

Harrison, B. (1993). Building our house from the rubbish tree: Minority directed education. In E. Jacob and C. Jordan (Eds.), *Minority education: Anthropological perspectives* (pp. 147–164). Norwood, NJ: Ablex.

Heath, S. B. (1983). *Ways with words: Language, life and work in communities and classrooms.* New York: Cambridge University Press.

Hillard, A. (1974). Restructuring teacher education for multicultural imperatives. In W. A. Hunter (Ed.), *Multicultural education through CBTE* (pp. 40–55). Washington, DC: AACTE.

Hixson, J. (1991, April). *Multicultural issues in teacher education: Meeting the challenge of student diversity.* Paper presented at the annual meeting of the American Educational Research Association, Chicago, IL.

Hixson, J. (1992). Multicultural issues in teacher education: Meeting the challenge of student diversity. In C. Grant (Ed.), *Toward education that is multicultural: Proceedings of the first annual meeting of the National Association for Multicultural Education* (pp. 139–147). New York: Silver Burdett.

Hodge, C. (1990). Educators for a truly democratic system of schooling. In J. Goodlad & P. Keating (Eds.), *Access to knowledge: An agenda for our nation's schools* (pp. 259–272). New York: The College Board.

Hollins, E. (1982). The Marva Collins story revisited: Implications for regular classroom instruction. *Journal of Teacher Education, 33*(1), 37–40.

Hollins, E. (1990). Debunking the myth of a monolithic white American culture: Or moving toward cultural inclusion. *American Behavioral Scientist, 34*(2), 201–209.

Hollins, E., & Spencer, K. (1990). Restructuring schools for cultural inclusion: Changing the schooling process for African-American youngsters. *Journal of Education, 172*(2), 89–100.

Holmes Group. (1986). *Tomorrow's teachers.* East Lansing MI: Author.

Holmes Group. (1990). *Tomorrow's schools: Principles for the design of professional development schools.* East Lansing, MI: Author.

Howey, K. (1992). Teacher education in the U.S.: Trends and issues. *Teacher Educator, 27*(4), 3–11.

Huber, T. (1992). Culturally responsible pedagogy: The wisdom of multicultural education. In C. Grant (Ed.), *Toward education that is multicultural: Proceedings from the first annual meeting of the National Association for Multicultural Education* (pp. 28–35). New York: Silver Burdett.

Huber, T., & Pewewardy, C. (1990). *Maximizing learning for all students: A review of the literature on learning modalities, cognitive styles and approaches to meeting the needs of diverse learners.* Washington, DC: ERIC Clearinghouse on Teacher Education. (ERIC Document Reproduction Service No. ED 324–289)

Hunter, W. (1974). *Multicultural education through competency-based teacher education.* Washington, DC: American Association of Colleges for Teacher Education.

Irvine, J. J. (1989). *Cultural responsiveness in teacher education.* Paper presented at the Annual Meeting of Project 30, Monterey, CA.

Kennedy, M. (1991). Some surprising findings on how teachers learn to teach. *Educational Leadership, 49*(3), 14–17.

King, J., & Ladson-Billings, G. (1990). The teacher education challenge in elite university settings: Developing critical perspectives for teaching in a democratic & multicultural society. *European Journal of Intercultural Studies, 1*(2), 15–30.

Kleinfeld, J. (1992). Learning to think like a teacher: The study of cases. In J. Shulman (Ed.), *Case methods in teacher education* (pp. 33–49). New York: Teachers College Press.

Knapp, M., & Turnbull, B. (1991). Alternatives to conventional wisdom. In M. Knapp & P. Shields (Eds.), *Better schooling for the children of poverty: Alternatives to conventional wisdom* (pp. 329–353). Berkeley, CA: McCutchan.

Ladson-Billings, G. (1990). Culturally relevant teaching. *The College Board Review, 155,* 20–25.

Ladson-Billings, G. (1991a). *Who will teach our children? Preparing teachers to successfully teach African-American students.* Paper presented at the California State University Teleconference on Cultural Diversity in Teacher Preparation and Assessment: A National Crisis, Hayward, CA.

Ladson-Billings, G. (1991b). *When difference means disaster: Reflections on a teacher education strategy for countering student resistance to diversity.* Paper presented at the annual meeting of the American Educational Research Association, Chicago, IL.

Ladson-Billings, G. (1991c). Like lightning in a bottle: Attempting to capture the pedagogical excellence of successful teachers of black students. *International Journal of Qualitative Studies in Education, 3,* 335–344.

Ladson-Billings, G. (1994). *The dream keepers: Successful teachers of African-American children.* San Francisco: Jossey-Bass.

LaFontaine, H. (1988). Educational challenges and opportunities in serving limited-English-proficient students. In Council of Chief State School Officers (Ed.), *School success for students at risk* (pp. 120–153). Orlando, FL: Harcourt Brace Jovanovich.

Lanier, J., & Little, J. (1986). Research on teacher education. In M. Wittrock (Ed.), *Third handbook of research on teaching* (pp. 527–569). New York: Macmillan.

Laosa, L. (1977). Cognitive styles and learning strategies research: Some of the areas in which psychology can contribute to personalized instruction in multicultural education. *Journal of Teacher Education, 28*(3), 26–30.

Larke, P. (1990a, April). *Cultural awareness inventory: Assessing the sensitivity of preservice teachers.* Paper presented at the annual meeting of the American Educational Research Association, Boston, MA.

Larke, P. (1990b). *The impact of cross cultural mentoring on the attitudinal changes of preservice teachers.* Paper presented at the annual meeting of the Association of Teacher Educators, Las Vegas, NV.

Law, S. G., & Lane, D. S. (1987). Multicultural acceptance by teacher education students. *Journal of Instructional Psychology, 14*(1), 3–9.

Lee, M. (1989). Making child development relevant for all children. Implications for teacher education. *Early-child Development and Care, 47,* 63–73.

Levin, H. (1987). Accelerated schools for disadvantaged students. *Educational Leadership, 44,* 19–21.

Liston, D., & Zeichner, K. (1991). *Teacher education and the social conditions of schooling.* New York: Routledge.

Lucas, T., Henze, R., & Donato, R. (1990). Promoting the success of Latino language-minority students: An exploratory study of six high schools. *Harvard Educational Review, 60*(3), 315–340.

Mahan, J. (1982). Native Americans as teacher trainers: Anatomy and outcomes of a cultural immersion project. *Journal of Educational Equity & Leadership, 2*(2), 100–110.

Maher, F., & Rathbone, C. (1986). Teacher education and feminist theory: Some implications for practice. *American Journal of Education, 94*(2), 214–235.

McCarthy, C. (1990). *Race and curriculum.* Bristol, PA: Falmer Press.

McCormick, J. (1991, December 23). A class act for the ghetto. *Newsweek,* pp. 62–63.

McDiarmid, G. W. (1989). What teachers need to know about cultural diversity: Restoring subject matter to the picture. In M. Kennedy (Ed.), *Competing visions of teacher knowledge: Proceedings from an NCRTE Seminar for educational policy makers* (pp. 91–106). East Lansing, MI: National Center for Research on Teacher Education.

McDiarmid, G. W. (1990). *What to do about differences? A study of multicultural education for teacher trainees in the Los Angeles Unified School District.* East Lansing, MI: National Center for Research on Teacher Learning.

McDiarmid, G. W., & Price, J. (1990). *Prospective teachers' views of diverse learners: A study of the participants in the ABCD project.* East Lansing, MI: National Center for Research on Teacher Learning.

McNeil, L. (1986). *Contradictions of control: School structure and school knowledge.* New York: Routledge.

Mehan, H., & Trujillo, T. (1989). *Teacher education issues* (Research & Policy series no. 4). Santa Barbara: University of California Linguistic Minority Research Project.

Moll, L. (1988). Some key issues in teaching Latino students. *Language Arts, 65*(5), 465–472.

Moll, L., & Diaz, R. (1987). Teaching writing as communication: The use of ethnographic findings in classroom practice. In D. Bloome (Ed.), *Literacy and schooling* (pp. 55–65). Norwood, NJ: Ablex.

Montecinos, C. (1995). Multicultural teacher education for a culturally diverse teaching force. In R. Martin (Ed.), *Practicing what we preach: Confronting diversity in teacher education.* Albany, NY: State University of New York Press.

Montero-Sieburth, M. (1989). Restructuring teachers—knowledge for urban settings. *Journal of Negro Education, 58*(3), 332–344.

Mungo, S. (1982). *Mental health and the intern: A teacher training model.* (ERIC Document Reproduction Service No. ED 240 121)

Murrell, P. (1990). Making uncommon sense: Critical revisioning professional knowledge about diverse cultural perspectives in teacher education. In M. Diez (Ed.), *Proceedings of the fourth national forum of the Association of Independent Liberal Arts Colleges for Teacher Education* (pp. 47–54). Milwaukee: Alverno College.

National Center for Research on Teacher Education. (1989). *Competing visions of teacher knowledge: Proceedings from an NCRTE seminar for education policymakers: Student diversity*, 2. East Lansing, MI: Author.

National Coalition of Advocates for Students. (1991). *The good common school: Making the vision work for all students*. Boston: Author.

Natriello, G., McDill, E., & Pallas, A. (1990). *Schooling disadvantaged children: Racing against catastrophe*. New York: Teachers College Press.

Nieto, C. (1986). The California challenge: Preparing teachers for a growing Hispanic population. *Action in Teacher Education, 8*(1), 1–8.

Nieto, S. (1992). *Affirming diversity: The sociopolitical context of multicultural education*. New York: Longman.

Noordhoff, K., & Kleinfeld, J. (1993). Preparing teachers for multicultural classrooms. *Teaching and Teacher Education, 9*(1), 27–39.

Oakes, J. (1986). Tracking, inequality, and the rhetoric of school reform: Why schools don't change. *Journal of Education, 168*(1), 60–80.

O'Hare, W. (1988). *The rise of poverty in rural America*. Washington, DC: Population Reference Bureau.

Olsen, L., & Mullen, N. (1990). *Embracing diversity: Teachers voices from California's classrooms*. San Francisco: California Tomorrow Project.

Ornstein, A., & Levine, D. (1989). Social class, race, and school achievement: Problems & prospects. *Journal of Teacher Education, 40*(5), 17–23.

Paine, L. (1989). *Orientation towards diversity: What do prospective teachers bring?* (Research report 89–9). East Lansing, MI: National Center for Research on Teacher Learning.

Paley, V. G. (1989). *White teacher*. Cambridge: Harvard University Press.

Pallas, A., Natriello, G., & McDill, E. (1989). The changing nature of the disadvantaged population. *Educational Researcher, 18*(5), 16–22.

Ptak, D. (1988). *Report on the achievement of black high school students in the Madison Metropolitan School District, 1987–1988*. Madison, WI: Urban League.

Quality Education for Minorities Project. (1990). *Education that works: An action plan for the education of minorities*. Cambridge, MA: Author.

Quintanar-Sarellana, R. (1991, April). *Training teachers for a multicultural society*. Paper presented at the annual meeting of the American Educational Research Association, Chicago, IL.

Reed, D., & Simon, D. (1991). Preparing teachers for urban schools: Suggestions from historically black institutions. *Action in Teacher Education, 13*(2), 30–35.

Reyes, M. (1992). Challenging venerable assumptions: Literacy instruction for linguistically different students. *Harvard Educational Review, 62*(4), 427–446.

Rist, R. (1970). Student social class and teacher expectations: The self-fulfilling prophecy in ghetto education. *Harvard Educational Review, 40*(3), 411–451.

Rivlin, H., & Sciara, F. (1974). A cross-cultural approach to multicultural teacher education. In W. Hunter (Ed.), *Multicultural education through competency-based teacher education* (pp. 243–251). Washington, DC: American Association of Colleges for Teacher Education.

Rodriguez, R. (1982). *Hunger of memory: An autobiography, the education of Richard Rodriguez*. Toronto: Bantam Books.

Rosewater, A. (1989). Child and family trends: Beyond the numbers. In F. Macchiarola & A. Gartner (Eds.), *Caring for America's children* (pp. 4–19). New York: Academy of Political Science.

Ross, D., Johnson, M., & Smith, W. (1991). *Helping preservice teachers confront issues related to educational equity: Assessing revisions in coursework and fieldwork*. Paper presented at the annual meeting of the American Educational Research Association, Chicago, IL.

Shulman, J., & Mesa-Bains, A. (1992). *Teaching diverse students: Cases and commentaries*. San Francisco: Far West Laboratory for Educational Research and Development.

Singer, E. (1988). *What is cultural congruence and why are they saying such terrible things about it?* (Occasional Paper No. 120). East Lansing: Michigan State University, Institute for Research on Teaching.

Slavin, R., & Madden, N. (1989). What works for students at risk. *Educational Leadership, 46*(5), 4–13.

Sleeter, C. (1985). A need for research on preservice teacher education for mainstreaming and multicultural teacher education. *Journal of Educational Equity and Leadership, 5*(3), 205–215.

Sleeter, C. (1988). *Preservice coursework and field experiences in multicultural education: Impact on teacher behavior*. Kenosha: University of Wisconsin–Parkside School of Education.

Sleeter, C., & Grant, C. (1988). *Making choices for multicultural education*. Columbus, OH: Merrill.

Smith, B. O. (1969). *Teachers for the real world*. Washington, DC: American Association of Colleges for Teacher Education.

Smith, W. (1980). The American teacher corps programme. In E. Hoyle & J. Megarry (Eds.), *World yearbook of education: Professional development of teachers* (pp. 204–218). New York: Nichols.

Tabachnick, B. R. (1991, November). *Learning to teach social studies from multicultural perspectives in multicultural classrooms*. Paper presented at the annual meeting of the College and University Faculty Assembly of the National Council of Teachers of Social Studies, Washington, DC.

Taylor, D., & Dorsey-Gaines, C. (1988). *Growing up literate: Learning from inner city families*. Portsmouth, NH: Heinemann.

Teitelbaum, K., & Britzman, D. (1991). Reading and doing ethnography: Teacher education and reflective practice. In B. R. Tabachnick & K. Zeichner (Eds.), *Issues and practices in inquiry-oriented teacher education* (pp. 166–185). Bristol, PA: Falmer Press.

Tharp, R., & Gallimore, R. (1988). *Rousing minds to life: Teaching, learning & schooling in social context*. New York: Cambridge University Press.

Tiedt, P., & Tiedt, I. (1990). *Multicultural teaching: A handbook of activities, information & resources*. Boston: Allyn & Bacon.

Tikunoff, W., & Ward, B. (1991). *Competencies of teachers of ethnolinguistically diverse student groups.* Los Alamitos, CA: The Southwest Regional Educational Laboratory.

Tippeconnic, J. W. (1983). Training teachers of American Indian students. *Peabody Journal of Education, 61*(1), 6–15.

Trent, W. (1990). Race and ethnicity in the teacher education curriculum. *Teachers College Record, 91,* 361–369.

Trueba, H. (1989a). Cultural embeddedness: The role of culture on minority students' acquisition of English literacy. In M. Kennedy (Eds.), *Competing visions of teacher knowledge: Student diversity* (pp. 77–90). East Lansing, MI: National Center for Research on Teacher Education.

Trueba, H. (1989b). *Raising silent voices: Educating the linguistic minorities for the 21st century.* New York: Newbury.

Trueba, H., Jacobs, L., & Kirton, E. (1990). *Cultural conflict & adaptation: The case of Hmong children in American society.* Bristol, PA: Falmer Press.

Valencia, R. (1991). *Chicano school failures and success: Research & policy agenda for the 1990's.* Bristol, PA: Falmer Press.

Villegas, A. M. (1988). School failures and cultural mismatch: Another view. *Urban Review, 20*(4), 253–265.

Villegas, A.M. (1991). *Culturally responsive pedagogy for the 1990's and beyond.* Princeton, NJ: Educational Testing Service.

Villegas, A. M. (1993, April). *Restructuring teacher education for diversity: The innovative curriculum.* Paper presented at the annual meeting of the American Educational Research Association, Atlanta, GA.

Wahab-Zaher, Z. (1989, April). *The melting pot revisited.* Paper presented at the annual conference of the Oregon Multicultural Association, Salem, OR.

Watson, D., Northcutt, Z., & Rydell, L. (1989). Teaching bilingual students successfully. *Educational Leadership, 46*(5), 59–61.

Wayson, W. (1988, April). *Multicultural education among seniors in the College of Education at Ohio State University.* Paper presented at the annual meeting of the American Educational Research Association, New Orleans, LA.

Weiner, K. (1989). Asking the right questions: An analytic framework for reform of urban teacher education. *The Urban Review, 21*(3), 151–161.

Wisconsin Department of Public Instruction. (1988). *Teacher education program approval rules.* Madison: Wisconsin Department of Public Institutions.

Zeichner, K. (1990a). Preparing teachers for democratic schools. *Action in Teacher Education, 11*(1), 5–10.

Zeichner, K. (1990b). Changing directions in the practicum: Looking to the 1990's. *Journal of Education for Teaching, 16*(2), 105–132.

Zeichner, K. (1991a). Contradictions and tensions in the professionalization of teaching and the democratization of schools. *Teachers College Record, 92,* 363–379.

Zeichner, K. (1991b, April). *Teacher education for social responsibility.* Paper presented at the annual meeting of the American Educational Research Association, Chicago, IL.

Zeichner, K. (1993). Connecting genuine teacher development to the struggle for social justice. *Journal of Education for Teaching, 19*(1), 5–20.

Zeichner, K., & Gore, J. (1990). Teacher socialization. In W. R. Houston (Ed.), *Handbook of research on teacher education* (pp. 329–348). New York: Macmillan.

Zeichner, K., & Hoeft, K. (in press). Teacher socialization for cultural diversity. In J. Sikula (Ed.), *Handbook of research on teacher education* (2nd ed.). New York: Macmillan.

Zeichner, K., & Melnick, S. (1995). *The role of community experiences in preparing teachers for cultural diversity.* East Lansing, MI: National Center for Research on Teacher Learning.

Zimpher, N. (1989). The RATE project: A profile of teacher education students. *Journal of Teacher Education, 40*(6), 27–30.

Zimpher, N., & Ashburn, E. (1992). Countering parochialism among teacher candidates. In M. Dillworth (Ed.), *Diversity in teacher education* (pp. 40–62). San Francisco: Jossey-Bass.

CHAPTER 8

The Role of Community Field Experiences in Preparing Teachers for Cultural Diversity

Ken Zeichner and Susan Melnick

The idea of community field experiences in the education of teachers has a long history in U.S. teacher education. In the Flowers Report (Flowers, Patterson, Stratemeyer, & Lindsey, 1948), which initiated the modern era of school-based experiences in U.S. teacher education, schools and their communities were defined as sites for field experiences in teacher education programs, and much attention was given to providing various kinds of community experiences for prospective teachers to enable them to better utilize community agencies and resources in the school program, to help them learn about their students and their families, to foster a greater sense of community service among both teachers and students, and to generally help to break down the barriers between schools and communities by creating more community-responsive schools.

> Modern educators are hopeful of abandoning the concept of the school as an isolated agency in society. They would like to see the school become a community-centered activity. This places new responsibilities on the shoulders of teachers and/or those responsible for their preservice education. It means professional laboratory experiences directed toward helping the intending teacher understand what is involved in building effective community relationships both as a teacher and as a citizen of the community. For a prospective teacher these may include experiences in working with parents, using community agencies and resources as they contribute to the ongoing activities of the group, studying the community to better understand learners' needs and backgrounds, working cooperatively with other educational agencies in the interests of children, contributing with children or youth to community activities. (Flowers et al., 1948, p. 27)

Since 1948, the idea of community experiences in teacher education has received only sporadic attention in the literature and in practice. In a few of the major reports on teacher education in the United States, such as Smith's (1980) *A Design for a School of Pedagogy*, schools and their communities were defined as "pedagogical training laboratories" and the idea of teacher education field experience as existing totally within schools was rejected (see also Blair & Erickson, 1964; Hodgdon & Saunders, 1951). In the National Teacher Corps, which educated thousands of teachers between 1966 and 1982 to teach in schools in poverty areas, community experiences were a central part of the education of all interns (W. Smith, 1980; Weiner, 1993). Over 25 years ago, Cuban (1969) argued that teacher education programs must shift their center of gravity from the university to the classroom and community and give more serious attention to the issue of preparing teachers to build bridges between home and school, to link schooling to the child's existence beyond the school walls. Today there is much evidence that students' educational and psychological growth occurs most fruitfully in settings that draw on family and community strengths (e.g., Au & Kawakami, 1994; Ladson-Billings, 1994; Moll, 1992).

Despite this attention to community field experiences in teacher education, the idea of community-based teacher education has mostly been ignored by teacher educators and by teacher education researchers. For example, in the *Handbook of Research on Teacher Education*, sponsored by the Association of Teacher Educators and billed as a comprehensive analysis of the research literature in teacher education (Houston, 1990), there is only one brief note about the idea of community field experiences in its 900 pages, a reference to the National Teacher Corps that is not explained. The chapter on student teaching and school experiences makes no mention of community experiences.

THE POTENTIAL VALUE OF COMMUNITY FIELD EXPERIENCES

As we think about the task of preparing teachers to educate all students to high academic standards in our increasingly culturally diverse and unequal society, the idea of community field experiences and the use of community people as teacher educators become crucial. It is thought by some that community field experiences in teacher education programs can help prospective teachers begin to view pupils not as isolated individuals in classrooms but as members of total family and community environments (e.g., Mahan, Fortney, & Garcia, 1983). The literature in multicultural teacher education has clearly shown the inadequacy of course work and intellectual analysis alone in preparing culturally sensitive and interculturally competent teachers who are committed to educating all students to high academic standards (Grant & Secada, 1990; Ladson-Billings, in press; Zeichner & Hoeft, 1996).

There is a widespread problem of low expectations for the achievement of poor students of color, and prospective teachers are often reluctant to teach students with backgrounds different from their own and to interact with the parents of these students (Zeichner, 1993). Many teacher education students come to their teacher education programs viewing diversity as a problem rather than as a resource (Paine, 1989), and generally have little knowledge beyond stereotypes about different groups in the United States, their cultures, their histories, and their participation in and contributions to life in the United States (Lauderdale & Deaton, 1993; Wayson, 1988).

According to recent demographic analyses of teacher education institutions, faculty in teacher education programs often lack the same kind of diverse cultural experiences that their students lack, including teaching experience in culturally diverse or culturally different schools (e.g., Haberman, 1987; Howey & Zimpher, 1990). Some have argued for many years that teacher education programs must expand their vision and consider teachers with experience in culturally diverse or culturally different schools and noncertified laypeople in the community as key part-time members of the staff of teacher education programs (e.g., Mahan, 1982b).

> Teacher education institutions can employ part-time faculty members with special competence not represented on the regular staff. . . . Persons with particular knowledge of the languages and dialects of Native American tribes, Asian, and Hispanic Americans could train students to levels of proficiency in those languages. Public school teachers who have successfully taught and worked with minority students and communities could present information about the diverse behavior patterns and learning characteristics of minority populations. Curriculum specialists can instruct teachers in the processes of developing units focusing on subject areas with content related to cultural and ethnic minorities. Artists and musicians who know the history, content, and form of traditional and contemporary expressions of the cultures can provide the background needed to expand traditional school curricula. With the combined efforts of regular and part-time faculty and community resource persons, colleges of education can enhance the training of their students to serve diverse cultural and ethnic communities. (Hayes, 1980, p. 107)

The literature strongly indicates the need for an experiential component in teacher education programs that helps prospective teachers examine themselves and their attitudes toward others, and helps them develop greater intercultural competence. The preparation of teachers for cultural diversity involves a fundamental transformation of people's world views and goes far beyond giving information about cultures, curriculum, and instruction (Nieto, 1992).

One response to this need for an experiential component that addresses issues of cultural competence has been to increase the placement of practicum students and student teachers in schools serving culturally diverse or different student populations. Because many schools are isolated from their communities and not responsive to community cultures, these school placements often do not provide the kind of contact that is needed to overcome negative attitudes toward culturally different students, their families, and communities (Zeichner, 1992) and sometimes end up strengthening and reinforcing stereotypes rather than stimulating their reexamination (Haberman & Post, 1992).

There is some evidence that certain kinds of community experiences facilitate the development of positive attitudes toward poor parents that are contrary to the deficit attitudes that still are dominant in many public schools. Sabrina, a graduate student teacher in the Teach for Diversity program at the University of Wisconsin–Madison, comments on how her experience of participating in a weekly parenting group composed mostly of poor young mothers influenced her understanding of these parents.[1]

> You gain insight into where your families are under stress, the kinds of stresses that are in their lives. It's hard to imagine I think, for people from a middle class, upper middle class background, what these people can be up against. And it's quite overwhelming at times. So you get a lot of insight into what their daily lives are and what their struggles are . . . what I was struck by again and again was their concern for their children. They want the best for their children. . . . I was just blown away by the articulateness of these people, how they could articulate their issues and problems, how they could articulate their concern and their love for their children. . . . They are under so much stress and they are not getting what they want as adults, as people, and as women. That makes it very hard to be able to do all of the best things for your children. But I was impressed by their intelligence, articulateness, and concern again and again.

Kathy, an undergraduate student teacher at the University of Wisconsin–Madison, describes how her deficit views of poor parents changed as a result of participating in two dialogues between school staff and parents in a government-subsidized housing project that were initiated by the parents. There were some very candid discussions during these meetings about the lack of achievement of some African-American students in the school.

> The two meetings had me thinking. Previously, I had the impression that most Southgate parents did not care very much about their children's education. It was very hard to get many of these parents to participate in school conferences or sign permission slips on time. From these meetings, I saw other possible explanations for their lack of participation. For many parents, time, money, and other stresses may get in the way. Lots of parents are working long days on the job just to

make ends meet. Others are struggling to find a job which we all know can be very difficult in today's economy. But overall, it sounds like many are doing the best they can to survive and support their children. I will not be so quick to judge parents when they don't show up for appointments or participate in their child's academic life.

The currently popular idea of professional development schools as they have been reported in the literature (e.g., Darling-Hammond, 1994; Levine, 1992) does not guarantee that these kinds of issues will be addressed by student teachers. There is little or no discussion in the professional development school literature of efforts to help prospective teachers become more knowledgeable about the communities in which they teach and about how to use this knowledge in their teaching (Zeichner, 1992) even by those who emphasize the importance of locating professional development schools in culturally diverse schools (Pugach & Pasch, 1994).

VARIETIES OF COMMUNITY FIELD EXPERIENCE

Despite the general neglect of community-based teacher education, various kinds of community field experience have been implemented by teacher educators. These include very brief experiences associated with particular courses such as the "cultural plunges" in the Introduction to Multicultural Education course at San Diego State University (Nieto, 1994; Tran, Young, & DiLella, 1994), early field experience practicums that precede student teaching (Mungo, 1980), and living and student teaching for a semester in culturally different communities (Mahan, 1982a; Mahan, Fortney, & Garcia, 1983).

Sometimes the focus of these experiences is on community service or on learning more in a general way about a culture different from one's own and about oneself (e.g., Anderson & Guest, 1994). This includes learning about what a particular community thinks about specific educational issues (Narode, Rennie-Hill, & Peterson, 1994) At other times, the focus is more directly on the classroom implications of these experiences (e.g., the skills of translating cultural knowledge into culturally relevant pedagogy, the skills of relating to culturally different parents). Other varieties of community experience in teacher education have emphasized developing prospective teachers' abilities to engage their pupils in community-action projects. Some community field experiences have emphasized more than one of these different purposes in various combinations of emphasis.

Community field experiences have also varied according to how structured or unstructured they are for prospective teachers. An example of a structured experience is the placement of student teachers in community agencies for a

specified number of hours per week to engage in specific tasks that are determined ahead of time. Unstructured community experiences sometimes involve
asking student teachers who are living in communities to arrange their own
community projects in consultation with community members. Community field
experiences also vary according to how closely they are supervised by representatives of the teacher education program and according to the degree of preparation, and the degree to which venues for structured reflection about the
experiences are provided in teacher education programs (Mahan, Fortney, &
Garcia, 1983).

Despite the potential benefits for prospective teachers in community work,
the use of community experiences in teacher education programs does not have
an unproblematic history. For example, in the National Teacher Corps, where
community work was a central feature of the preparation of teachers, the community experiences were considered by some to be the most varied, difficult,
and controversial aspects of the program. Often adequate time was not provided
to complete these experiences and cooperating teachers sometimes exerted
pressures on interns to keep them in the classroom and away from the outside
community (Corwin, 1973).

THE AMERICAN INDIAN RESERVATION PROJECT

We have chosen to present, as one example of a program that provides community field experiences to prospective teachers with the goal of developing greater
cultural sensitivity and intercultural teaching competence, The American Indian Reservation Project (AIRP) at Indiana University. This program, examined
as part of a 5-year study funded by the U.S. Department of Education, Office of
Educational Research and Improvement (OERI) and the National Center for
Research on Teacher Learning (NCRTL) at Michigan State University (Melnick
& Zeichner, 1994), involves a semester-long immersion experience of living and
student teaching on a Native American reservation in the southwest United
States.[2] NCRTL researchers visited the program twice (3 days per visit) to observe
various program activities, to interview program staff and students, and to interview graduates of each program. We also examined both published and unpublished literature that was available on the program (e.g., Mahan, 1982a, 1982b,
1993a, 1993b), as well as internal program documents such as course syllabi
and reports.

The American Indian Reservation Project is a semester-long cultural immersion program for student teachers at Indiana University and elsewhere, that
fulfills the student teaching requirement in whatever program the students are
enrolled.[3] Students, who have mostly been young white females, participate in
a year-long structured preparation for the immersion experience, a 17–18 week

student teaching experience in a school on a Native American reservation in the southwest United States (mostly Navajo, Tohono O'Odham, or Apache), and various kinds of community activities that evolve from their living in Bureau of Indian Affairs (BIA) dormitories with Native American students and working with Native American dormitory staff.[4]

Program Overview

The emphasis in the AIRP is on helping student teachers to become more culturally sensitive and interculturally competent teachers who are able to adapt themselves and their instruction to be successful in any type of cross-cultural teaching situation. According to Jim Mahan, who developed the program for the 1973–1974 academic year and directed it until his retirement in 1994:

> We want the students to learn about the culture of another group. We want them to adapt to the culture of that group, while they are student teaching in it. We want them to try to adjust and to modify their teaching procedures and their choices of curricular units to whatever degree they can to be more sensitive teachers. I would hope that after they've gone through the American Indian Reservation Project . . . that if they end up in schools in Detroit or Indianapolis, they would be more sensitive, more adapting teachers there too.

The goals of the program extend beyond the desire to create more culturally relevant schooling in Native American contexts. Mahan and his staff hope that AIRP graduates will also teach non–Native American students better about Native Americans (Interview with Mahan, 2/15/93). Finally, the goals of the program go beyond the promotion of more culturally relevant and culturally accurate teaching practices and seek the development of more culturally sensitive people who know more both about themselves and about a particular Native American community. One of the major goals of the program, for example, is for AIRP student teachers to forge a few close friendships during the semester with Native American adults (Mahan, 1982a). According to Mahan, living in the community and making friends are key elements in overcoming stereotypes about culturally different people.

> Once you've got 8, 10, or 12 close Navajo friends and know 2 or 3 Navajo families, and know their children and maybe have babysat the children a time or two, and gone off shopping all day with them on 4 or 5 different weekends—while you are doing it, you learn an awful lot about Navajo people. This is the kind of teacher preparation experience that defeats some stereotypes often held by preservice teachers.

Program Opportunities for Learning from and About Communities

The first aspect of the AIRP program that students experience is a year-long orientation program that culminates in an intensive 2½-day workshop on the Indiana University campus. During this year-long cultural preparation, which is used as a screening device for the program, students are required to read, from a collection supplied by the program, over 30 articles and at least two books about various aspects of Native American cultures (e.g., history, religion, economics, political and educational issues, current events). This activity, like most every other aspect of AIRP, has been very carefully structured by the project staff. Students are required to write a brief analysis of each article and book that they read, which includes a summary, their personal reaction to the piece, and a discussion of the classroom implications of the reading. Project staff respond to these student analyses in writing and hold regular evening discussion sessions with the students during the academic year preceding their student teaching for students who are located on the Indiana University campus.

In addition, students are required to complete one major project during the preparation period that represents something that they learned from their cultural preparation and that will be useful to their teaching during their student teaching semester. During the preparation period the year that we studied the program, these curriculum unit projects included such things as the development of thematic units about various aspects of Navajo culture and religion, the development of an anthology of Native American literature for use in the classroom, the development of units on teenage pregnancy and fetal alcohol syndrome, and the performance of a ceremony at the workshop that indicated what students had learned about Native American culture. This ceremony included the reading of the poem "Indian Education Blues," written by one of the students, which expressed her concern with the BIA boarding school system and the general state of Native American education in the United States.

During the intensive 2½-day orientation program that is conducted in Bloomington each spring, all of the students who will be student teaching in the AIRP program the following academic year gather with the program staff, several graduates of the program, and several consultants who are noncertified Native American adults from the communities where the students will teach. This workshop includes films, discussions, lectures, and simulations designed to help the prospective teachers become more aware of their own values, more knowledgeable about the complexities of the histories and contemporary situations of the Native American peoples in the areas where they will teach, and more informed about the situation in the schools in which they will work. Students are also given a lot of information about the details of student teaching requirements, including detailed information about the community experiences that will be a central feature of their student teaching semester.

One of the most important dimensions of this workshop from the perspective of both students and staff is the time that students spend with the Native American consultants. During the spring 1993 workshop that we observed, the consultants included a Navajo poet who also worked as director in one of the BIA dormitories in which AIRP students live, and a husband and wife who also worked in BIA dormitories on the Navajo reservation and who were artists. These consultants shared aspects of Navajo language and culture and gave students advice on how to make Navajo friends and about how to make meaningful contributions to dormitory and community life. They also shared how important their cultural identity is to them and the importance of incorporating cultural elements into the school program.

During the student teaching semester students are required to live and work in BIA dormitories and to engage in various community activities (Mahan, 1982a). Their activities in the dormitories include such things as serving meals, helping to prepare children for bed, organizing and leading various informal recreational activities, tutoring and helping children with their homework, chaperoning children to various events, and providing emotional support to children (Willison, 1989). Project participants also frequently report sponsorship of dormitory, art, dance, and other clubs. The Native American dormitory aides are the key instructors in this aspect of AIRP. It is by making friends with these aides that student teachers gain access to events and practices in the larger community.

> Your main contact in that building is going to be the dorm aides. Their grass roots are Indian people. They usually do not have college degrees. Many of them don't have a very high salary. Their parents, or maybe they themselves, are still raising sheep or still weaving rugs. . . . The students get to know these folks in the dorm very well before it's all over. And they start going home with them. They start getting involved in the daily activities of the dormitory personnel. They hear these people talk and they learn from them informally.

Throughout the life of AIRP, student teachers have been required to complete biweekly cultural reports (eight per semester) in which they identify and discuss significant cultural events and cultural values, and explain the implications for their teaching of what they have learned. These reports take about 3 hours to complete each time and are responded to in writing by program staff based on the Indiana University campus.[5] The requirement of writing cultural reports has ensured that student teachers become involved in the larger community.

> To complete these reports, students must become involved in the life of the cultural community in which they are placed, observe events,

conditions, attitudes in that community, find meaning in the cultural phenomena around them, and utilize those meanings and learnings to modify personal teaching procedures. (Mahan, 1990, p. 4)

On average, students in AIRP spend about 15 hours per week in nonschool activities in the dorms and the larger community. Students have been invited into Native American homes for meals and to play games; have participated with their new Native American friends in various community activities such as chapter house meetings and ceremonies and dances; and have volunteered their time to work in libraries and to assist in sheep herding, in making baskets and jam, in handling hay to be distributed to snow-threatened sheep, and in raising money for community needs.

A key aspect of the AIRP project, according to Mahan, is the careful way in which it has been structured to provide for cultural learning.

The reservation project is not a "throw the student teachers into the culture and hope for the best" endeavor. Considerable study of Native American people and conditions is a prerequisite for participation. Involvement in community and dormitory activities outside classroom walls and beyond the classroom day is required. Detailed reflection followed by interpretative writing on Native American values, issues, conditions, aspirations and learning are completed on a biweekly basis. Project faculty and former participants share successful ways for gaining community involvement and understanding. The structure and requirements of a student teaching experience play major roles in determining what student teachers learn and what sources provide impetus for that learning. (Mahan, 1993b, p. 12)

Impact on Students

Throughout the orientation and student teaching periods, there is a continual emphasis on the importance of adapting one's teaching to reflect, utilize, and build on cultural values and learning patterns. In our interviews with program graduates and student teachers, we found much evidence of student teachers' making efforts to connect their classrooms to community people, practices, and values, even when cooperating teachers did not support these practices. Our interviewees spoke frequently of how they learned the value for teachers of acquiring cultural knowledge of the community. For example, Susan, an AIRP graduate, was involved in a variety of community activities during her student teaching semester that included sheepherding and volunteering at a community library. She attended many community events such as pow wows, dances, and ceremonies; visited all of the homes of her pupils; and commented on the value of these experiences as follows:

> You don't really take into account what the kids do all weekend when they're home. Around where I live, the kids will go to a soccer game or go out with their parents to a movie or do the normal little white kid thing, the normal "American" things to do. . . . But these kids don't do these kinds of things. Some of them are home all alone all weekend, some of them have to go straight home from school and herd the sheep, some of them are involved in dance competitions with their pow wows and every weekend travel for that kind of thing. Some of them are real talented artists.
>
> Getting to know my students' families changed how I taught things. The more that you learn about the family and the way that they do things at home, the easier it is to teach the students the way they're used to being taught. For example, I didn't know that some of the kids in my kindergarten class spoke only Navajo at home. It was real hard for them to come in the morning and have to go from Navajo to English and back and forth and I would do as much as I could in Navajo even if it was just the days of the week and the months of the year.
>
> I also visited their homes. I saw how many kids were around the house, how much of the extended family was living with the kids. They would introduce me to their families and each kid would have something they'd want to show us at home. Most of the parents were really receptive. Back in the classroom, rather than saying "Did Mom help you with this, or did Dad say you could do that?" I could say "Oh, your uncle Joe was there. Did he talk with you about this at all? Did you ask him about this kind of thing?" And they would know that I was making the effort.
>
> The more I got involved in the community, the more it made me realize these students bring so much into the classroom. It really helps me to be a more effective teacher when I can relate things to what I know kids are doing. Most of my kids lived in hogans with no electricity or running water or anything, and just to see it helped me to understand what they went through every morning just to get to school.
>
> Learning about my students has done wonders. It has made me see things through other people's eyes. I take more time now to sit and say "Why are they doing it this way, or why are they thinking this way?" It has made me much more patient, because I had to do a lot more waiting, listening, and learning, rather than the "go get em" kind of thing that I'm used to doing.

Another program graduate, Judy, commented on how community experience helped her understand the cultural meaning of community practices that would otherwise be looked down on by outsiders like herself, and to gain the respect of the community.

> As a teacher you need to possess a knowledge of where your students are coming from—what their lives are like, or just really what their everyday existence is so that you're able to relate to them. I think community experience gave me terrific insights into what their cultures and traditions were. For example, they use a cactus and they dry it out, and it is medicinal, like an herb. However, it is also kind of like a hallucinogenic drug. I think the Anglo culture would be very quick to shun its use, especially with children, or in a religious way, because we would say that it is a drug. However, in their belief system, it is an integral part of their religion and so it is very hurtful to them when you say it is not good for you or it is a drug. They actually use it to stop babies from crying and, of course, in their ceremonies. . . . By interacting with the families on the weekends or in off time you can kind of bring that to your teaching. . . . when you show that you have an interest in the people and that you're not just this teacher who has descended upon them from wherever and is there to show them the right way like a missionary type of attitude. I think that means a lot to them in terms of gaining their respect as a community. . . . You really need that to be an effective teacher.

These comments were echoed by Donna, another program graduate, who became convinced of the importance of learning from the community and of using this knowledge to make the classroom experience relevant to children's lives outside of school.

> I think it really helped to know what the kids were talking about. I mean when they say "squaw dance." When I first got here, I'm like "squaw dance? What's this all about?" Through meeting community members and the ladies in the dorms, the dorm mothers, I was able to find out what it is all about. Sometimes the kids come in and they're really tired and you think, "Oh, my gosh, these parents are not taking care of their kids." I would think "What's going on here." . . . And actually it would be some kind of ceremony or special things like that. After a family member dies, they are not to bathe for four days. The ceremony goes on for four nights in a row. It really helps to be aware of what's going on in the child's life and to understand what the requirements are at home.

Many of them go home and herd sheep on the weekends or in the evening or chop wood or carry water. It really helps me to bring that into my classroom rather than to push it away and teach like I was in suburban Cincinnati where all of the families are lily white. It gave me a better way to present problem solving to them in math or science. Experiments will have something to do with their experience at home to bring it together. Trying to make school not a totally foreign experience, a totally anglo experience for them.

While reading the literature on the AIRP program and during our site visits, we were presented with many examples of student teachers making connections to the community and using community "funds of knowledge" (Moll, Amanti, Neff, & Gonzalez, 1992) in their teaching. These included two student teachers who reported bringing Navajo grandmothers into their classrooms to help pupils dye wool as part of a unit on changes, and to teach weaving to the class. Others incorporated Navajo language into their classrooms, used Native American literature in instruction, made up word problems in math with things from the Navajo culture to substitute for those in the book, and encouraged their pupils to bring elements of their cultures into the classroom through their writing about community issues or in art projects such as quilt making. One program graduate, Carmen, reported basic adjustments that she made in her teaching style in her efforts to become a more culturally relevant teacher. For example:

I was the coach for the volleyball team. When we first started volleyball, I got the ball and the net and I started yelling like a coach. . . . I was acting like a typical coach. They all walked off the volleyball court and went playing and whatever. . . . I sat there . . . not knowing what to do. That night I was really upset and I sat in my room and thought about it and I remembered that competition and outside authoritarian behavior are not the style of their upbringing or their culture. So rather than yell to them, "This is what you're going to do," the next day I realized that I just have to go out there and sit there and see what they do. So I went out there, and I took the ball and sat there with the ball bouncing it. And eventually some of the Navajo girls came over . . . and they took the ball. I passed it to them and they started bouncing it over the net and some of the guys came over and some more and finally enough for two teams. And while they were playing, I just sat there for the longest time, not saying a word and they would joke to each other in Navajo, having fun and not really paying attention to me. The second day I started saying "Well, stand back a little bit more" or "Try to hit it this way." But it was very low key, no yelling out "Hey go do this, go do that" because it just wasn't the way to approach it.

There is some limited evidence that the impact of the program on encouraging a more culturally relevant approach to teaching persists beyond student teaching. First, there is some evidence presented by Mahan and Lacefield (1982) that graduates of AIRP and other cultural immersion projects at Indiana University often take teaching positions in schools serving ethnic minority populations. However, even when they do not do so and instead go to relatively nondiverse schools in suburbia, there is some evidence that they become advocates for a more multicultural approach to teaching than is common in those schools. For example, Carmen, who at the time of our interview was back teaching first grade in a predominately white elementary school in Indiana, told us that she brings many cultural ideas and concepts into her class, especially with regard to Native Americans. She claimed that her teaching about Native Americans has countered many stereotypes that her first graders had about Native Americans.

Judy, another program graduate, also claimed that she is the outspoken one in her school for examining curriculum from cultural viewpoints. Mahan cited many instances to us of program graduates who have gone back to nondiverse schools and created Native American literature courses at the secondary level or Native American units in elementary schools. While we have not directly observed the classrooms of program graduates, the belief that AIRP graduates teach multiculturally and "against the grain" is very pervasive among many of those who have been associated with the program.

Another influence of the program on students goes beyond its effects on teaching style and content and suggests that, to some degree, a fundamental personal transformation takes place in AIRP students as people. Most of the program graduates that we interviewed spoke to us with enthusiasm about how AIRP had changed their lives and made them better people—more patient, less selfish, more understanding and open-minded and more aware of their privileged position in the world. This same tendency is also present in student reactions reported by Mahan (1982a). For example,

> I used to be very selfish, but the Navajo people I worked with have somehow changed that part of me.

> It's just amazing the type of transformation that takes place over the time frame that you're there. . . . I wouldn't change my time out there for anything in the world. . . . The truth of the matter is that as much as you learn about them, you're going to learn about yourself, if not more.

> In terms of how did it change me—how did it change my world view, it was pretty significant . . . as a teacher you look at how you are teaching things . . . you examine your position of privilege in relation to other

people and you have to understand that before you can understand where they're coming from.

The experience of living and teaching in a Native American community for a full semester seems to have developed more cultural sensitivity and intercultural competence, despite the fact that many of the cooperating teachers often did not model or support a culturally relevant approach to teaching. In Willison's (1989) case studies of five AIRP student teachers on the Navajo Reservation, the student teachers reported that some of the non-Indian staff made them feel guilty for participating in and learning about the Navajo culture. Some of the cooperating teachers in this study disagreed with the idea of integrating culture into the classroom.

> Believe it or not, some of the Anglo people I worked with out on the Navajo reservation seemed to have a very limited view of the students they were teaching and seemed to have very anglicized views about the educational processes that these Navajo students should undertake. I think that they were almost like strangers in a strange land. They were living amongst these people but they knew almost nothing about them and didn't care to know anything about them. To me that just seemed wrong.

One of the most significant aspects of AIRP for prospective teachers seems to be the experience that many of them had for the first time in their lives "of being a minority, of being watched, of not knowing exactly how to act or interact, and of not necessarily being accepted" (Willison, 1989, p. 216).

> I went to a pow wow a couple of weeks ago. And in the pow wow, they had these things called inter tribals which are dances where one of the drum groups dances and the head male and female dancers go out and lead the dance. It's a really simple traditional Indian dance. All it is, is like a little bobbing walking step. And my friend who took me said, "Come on Dara, let's go and dance." So I went out there and everybody was watching me. I mean I never had that experience before. My skin was just crawling and literally everybody was watching me. I [now] know what friends of mine who are black say whenever they've had this experience.

Despite the positive effects that AIRP seems to have had on many students, not all students became fully involved in community activities and not all students integrated cultural elements into their teaching. For example, Willison

(1989) concluded in his case studies that "while all the students gained insight into the Navajo culture, they did not necessarily demonstrate that the cultural insights affected their actual instructional strategies" (p. 222). Amy, Peg, and Rea, three of the five student teachers, were singled out for their lack of culturally relevant teaching at particular points in the semester.

> Although Rea was capable of suggesting ways in which the curriculum could be changed, she never demonstrated a strong desire or conviction to implement changes in either of her student teaching placements. (p. 182)

> Peg did not develop a single lesson which incorporated a culturally relevant topic. (p. 163)

> In discussing how the Navajo culture was integrated into the classroom, Amy stated that because she allowed the students to choose their own writing topics she was in a sense integrating culture into the classroom. (p. 194)

So while most of the students who participated in AIRP gained insights into the Native American culture in which they were immersed, they did not all demonstrate adaptations of their teaching based on these cultural insights (Willison, 1989). Although the lack of support for culturally relevant instruction by some cooperating teachers was a factor in the lack of classroom actions based on cultural insights, it was not the determining factor. In some of the cases reported by Willison and in some of our interviews, there is evidence that student teachers sometimes became *more determined* to teach in a culturally relevant way because of the cultural insensitivity of their cooperating teachers. For example, Willison (1989) reported:

> Sue's negative comments dealt with her supervisor's lack of cultural sensitivity. Because this lack of sensitivity was so prevalent . . . Sue stated that she became more determined and interested in representing the culture in the curriculum. (p. 126)

The degree to which student teachers are fully involved in the community and make friends in the community seems to be a critical factor in determining the degree to which adaptations are made in the classroom based on cultural insights about one's pupils and their lives outside of school. Despite the careful structure of the program to provide for community experiences and cultural learning, some student teachers seem to be able to minimize their contacts outside of school to superficial relationships and do not develop the support network to enable them to teach against the grain in a culturally relevant way. Other student teachers take full advantage of the opportunities presented in the community and develop support systems to sustain them in the face of cooperating teachers who criticize a culturally relevant approach to teaching.

All AIRP student teachers suddenly find themselves geographically and culturally isolated for a substantial period of time, initially unable to rely on a support system of family, friends, and university staff. Because models of culturally relevant teaching are not widespread in Native American schools, and particularly in the BIA schools that are used a lot by AIRP, some support system is needed to encourage student teachers to incorporate cultural knowledge into the curriculum. A few student teachers are able to get this encouragement from the staff in the schools in which they are working. Most students, however, must find this support in their "cultural correspondence" with program staff in Indiana or through friendships made with local community members.

CONCLUSION

The carefully structured community experiences in AIRP serve to promote greater self-understanding and cultural learning on the part of most students. The experience of being a minority in a culturally different context seems to have had a tremendous impact on some students. Whether these insights are translated into adaptations in classroom practice seems to depend on the degree to which student teachers take full advantage of the program's opportunities and extend themselves into the community in more than a superficial way, to make close friends and to actively participate in community activities.

When community participation is great, student teachers are more likely to engage in culturally relevant teaching, even when it is not supported by their cooperating teachers. The careful structure of the program in preparing students for the experience, and in monitoring their community work and their reflection about that work through the interactive process of writing and responding to cultural reports, is a key feature of this program. The Native Americans who serve as paid part-time consultants in the program to help prepare student teachers for the 4-month immersion experience are seen by student teachers as the most valuable part of their preparation.

Also, while there is limited evidence that the effects of AIRP on student teachers carries over into the early years of teaching, we do not know all that much at present about the impact of community field experiences over time.

The fact that some of the schools associated with AIRP did not offer student teachers models of high expectations for pupils and the incorporation of cultural content into the classroom has reinforced for us the inadequacy of school-based experiences alone in culturally different communities in developing cultural sensitivity and intercultural teaching competence.

Our findings underline the importance of teacher education programs' employing community members in both the preparation for and instruction during community experiences. Teacher education institutions as a whole lack faculty who have the knowledge and ability to implement community field experiences on their own. The new partnerships between schools and universities that are receiving so much attention today in the literature are not sufficient for developing the cultural competence needed by today's teachers unless these partnerships also extend to the communities in which the schools exist.

Community field experiences are not a panacea for the failure of teacher education programs to prepare teachers for cultural diversity. They are difficult to initiate and sustain and have as little status as school-based experiences within teacher education institutions. They are also often resisted by schools that are unresponsive to the communities in which they exist.

Given the scope of the task before us today in preparing teachers to teach many students who have backgrounds and life experiences different from their own, it seems important for the teacher education community to further explore ways to make community experiences an integral part of the preparation of all teachers.

NOTES

1. Since the fall of 1992, some faculty and graduate students in the elementary student teacher program at the University of Wisconsin–Madison have been studying various kinds of community experiences for student teachers. The data from this work cited in this chapter come from ongoing research projects conducted by Luann Duesterberg and Ken Zeichner.

2. For examples of other teacher education programs that have included community field experiences as central figures see Clothier & Hudgins, 1971; Ellner & Barnes, 1977; Kapel & Kapel, 1982; Lebaron & Royster, 1974; Soptick & Clothier, 1974; and Zeichner & Melnick, 1995.

3. Students from other universities can apply for AIRP and if admitted complete a modified orientation program. Over the life of the program, about 65% of the 800+ students who have completed AIRP have come from Indiana University.

4. Not all of the students are placed in BIA schools. Some are placed in public schools but still live in BIA dormitories. The only individuals who live in the dormitories are the Native American pupils and the student teachers, although several Native American adults work as dormitory aides.

5. In 1994, this aspect of the program was changed and students were required to engage in and write up three on-site community service projects during the student teaching semester. This new assignment increases community involvement and expands the number of nonschool Navajo people met by the preservice teachers.

REFERENCES

Anderson, J., & Guest, K. (1994). Service learning in teacher education at Seattle University. In R. Kraft & M. Swedener (Eds.), *Building community: Service learning in the academic disciplines.* Denver: Colorado Campus Compact.

Au, K., & Kawakami, A. (1994). Cultural congruence in instruction. In E. Hollins, J. King, & W. Hayman (Eds.), *Teaching diverse populations* (pp. 5–24). Albany, NY: State University of New York Press.

Blair, L., & Erickson, P. (1964). *The student teacher's experiences in the community.* Reston, VA: Association of Teacher Educators.

Clothier, G., & Hudgins, B. (1971). *Unique challenges of preparing teachers for inner-city schools.* Kansas City, MO: Mid-continent Regional Educational Laboratory. (ERIC Document Reproduction Service No. ED 056 971)

Corwin, R. (1973). *Reform and organizational survival: The Teacher Corps as an instrument of educational change.* New York: Wiley.

Cuban, L. (1969). Teacher & community. *Harvard Educational Review, 39*(2), 253–272.

Darling-Hammond, L. (Ed.). (1994). *Professional development schools: Schools for developing a profession.* New York: Teachers College Press.

Ellner, C., & Barnes, B. J. (1977). *School making: An alternative in teacher education.* Lexington MA: Lexington Books.

Flowers, J. G., Patterson, A., Stratemeyer, F., & Lindsey, M. (1948). *School and community laboratory experiences in teacher education.* Oneata, NY: American Association of Teachers Colleges.

Grant, C., & Secada, W. (1990). Preparing teachers for diversity. In W. R. Houston (Ed.), *Handbook of research on teacher education* (pp. 403–422). New York: Macmillan.

Haberman, M. (1987). *Recruiting and selecting teachers for urban schools.* New York: ERIC Clearing House on Urban Education, Institute for Urban & Minority Education.

Haberman, M., & Post, L. (1992). Does direct experience change education students' perceptions of low-income minority children? *Midwestern Educational Researcher, 5*(2), 29–31.

Hayes, S. (1980). The community and teacher education. In H. P. Baptiste, Jr., M. Baptiste, & D. Gollnick (Eds.), *Multicultural teacher education: Preparing educators to provide educational equity* (pp. 94–108). Washington, DC: American Association of Colleges for Teacher Education.

Hodgdon, E. R., & Saunders, R. (1951). Using the community in teacher education. *Journal of Teacher Education, 2*(3), 216–218.

Houston, W. R. (Ed.). (1990). *Handbook of research on teacher education.* New York: Macmillan.

Howey, K., & Zimpher, N. (1990). Professors and deans of education. In W. R. Houston (Ed.), *Handbook of research on teacher education* (pp. 349–370). New York: Macmillan.

Kapel, D., & Kapel, M. (1982). *The preparation of teachers for urban schools: The state of the art in preservice and in-service education.* New York: Columbia University Institute for Urban & Minority Education. (ERIC Document Reproduction Service No. ED 219 482)

Ladson-Billings, G. (1994). *The dream keepers: Successful teachers of African-American children.* San Francisco: Jossey-Bass.

Ladson-Billings, G. (in press). Multicultural teacher education: Research, policy & practice. In J. Banks (Ed.), *Handbook of research on multicultural education* (pp. 747–762). New York: Macmillan.

Lauderdale, W. B., & Deaton, W. L. (1993). Future teachers react to past racism. *Educational Forum, 57*(3), 266–276.

Lebaron, W., & Royster, P. (1974). Community involvement: A perspective from Teacher Corps. *Community Education Journal, 4*(5), 53–55.

Levine, M. (Ed.). (1992). *Professional practice schools: Linking teacher education and school reform.* New York: Teachers College Press.

Mahan, J., (1982a). Community involvement components in culturally oriented teacher preparation. *Education, 102*(2), 163–172.

Mahan, J. (1982b). Native Americans as teacher trainers: Anatomy and outcomes of a cultural immersion project. *Journal of Educational Equity & Leadership, 2*(2), 100–109.

Mahan, J. (November, 1990). EDUC T550 Cultural Community Forces and the School Syllabus. Indiana University, School of Education.

Mahan, J. (1993a, February). *Native Americans as non-traditional usually unrecognized, influential teacher educators.* Paper presented at the annual meeting of the Association of Teacher Educators, Los Angeles, CA.

Mahan, J. (1993b). Teacher education in American Indian communities: Learnings from reservation sources. *Journal of Navajo Education, 11*(1), 13–21.

Mahan, J., Fortney, M., & Garcia, J. (1983). Linking the community to teacher education: Toward a more analytical approach. *Action in Teacher Education, 5*(1–2), 1–10.

Mahan, J., & Lacefield, W. (1982). Employability and multicultural teacher preparation. *Educational Research Quarterly, 7*(1), 15–20.

Melnick, S., & Zeichner, K. (1994, April). *Teacher education for cultural diversity: Enhancing the capacity of teacher education institutions to address diversity issues.* Paper presented at the annual meeting of the American Association of Colleges for Teacher Education, Chicago, IL.

Moll, L. (1992). Bilingual classroom studies and community analysis: Some recent trends. *Educational Researcher, 21*(2), 20–24.

Moll, L., Amanti, C., Neff, D., & Gonzalez, N. (1992). Funds of knowledge for teaching: Using a qualitative approach to connect homes & classrooms. *Theory into Practice, 31*(2), 132–141.

Mungo, S. (1980). *Experiential cross-cultural approaches in multicultural early field experiences in the small community.* (ERIC Document Reproduction Service No. ED 240 120)

Narode, R., Rennie-Hill, L., & Peterson, K. (1994). Urban community study by prospective teachers. *Urban Education, 29*(1), 5–21.

Nieto, J. (1994). *Using cultural immersion to heighten cultural sensitivity.* Unpublished paper, San Diego State University, School of Education.

Nieto, S. (1992). *Affirming diversity: The sociopolitical context of multicultural education.* New York: Longman.

Paine, L. (1989). *Orientation towards diversity: What do prospective teachers bring?* (Research report 89-9). East Lansing, MI: National Center for Research on Teacher Learning.

Pugach, M., & Pasch, S. (1994). The challenge of creating urban professional development schools. In R. Yinger & K. Borman (Eds.), *Restructuring education: Issues & strategies for schools, communities & universities* (pp. 129–156). Norwood, NJ: Ablex.

Smith, B. O. (1980). *A design for a school of pedagogy*. Washington, DC: U.S. Department of Education.

Smith, W. (1980). The American Teacher Corps Programme. In E. Hoyle & J. Megarry (Eds.), *World year book of education: Professional development of teachers* (pp. 204–218). New York: Nichols.

Soptick, J., & Clothier, G. (1974). *CUTE installation and diffusion project* (second phase). Kansas City, MO: Midcontinent Regional Educational Laboratory. (ERIC Document Reproduction Service No. ED 095 171)

Tran, M. T., Young, R., & DiLella, J. (1994). Multicultural education courses and the student teacher: Eliminating stereotypical attitudes in our ethnically diverse classroom. *Journal of Teacher Education, 45*(3), 183–189.

Wayson, W. (1988, April). *Multicultural education among seniors in the College of Education at Ohio State University*. Paper presented at the annual meeting of the American Educational Research Association, New Orleans, LA.

Weiner, L. (1993). *Preparing teachers for urban schools*. New York: Teachers College Press.

Willison, S. (1989). *Cultural immersion of student teachers on an American Indian reservation: A study of participants, experiences, activities, & resulting outcomes*. Unpublished doctoral dissertation, Indiana University.

Zeichner, K. (1990). Preparing teachers for democratic schools. *Action in Teacher Education, 11*(1), 5–10.

Zeichner, K. (1992). Rethinking the practicum in the professional development school partnership. *Journal of Teacher Education, 43*(4), 296–307.

Zeichner, K. (1993). *Educating teachers for cultural diversity*. East Lansing, MI: National Center for Research on Teacher Learning.

Zeichner, K., & Hoeft, K. (1996). Teacher socialization for cultural diversity. In J. Sikula, T. Buttery, & E. Guyton (Eds.), *Handbook of research on teacher education* (2nd ed.). New York: Macmillan.

Zeichner, K., & Melnick, S. (1995). *Preparing teachers for diversity through community field experiences*. East Lansing, MI: National Center for Research on Teacher Learning.

PART III

Promoting Reflective Practice in Teacher Education

CHAPTER 9

Teachers as Reflective Practitioners and the Democratization of School Reform

Ken Zeichner

During the last decade, the slogans "reflective teaching," "action research," and "teacher empowerment" have been embraced by teachers, teacher educators, and educational researchers all over the world (see Zeichner, 1994). From one perspective, this international movement that has developed in teaching and teacher education under the banner of reflection can be seen as a reaction against the increased attempts by governments in many countries to centralize control of schools and teacher education institutions (Gideonse, 1992; Popkewitz, 1993). With the increased centralization of control has come a view of teachers as technicians who are merely to carry out what others, removed from the classroom, want them to do, and an acceptance of top-down forms of educational reform that involve teachers only as passive participants. According to Paris (1993), "Teachers are considered to be consumers of curriculum knowledge, but are not assumed to have the requisite skills to create or critique that knowledge" (p. 149).

On the surface, the reflective practice movement involves a recognition that teachers should play active roles in formulating the purposes and ends of their work, and that teachers should play leadership roles in curriculum development and school reform. Reflection also signifies a recognition that the generation of new knowledge about teaching is not the exclusive property of colleges, universities, and research and development centers—a recognition that teachers too have theories that can contribute to a codified knowledge base for teaching. Even today, with all of the talk about teacher empowerment, we still see a general lack of respect for the craft knowledge of teachers in the educational research establishment, which has attempted to define a so-called knowledge base for teaching minus the voices and insights of teachers (Cochran-Smith & Lytle, 1993; Grimmett & MacKinnon, 1992).

In addition to the invisibility of teacher-generated knowledge in what counts as educational research, many staff-development and school-improvement initiatives still ignore the knowledge and expertise of teachers and rely primarily on top-down models of school reform, which try to get teachers to comply with some externally generated and allegedly research-based solution to school problems. The selling of educational solutions and gimmicks, what Canadians Massey and Chamberlin (1990) have referred to as "snake oil" staff development, is still big business today in many parts of the world despite all that the reform literature has told us over the last 30 years about the futility of attempting to reform schools when teachers are treated merely as passive implementors of ideas conceived elsewhere (e.g., Fullan, 1991; McLaughlin, 1987).

THE REFLECTIVE PRACTICE MOVEMENT

The concept of the teacher as a reflective practitioner appears to acknowledge the wealth of expertise that resides in the practices of teachers, what Schön (1983) has called "knowledge-in-action." From the perspective of the individual teacher, this means that the process of understanding and improving one's own teaching must start from reflection on one's own experience and that the sort of wisdom derived entirely from the experience of others (even other teachers) is impoverished (Winter, 1989).

Reflection as a slogan for educational reform also signifies a recognition that the process of learning to teach continues throughout a teacher's entire career, a recognition that no matter what we do in our teacher education programs, and no matter how well we do them, at best we can only prepare teachers to begin teaching. When embracing the concept of reflective teaching, there is often a commitment by teacher educators to help prospective teachers internalize during their initial training the disposition and skill to study their teaching and become better at teaching over time, a commitment to take responsibility for their own professional development (Korthagen, 1993).

Amid this explosion of interest in the idea of teachers as reflective practitioners there has been a great deal of confusion about what is meant in particular instances by the use of the term *reflective teaching* and whether the idea of teachers as reflective practitioners should be supported (e.g., Day, 1993; Feiman-Nemser, 1990; Valli, 1992). Although those who have embraced the slogan of reflective practice appear to share certain goals about the active role of teachers in school reform, in reality one cannot tell very much about an approach to teaching or teacher education from an expressed commitment to the idea of teachers as reflective practitioners. Underlying the apparent similarity among those who have embraced the slogan of reflective practice are vast differences in perspectives about teaching, learning, schooling, and the social order. It has come to the point now that the whole range of such beliefs have become incorporated into the discourse about reflective practice. It seems that everyone, regardless of ideological orientation, has jumped on the bandwagon at this point, and has committed his or her energies to furthering some version of reflective teaching practice. According to Calderhead (1989):

> Reflective teaching has been justified on grounds ranging from moral responsibility to technical effectiveness, and reflection has been incorporated into teacher education courses as divergent as those employing a behavioral skills approach, in which reflection is viewed as a means to the achievement of certain prescribed practices, to those committed to a critical science approach in which reflection is seen as a means toward emancipation and professional autonomy. (p. 43)

In this chapter,[1] I will argue that despite the lofty rhetoric surrounding efforts to help teachers become more reflective, in reality reflective teacher education has done very little to foster genuine teacher development and to enhance teachers' roles in educational reform. Instead, an illusion of teacher development has often been created that has maintained in more subtle ways the subservient position of the teacher. As part of my critique of the way in which the slogan of reflective practice has come to be used by teachers and teacher educators, I will discuss the need for reflective practice to be conceptualized in the service of genuine teacher development.

Even when reflection is used as a vehicle for genuine teacher development, however, teacher development often is seen as an end in itself, unconnected to broader questions about education in democratic societies. In its extreme form, we see an uncritical glorification of anything that a teacher does or says and an outright rejection of anything that is initiated outside the immediate context of classrooms.

I will argue that efforts to prepare teachers who are reflective must both foster genuine teacher development and support the realization of greater equity and social justice in schooling and the larger society. Kemmis (1985) has argued that reflection is inevitably a political act that either hastens or defers the realization of a more rational, just, and fulfilling society. The democratization of school reform through efforts to foster teacher reflection should not be supported as an end in itself without connecting these efforts to making a better society.

THE ILLUSION OF TEACHER EMPOWERMENT

Despite all of the talk about empowering teachers that emanates from reflective teacher education circles, we get a very different picture when we look more closely at the ways in which the concepts of reflection and the reflective practitioner have been employed in teacher education programs. During the last few years, I have been conducting analyses of the ways in which these concepts have been used by teacher educators in the United States (e.g., Zeichner, 1992). I have examined the writings of teacher educators who say that reflective inquiry is a central element in their preservice teacher education programs, and have attended conferences where these programs have been described. I have also examined a number of curricular materials that have been designed to assist teacher educators in encouraging reflective practice by their students.

As a result of analyzing all of this material, and of my discussions with teacher educators from across the United States, I have come to the conclusion that the ways in which the concepts of reflection and the reflective practitioner have come to be used in teacher education programs have done very little to foster genuine teacher development—that is, teacher development that truly democratizes the process of school reform and gives teachers an important role in determining its direction. Instead, an illusion of teacher development is often created that maintains in more subtle ways the subservient position of the teacher in relation to those removed from the classroom. There are four ways the concept of reflection has been employed in preservice teacher education that undermine the expressed emancipatory intent of teacher educators. Although my analysis focuses on teacher education in the United States, I think it is likely that the trends I describe are true in other countries as well.

Replicating Research Practices

First, one of the most common uses of the concept of reflection has involved helping teachers reflect about their teaching with the primary aim of better replicating in their practice that which university-sponsored empirical research has allegedly found to be effective. Such research has often been packaged and sold to schools and teacher education institutions as part of expensive school-improvement programs, complete with checklists and observation forms for supervisors to use in determining the degree of congruence between teachers' practices and what the research says they should be doing. Sometimes the creative intelligence of the teacher is allowed to intervene, to determine the situational appropriateness of employing particular strategies, but oftentimes not. Canadian Peter Grimmett and his colleagues (Grimmett, MacKinnon, Erickson, & Riecken, 1990) refer to this perspective as one in which reflection serves merely as an instrumental mediator of action, where knowledge is used to try to direct practice. What is absent from this very prevalent conception of reflective teaching practice is any sense of how the practical theories that reside in the practices of teachers (knowledge-in-action) are to contribute to the process of teacher development.

Ironically, despite Schön's very articulate rejection of this technical rationality in his presentation of the case for an epistemology of practice in his highly influential books (Schön, 1983, 1987), "theory" is still seen by many to reside exclusively within universities and "practice" to reside only within elementary and secondary schools. The problem is still wrongly cast by many as merely translating or applying the theories of the universities to classroom practice. The fact that theories are always produced through practices and that practices always reflect particular theoretical commitments is ignored.

There are many instances of this technical rationality in U.S. teacher education programs today. In many programs there is a great deal of emphasis on the so-called knowledge base of teaching produced through university research, and on getting student teachers to base their practice on an application of this research. For example, a description of a teacher education program at the University of Maryland (McCaleb, Borko, & Arends, 1992) states:

> A reflective teacher is a teacher who has command of the knowledge base for teaching. This teacher can: (1) explain the core ideas emanating from the knowledge base and cite appropriate best practices associated with them; (2) cite key pieces of research associated with the knowledge base and provide thoughtful critique of the research; (3) execute effectively (at a novice level) selected best practices which grow out of the research in simulated and laboratory settings and in real classrooms and (4) engage in critical reflection and intellectual dialogue about the knowledge base and understand how the various ideas are connected and how they interact to inform (situationally) a particular teaching/school event or episode. (pp. 57–58)

Although here and in many similar programs we see language that emphasizes the empowering effects of reflecting on an externally generated knowledge base of teaching, and a clear message to teachers that they should engage in thoughtful and critical use of the research by engaging in problem solving, decision making, and critical analysis, the fact is that this conception of reflective practice denies teachers the use of the wisdom and expertise embedded in their own practices and in the practices of their colleagues. They are merely to fine-tune and/or adapt knowledge that was formulated elsewhere by someone unfamiliar with the teachers' particular situations. The relationship between theory and practice is seen as one-way instead of as dialogic. In a dialogic relationship, theory and practice inform each other.

Avoiding Ethical and Moral Implications

Closely related to this persistence of technical rationality under the banner of reflective teaching is the limitation of the reflective process to consideration of teaching skills and strategies (the means of instruction) and the exclusion from the process of defining the ends of teaching—the exclusion of the ethical and moral realms of teaching from the teacher's purview. Here again teachers are denied the opportunity to do anything but fine-tune and adjust the means for accomplishing ends determined by others. Teaching becomes merely a technical activity. Important questions related to values such as what should be taught to whom, and why, are defined independently and relegated to others removed from the classroom.

One of the clearest examples of limiting teachers to instrumental reasoning, while claiming to liberate them, can be found in the "Reflective Teaching" materials developed at Ohio State University and disseminated throughout the world by *Phi Delta Kappan* (Cruickshank, 1987). On the one hand, these materials speak very eloquently about the empowerment of teachers through reflective teaching:

> The point is that teachers who study teaching deliberately and become students of teaching can develop life-long assurance that they know what they are doing, why they are doing it, and what will happen as a result of what they do. Foremost they can learn to behave according to reason. To lack reason is to be a slave to chance, irrationality, self-interest, and superstition. (p. 34)

On the other hand, when teachers use these materials in teacher education programs, the content of what is to be taught is provided to student teachers in 36 reflective teaching lessons, 32 of which are actually described as "content free." Not surprisingly, what results from this structure and from the discussion questions that are provided with the materials is a lot of thinking and discussion about teaching techniques and strategies divorced from ethical questions about what is taught.

Avoiding Social Considerations

A third aspect of the recent proliferation of the teacher education literature and programs with material related to reflective teaching is a clear emphasis on focusing teachers' reflections inwardly on their own teaching and/or students, to the neglect of any consideration of the social conditions of schooling that influence the teacher's work within the classroom. This individualist bias makes it less likely that teachers will be able to confront and transform those structural aspects of their work that hinder the accomplishment of their educational goals. The context of the teacher's work is to be taken as given. Now while teachers' primary concerns understandably lie within the classroom and with their students, it is unwise to restrict their attention to these concerns alone. As the U.S. philosopher Israel Scheffler (1968) has argued:

Teachers cannot restrict their attention to the classroom alone, leaving the larger setting and the purposes of schooling to be determined by others. They must take active responsibility for the goals to which they are committed and for the social setting in which these goals may prosper. If they are not to be mere agents of others, of the state, of the military, of the media, of the experts and bureaucrats, they need to determine their own agency through a critical and continual evaluation of the purposes, the consequences, and the social context of their calling. (p. 11)

We must be careful here that teachers' involvement in matters beyond the boundaries of their own classrooms does not make excessive demands on their time, energy, and expertise, diverting their attention from their core mission with students. In some circumstances, creating more opportunities for teachers to participate in schoolwide decisions related to curriculum, instruction, staffing, budgeting, and so on, can intensify their work beyond the bounds of reasonableness and make it more difficult for them to accomplish their primary task of educating students (see Apple, 1986). It does not have to be this way, of course, but it can unless efforts are made to incorporate teachers' participation in school leadership into their work.

Isolating Individual Teachers

A fourth and closely related aspect of much of the material in the reflective teaching movement is a focus on facilitating reflection by individual teachers, who are meant to think by themselves about their work. There is very little sense, in a lot of the discourse on reflective teaching, of reflection as a social practice, where groups of teachers can support and sustain each other's growth. This definition of teacher development as an activity to be pursued by individual teachers greatly limits the potential for teacher growth. The challenge and support gained through social interaction is important in helping us clarify what we believe and in gaining the courage to pursue our beliefs (Solomon, 1987).

One consequence of this isolation of individual teachers and the lack of attention to the social context of teaching in teacher development is that teachers come to see their problems as their own, unrelated to those of other teachers or to the structure of schools and school systems; thus we have seen the emergence of terms such as "teacher burnout" and "teacher stress." The attention of teachers is directed away from a critical analysis of schools as institutions and toward a preoccupation with their own individual failures. If we are to have genuine teacher development in which teachers are truly empowered, then we must turn away from this individual approach and heed the advice of the teachers who were members of the Boston Women Teachers Group in the 1980s. These teachers argued that teachers must now begin to turn the investigation of schools away from scapegoating individual teachers, students, parents, and administrators toward a system wide approach. Teachers must recognize how the structure of schools controls their work and deeply affects their relationships with their fellow teachers, their students, and their students' families. Teachers must feel free to express these insights and publicly voice their concerns. Only with this knowledge can they grow into wisdom and help others to grow. (Freedman, Jackson, & Boles, 1983, p. 299)

In summary, when we examine the ways in which the concept of reflective teaching has recently been integrated into preservice teacher education programs in the United States, we find four themes that undermine the potential for genuine teacher development: (1) a focus on helping teachers to better replicate practices suggested by research conducted by others and a neglect of the theories and expertise embedded in teachers' practices; (2) a means–end thinking that limits the substance of teachers' reflections to technical questions of teaching techniques and internal classroom organization and a neglect of questions of curriculum; (3) facilitating teachers' reflections about their own teaching while ignoring the social and institutional context in which teaching takes place; and (4) an emphasis on helping teachers reflect individually.

All of these practices help create a situation in which there is merely the illusion of teacher development and teacher autonomy. It is not inevitable, however, that efforts to foster reflection by teachers will reinforce the subservient position of teachers. There are examples in the literature from several countries, including the United States, of efforts by teacher educators to encourage reflective practice by teachers that focus on the ends as well as the means of instruction, that focus on the social conditions of schooling as well as on the teaching itself, and that emphasize reflection as a social practice within communities of teachers (e.g., see the different efforts described in Tabachnick & Zeichner, 1991). These efforts support the genuine empowerment of teachers to play important roles in school reform. I want to argue, though, that even if the teacher development we foster is genuine and not a fraud, it should not necessarily be supported. Reflective teacher education that fosters genuine teacher development should be supported only, in my view, if it is connected to the struggle for greater social justice and somehow contributes to the lessening of the pain and suffering associated with the unjust distribution of entitlements, including education, in many countries. I want to spend the rest of this chapter discussing how I think we can connect the idea of teachers as reflective practitioners, and the democratization of school reform associated with it, to the struggle for social justice.

DIFFERENT CONCEPTIONS OF REFLECTIVE PRACTICE
IN TEACHING AND TEACHER EDUCATION

First, one must recognize that all teachers are reflective in some sense. There is no such thing as an unreflective teacher. We need to move beyond the uncritical celebration of teacher reflection and teacher empowerment and focus our attention on what kind of reflection teachers are engaging in, what it is teachers are reflecting about, and how they are going about it (Zeichner & Liston, in press). Reflective teaching is not necessarily good teaching and uncritically privileging knowledge generated through teacher reflection is problematic because, under some circumstances, more reflection may actually serve to legitimate and strengthen practices that are harmful to students (Ellwood, 1992).

Giving teachers responsibility for designing their own professional development programs and for the reform of curriculum and instruction in schools when they might not have a vision of teaching that includes provisions for the learning of all students presents teacher educators and policymakers with a serious dilemma. While teacher educators and policymakers might want to encourage teachers to be leaders in various aspects of school reform, they must also consider their obligation to provide some direction to the process, so that issues of equity and social justice are addressed. In the end, there probably should be a balance between the setting of broad goals by policymakers that lay out a direction for school reform and giving teachers a lot of power to figure out how to meet those goals. Teacher power is a complex and contradictory process that is not necessarily exercised in the interests of all students and families (Ayers, 1992).

One example of what I have in mind is a school district establishing a clear focus on improving the achievement of poor students of color who are typically underserved by public schools and then giving teachers a lot of flexibility to produce results. A number of school districts across the United States have used the idea of organizing teacher research groups to address these gaps in achievement. Teachers are given released time and facilitative support to plan and carry out specific improvement projects in their classrooms to address issues of equity in achievement and then the school district publishes and disseminates what teachers have learned (e.g., Fairfax County Public Schools, 1991).

There are many ways in which different approaches to the idea of teachers as reflective practitioners have been conceptualized in the literature (see Zeichner, 1994). Here I would like to describe a heuristic that I have used to help me understand the different commitments underlying approaches to reflective practice. Several years ago Dan Liston and I (Liston & Zeichner, 1991), building on the work of our colleague Herb Kliebard (1986) on the development of the public school curriculum in the United States, developed a framework describing different traditions of practice in teacher education. Later Bob Tabachnick and I (Tabachnick & Zeichner, 1991) extended this analysis to describe different traditions of reflective practice in teaching and teacher education.

This framework, which is situated within the history and culture of the United States, includes four approaches to the idea of reflective practice:

1.   An *academic* tradition, which stresses reflection by teachers on subject matter and the representation and translation of that subject-matter knowledge to promote student understanding. The work of Shulman (1987) and his colleagues is a prominent example of this tradition.

2.   A *social efficiency* tradition, which emphasizes the application by teachers of teaching strategies suggested by research on teaching. Here teachers' reflections are to focus on how well their practices match what the research says they should be doing. Historically, the research knowledge base has not included any knowledge produced by teachers themselves (Cochran-Smith & Lytle, 1993).

3.   A *developmentalist* tradition, which prioritizes teaching that is sensitive to students' interests, thinking, and patterns of developmental growth. The distinguishing characteristic of this tradition is the belief that classroom practice should be grounded in the close observation and study of students by the teacher. Duckworth's (1987) work on teaching as research is illustrative of this tradition.

4.   A *social-reconstructionist* tradition, which views reflection as a political act that either contributes to or hinders the realization of a more just and humane society. The teacher's attention is focused both inwardly at his or her own practice and outwardly at the social conditions in which this practice is situated. A second characteristic of this approach to reflective practice is its democratic and emancipatory impulse, and the corresponding focus of teachers' deliberations on substantive issues that address the social and political dimensions of their teaching. For example, here teachers would consider issues such as gender, race, and social class that are embedded in everyday classroom practices (Liston & Zeichner, 1990). The third characteristic of a social-reconstructionist conception of reflective practice is its commitment to the idea of reflection as a social practice; the intent is to create learning communities in which teachers support and sustain each other's growth. This commitment to collaborative modes of learning indicates a dual commitment by teacher educators to an ethic where social justice on the one hand and care and compassion on the other are valued. Contemporary examples of an emphasis on a social reconstructionist conception of reflective practice include teacher education programs that have incorporated feminist and antiracist perspectives into their curricula (see Tabachnick & Zeichner, 1991).

In identifying these different approaches to reflective practice in teaching and teacher education in the United States, I am not suggesting that individual instances of teacher reflection or individual teacher education programs can be viewed as pure examples of any of the orientations. On the contrary, all teacher education programs in the United States reflect some pattern of resonance with all of the value orientations, emphasizing some traditions and marginalizing others, and defining each tradition in a way that reflects the particular priorities of teachers and teacher educators in a given situation. I am also not trying to imply that these same traditions of reflective practice exist in other countries. The identification of approaches to reflective practice in other countries must take into account the particular histories and cultural elements in those countries.

This framework can help us see that reflective teaching is not, by itself, a distinct conceptual orientation to teaching or teacher education without further elaboration of the assumptions and commitments associated with particular projects of work. It can help us determine how particular conceptions of reflective practice have become dominant or have been suppressed in specific situations. In many places, including the United States, what I have called a social-reconstructionist orientation to reflective practice has been marginalized, and other allegedly politically neutral conceptions have been dominant.

CONNECTING TEACHER REFLECTION WITH THE STRUGGLE FOR SOCIAL JUSTICE

It has become common in some of the most recent literature on reflective practice to argue that teacher educators who try to help teachers reflect on the social and political dimensions of their teaching and the contexts in which that teaching takes place are wasting their time either because the teachers are not up to the demands of this kind of critical inquiry or because the institutions of schools and universities are so hostile to it. For example, Calderhead and Gates (1993) of the United Kingdom have argued with respect to initial teacher education that

> the aims of preservice reflective teaching programs are quite often highly ambitious and set targets that are probably impossible to achieve with the majority of students in the time available. Becoming a teacher who is aware of one's own values and beliefs, able to analyze their own practice and consider its ethical basis and its social and political context involves considerable ability and experience and may well be beyond the capabilities of most student teachers in the span of a preservice program. (pp. 4–5)

One approach that is often proposed is a kind of depoliticized teacher education in which serious questions about equity and social justice are not part of the education of teachers. It concerns me a great deal that many who identify with the reflective practice movement in teaching and teacher education seek to be politically neutral and often give very little attention in their work to issues of social continuity and change. Contrary to this popular view—that teacher educators can somehow maintain political neutrality—is the view to which I subscribe: that every plan for teacher education necessarily takes a position, at least implicitly, on the current institutional form and social context of schooling (Crittenden, 1973). In societies that profess to be democratic, teacher educators are morally obligated to attend to the social-reconstructionist dimension of teaching practice despite any practical difficulties involved in doing so.

It has become very clear in many countries that the gap between the concept of democracy and the reality of domination and oppression is growing greater. In the United States, there is irrefutable evidence that social-class background, race, gender, sexual orientation, and so on, continue to play strong roles in determining access to a variety of things in addition to a quality education—quality housing, health care, rewarding work that pays a decent wage—and that they affect a whole host of "rotten outcomes" such as the incidence of child abuse, malnutrition, childhood pregnancy, violent crime, and drug abuse. Over 13 million children in the United States currently live in conditions of poverty that make them highly vulnerable to these factors. An African-American male child born in California in 1988 is three times more likely to be murdered than to be admitted to the University of California (Ladson-Billings, 1991).

The point that I want to make is that this growing gap between the rich and the poor has proceeded despite the growing democratization of the educational reform process during the so-called second wave of educational reform and the explosion of rhetoric about the greater professionalization of teaching and reflective teaching practice. Decentralization of control to the local level, giving more power over schooling to teachers and communities, is no guarantee that greater equity and social justice will be sought or achieved. In fact, in some cases, there is evidence that greater teacher empowerment has undermined important connections between schools and their communities as teachers have used their greater power to justify keeping parents and communities outside of the decision-making process in schools (see Zeichner, 1991). Despite all of the attention to allegedly enlightened teaching practices such as whole-language instruction, conceptual-change teaching, and "teaching for understanding," gaps in achievement between students of different racial and social-class backgrounds continue to exist. We must look very critically at proposals that would have us accept reflective teaching and associated concepts like action research and teacher empowerment as panaceas for educational, social, and economic ills.

This critical appraisal of recent efforts to enhance teacher autonomy should not be interpreted as an argument against greater professionalization of teaching. On the contrary, we should be doing all that we can to support efforts to give teachers, as well as parents, greater voices in educational reform, and to combat efforts by governments or by reform entrepreneurs to control educational reform from the outside. But, as I have tried to show, there are many different versions of the idea of teachers as reflective practitioners, some of which are disingenuous, and most of which do not even begin to confront the serious problems of inequity and injustice plaguing many countries. We must support efforts to preserve and enhance teacher autonomy and local control, but we must ensure that these potentially progressive processes become explicitly connected to the struggle for greater social justice.

OVERCOMING RESISTANCE IN TEACHER EDUCATION PROGRAMS

For teacher educators like myself, there is an important strategic issue involved in this, because many of the prospective teachers we work with do not want to think about the kinds of issues raised in the social-reconstructionist dimension or do not want to work with the disenfranchised poor children of color who increasingly populate our public schools (Zeichner, 1993). How to pursue a teacher education agenda that openly addresses the social and political dimensions of teaching and contributes to the amelioration of social ills in an environment like this is a difficult matter, ethically as well as practically.

There is a lot of debate right now among social reconstructionist–oriented teacher educators about how best to pursue a socially progressive agenda in a hostile environment (e.g., McIntyre, 1993). One point of debate, for example, is whether the process of teacher reflection in teacher education programs should begin with reflection about public theories and the practices of others, or with reflection about one's own practices. The vast majority of discourse, however, even in the supposedly progressive reflective practice movement, is either silent on the social and political dimensions of teaching or is critical of efforts to address social ills through teacher education.

We must begin by adopting a supportive yet critical stance toward proposals that seek to enhance the autonomy of teachers (and often parents) through the democratization of school reform. While supporting the direction these proposals suggest, we must push those who offer them to go beyond an exclusive concern with individual empowerment and personal transformation to include an explicit concern for social reconstruction, a reconstruction that will help us move closer to a world in which what we want for our own children is available to everybody's children. This is the only kind of world with which we should be satisfied, and no movement or approach to teacher education is worthy of our support unless it can help move us closer to this kind of world.

NOTE

1. This chapter is a revised version of a lecture given at the Congreso Internacional de Didactica Volver a Pensar, La Coruña, Spain, September 1993.

REFERENCES

Apple, M. (1986). *Teachers and texts: A political economy of class & gender relations in education.* New York: Routledge.

Ayers, W. (1992). Work that is real: Why teachers should be empowered. In G. A. Hess (Ed.), *Empowering teachers and parents: School restructuring through the eyes of anthropologists* (pp. 13–28). Westport, CT: Bergin & Garvey.

Calderhead, J. (1989). Reflective teaching and teacher education. *Teaching and Teacher Education, 5*(1), 43–51.

Calderhead, J., & Gates, P. (Eds.). (1993). Introduction. In *Conceptualizing reflection in teacher development* (pp. 1–10). London: Falmer Press.

Cochran-Smith, M., & Lytle, S. (1993). *Inside-out: Teacher research and knowledge.* New York: Teachers College Press.

Crittenden, B. (1973). Some prior questions in the reform of teacher education. *Interchange, 4*(2–3), 1–11.

Cruickshank, D. (1987). *Reflective teaching.* Reston, VA: Association of Teacher Educators.

Day, C. (1993). Reflection: A necessary but not sufficient condition for professional development. *British Educational Research Journal, 19*(1), 83–93.

Duckworth, E. (1987). *The having of wonderful ideas.* New York: Teachers College Press.

Ellwood, C. (1992, April). *Teacher research: For whom?* Paper presented at the annual meeting of the American Educational Research Association, San Francisco, CA.

Fairfax County Public Schools. (1991). *Classroom research on students in the middle.* Fairfax, VA: Author.

Feiman-Nemser, S. (1990). Teacher preparation: Structural and conceptual alternatives. In W. R. Houston (Ed.)., *Handbook of research on teacher education* (pp. 212–233). New York: Macmillan.

Freedman, S., Jackson, J., & Boles, K. (1983). Teaching: An imperiled profession. In L. Shulman & G. Sykes (Eds.), *Handbook of teaching & policy* (pp. 261–299). New York: Longman.

Fullan, M. (1991). *The new meaning of educational change.* New York: Teachers College Press.

Gideonse, H. (Ed.). (1992). *Teacher education policy: Narratives, stories & cases.* Albany, NY: State University of New York Press.

Grimmett, P., & MacKinnon, A. (1992). Craft knowledge and the education of teachers. In A. Grant (Ed.), *Review of research in education* (pp. 385–456). Washington, DC: American Educational Research Association.

Grimmett, P., MacKinnon, A., Erickson, G., & Riecken, T. (1990). Reflective practice in teacher education. In R. Clift, W. R. Houston, & M. Pugach (Eds.), *Encouraging reflective practice in education* (pp. 20–38). New York: Teachers College Press.

Kemmis, S. (1985). Action research and the politics of reflection. In D. Boud, R. Keogh, & D. Walker (Eds.), *Reflection: Turning experience into learning* (pp. 139–164). London: Croom Helm.

Kliebard, H. (1986). *The struggle for the American curriculum, 1893–1958*. Boston: Routledge & Kegan Paul.

Korthagen, F. (1993). The role of reflection in teachers' professional development. In L. Kremer-Hayon, H. Vonk, & R. Fessler (Eds.), *Teacher professional development: A multiple perspective approach* (pp. 133–145). Amsterdam: Swets & Zeitlinger.

Ladson-Billings, G. (1991). *Who will teach our children? Preparing teachers to successfully teach African-American students*. Paper presented at the California State University Teleconference on Cultural Diversity, Hayward, CA.

Liston, D., & Zeichner, K. (1990). Teacher education and the social context of schooling: Issues for curriculum development. *American Educational Research Journal, 27*(4), 610–636.

Liston, D., & Zeichner, K. (1991). *Teacher education and the social conditions of schooling*. New York: Routledge.

Massey, D., & Chamberlin, C. (1990). Perspective, evangelism and reflection in teacher education. In C. Day, M. Pope, & P. Denicolo (Eds.), *Insight into teachers' thinking and practice* (pp. 133–154). London: Falmer Press.

McCaleb, J., Borko, H., & Arends, R. (1992). Reflection, research & repertoire in the Masters certification program at the University of Maryland. In L. Valli (Ed.), *Reflective teacher education: Cases and critiques* (pp. 40–64). Albany, NY: State University of New York Press.

McIntyre, D. (1993). Theory, theorizing & reflection in initial teacher education. In J. Calderhead & P. Gates (Eds.), *Conceptualizing reflection in teacher development* (pp. 39–52). London: Falmer Press.

McLaughlin, M. W. (1987). Learning from experience: Lessons from policy implementation. *Educational Evaluation & Policy Analysis, 9*, 171–178.

Paris, C. (1993). *Teacher agency and curriculum making*. New York: Teachers College Press.

Popkewitz, T. (1993) (Ed.). *Changing patterns of power: Social regulation and teacher education reform*. Albany, NY: State University of New York Press.

Scheffler, I. (1968). University scholarship and the education of teachers. *Teachers College Record, 70*, 1–12.

Schön, D. (1983). *The reflective practitioner*. New York: Basic Books.

Schön, D. (1987). *Educating the reflective practitioner*. San Francisco: Jossey-Bass.

Shulman, L. (1987). Knowledge and teaching: Foundations of the new reform. *Harvard Educational Review, 57*, 1–22.

Solomon, J. (1987). New thoughts on teacher education. *Oxford Review of Education, 13*(3), 267–274.

Tabachnick, B. R. & Zeichner, K. (1991). *Issues and practices in inquiry-oriented teacher education*. London: Falmer Press.

Valli, L. (1992). Introduction. In L. Valli (Ed.), *Reflective teacher education: Cases and critiques* (pp. xi–xxv). Albany: SUNY Press.

Winter, R. (1989). *Learning from experience: Principles & practice in action research*. London: Falmer Press.

Zeichner, K. (1991). Contradictions and tensions in the professionalization of teaching and the democratization of schools. *Teachers College Record, 92*, 363–379.

Zeichner, K. (1992). Conceptions of reflective teaching in contemporary U.S. teacher education programs. In L. Valli (Ed.), *Reflective teacher education: Cases and critiques* (pp. 161–173). Albany, NY: State University of New York Press.

Zeichner, K. (1993). *Educating teachers for cultural diversity*. East Lansing, MI: National Center for Research on Teacher Learning.

Zeichner, K. (1994). Conceptions of reflective practice in teaching and teacher education. In G. Harvard & P. Hodkinson (Eds.), *Action and reflection in teacher education* (pp. 15–34). Norwood, NJ: Ablex.

Zeichner, K., & Liston, D. (in press). *Reflective teaching*. Hillsdale, NJ: Erlbaum.

CHAPTER 10

Designing Educative Practicum Experiences for Prospective Teachers

Ken Zeichner

In this chapter I will share some of my thoughts about the design of practicum experiences in initial teacher education.[1] I am using the term *practicum* in a general sense to refer to all varieties of observational and teaching experiences in a preservice teacher education program, field experiences that precede professional education course work, early field experiences that are tied to particular courses, and student teaching and internship experiences.

DEFINING AN EDUCATIVE PRACTICUM

First, I will define the kind of practicum that I think we should be aiming for in our teacher education programs, regardless of the organizational and structural arrangements we choose to employ (its length, who supervises it, and whether it takes place in one of the newer professional development school [PDS] partnerships that are now emerging in some parts of the world). I refer to this practicum very simply as an "educative practicum." Feiman-Nemser and Buchmann (1985) argue that at least three questions must be asked about the role of any practicum in learning to teach:

1. What is the preservice teacher learning in the here and now about being a teacher, about pupils, classrooms, and the activities of teaching?
2. How do these lessons of experience relate to the central purpose of teaching, helping pupils learn?
3. To what extent do these lessons of experience foster the student's capacity to learn from future experience?

I believe that these three questions capture the essence of the task facing those of us who must design a curriculum for practicum experiences. It is very clear from the literature in this area that some lessons will be learned by student teachers during the practicum. We must therefore view the practicum as an important occasion for teacher learning and not merely a time for the demonstration of things previously learned. Whether what student teachers learn is consistent with what we would hope that they learn is beside the point. They will learn something, and if we are to take the reports of graduates of teacher education programs seriously (e.g., Lamm, 1988), these lessons will be crucial in helping to form the teachers who go into our schools.

We also know from research on teacher learning that the lessons of experience that student teachers learn during the practicum will be strongly influenced by the assumptions, conceptions, beliefs, dispositions, and capabilities that they bring to the practicum (Zeichner & Gore, 1990). Teacher learning during the practicum is filtered through these lenses, and how well our teacher education programs help student teachers uncover and examine what they bring to the classroom will greatly influence our ability to achieve our goals (Wubbels, 1992). According to the literature, many of the ideas that student teachers bring to the practicum are problematic: that teaching is telling, for example, or that some pupils just can't learn because of their socioeconomic backgrounds (Calderhead, 1991). Unless these ideas are reexamined, they will interfere with teachers' learning things during the practicum that will contribute to the accomplishment of the central purposes of schooling.

For example, few people would argue that the practicums in the 1,200 or so teacher education institutions in the United States are helping to prepare teachers to teach all children. Most teacher education students in the United States are culturally encapsulated, white, and monolingual, and are being prepared to teach pupils just like themselves in communities they are familiar with (Zimpher & Ashburn, 1992). Given the current explosion of cultural and linguistic diversity in the United States, this leaves vast numbers of students of color, many of them poor, without the benefit of teachers who have been especially prepared for the cross-cultural encounters that are a fact of life in many schools.

We also know, because of the narrow focus of most practicums on the classroom and the lack of attention to school and community contexts, that the practicum often fails to prepare student teachers for the full scope of the teacher's role. Unless the practicum gives student teachers a direct understanding of how their work in the classroom fits into the larger contexts of school and community, and the capability to deal effectively with colleagues, administrators, parents, and community people, their effectiveness in the classroom will be severely compromised.

Goodlad (1990) argues that prospective teachers typically learn a great deal about how to go it alone within a classroom, and, like many others who have examined the scope of the practicum in a number of countries (Cochran-Smith, 1991; Koetsier, Wubbels, & van Driel, 1992), he concludes that the practice of placing student teachers in a single classroom with one teacher is seriously flawed, because it fails to prepare teachers for the full range of responsibilities they have to assume even as beginning teachers, including their role as stewards of schools. In many places in North America, teachers are assuming new responsibilities for school-based curriculum development, staff development, school governance, and new forms of collaborative relations with colleagues and parents (Lieberman, 1989). A focus in the practicum only on instruction with children in the classroom, although important, does not prepare teachers for the full range of their responsibilities or for the leadership roles they will be expected to play in many places.

Feiman-Nemser and Buchmann's (1985) third question—about the extent to which lessons of experience during the practicum live on in further experience and foster the student teacher's capacity to learn from future experience—is critical, and takes us back to John Dewey's work in examining the relationships between experience and education (e.g., Dewey, 1938). Dewey argued that while firsthand experience in schools is critical to the education of teachers, not all experience is necessarily beneficial:

> The belief that all genuine education comes about through experience does not mean that all experiences are genuinely or equally educative. Experience and education cannot be directly equated to each other. For some experiences are miseducative. Any experience is miseducative that has the effect of arresting or distorting the growth of further experience. (p. 25)

No matter what we do in our preservice teacher education programs and no matter how well we do it, at best we can only prepare teachers to begin teaching. Unless the practicum helps to teach prospective teachers how to take control of their own professional development and to learn how to continue learning, it is miseducative, no matter how successful teachers might be in the short run. Dewey (1904/1965) criticized the tendency in teacher education of his day to place too much emphasis on the immediate proficiency of the teacher, and too little emphasis on preparing students of education who have the capacity and disposition to keep on growing.

> Practical work should be pursued primarily with reference to its reaction upon the professional pupil in making him a thoughtful and alert student of education, rather than to help him get immediate proficiency. For immediate skill may be got at the cost of power to go on growing. Unless a teacher is . . . a student [of education] he may continue to improve in the mechanics of school management, but he cannot grow as a teacher, an inspirer and director of soul-life. (p. 151)

It is my belief that a worthwhile practicum experience, what I am calling here an educative practicum, responds in an acceptable way to all three of Feiman-Nemser and Buchmann's (1985) queries. We need to be able to exam-

ine our practicums and be able to say that the lessons student teachers are learning in them are helping to prepare them for the full scope of the teacher's role,
for accomplishing the central purposes of schooling with all students, and that
these lessons are helping to foster the ability and disposition to learn from further experience.

THREE CONCEPTIONS OF THE PRACTICUM

Although there are many different structural and organizational forms of the
practicum across the world (e.g., Buchberger & Busch, 1988), I think there have
been essentially three major conceptual approaches to designing practicum
experiences in initial teacher education programs. These different conceptual
orientations—the apprenticeship practicum, the applied-science practicum, and
the inquiry-oriented practicum—reflect different ideas about the source of teaching expertise and respond in different ways to the three key questions that must
be asked of all practicum courses.

The Apprenticeship Practicum

In the apprenticeship approach, the source of teaching expertise is thought to
lie in the heads of experienced practitioners who need only show the novice
how to do what they are able to do well. Despite all the bad press that the notion of apprenticeship has received in teacher education, and the position
expressed by some teacher education organizations that classroom experience
by itself cannot be trusted to foster dispositions that will lead to good teaching
and the ability to become better at teaching over time, it is generally acknowledged that an apprenticeship model is still dominant in many countries throughout the world (Buchberger & Busch, 1988; Stones, 1987).

I want to draw a distinction between the "sink-or-swim" apprenticeship
model, where student teachers are essentially turned loose in schools and left
entirely in the hands of collaborating teachers,[2] and an apprenticeship experience, where there is more of a planned effort by college and university teacher
educators to tap into the expertise of experienced teachers and to coordinate
practicum work with academic course work. Unfortunately, the most common
form of the apprenticeship in initial teacher education, especially in universities, has been the sink-or-swim version. In this model, it is implicitly assumed
that good teaching is caught and not taught, that good things happen more by
accidental fortune than by deliberate design (Stones, 1984), and that the hall-
mark of success is the assumption of independent teaching performance
(Feiman-Nemser & Beasley, 1993). For a variety of reasons related to the low
status and prestige associated with practicum and the labor-intensive nature of

practicum supervision, college and university teacher educators throughout the world have abandoned responsibility for trying to ensure that the practicum experience is an educative one for student teachers.

Relying in a simple way on the unmediated mentoring of experienced teachers during the practicum interferes with student teacher learning. One major problem is that the placement of student teachers into particular classrooms and schools has often been made on the basis of administrative convenience and political advantage rather than on the basis of which settings can provide the best learning experience for student teachers (Zimpher, 1990). Student teachers throughout the world are frequently placed in classrooms where the teaching they are exposed to contradicts what they are taught in the colleges. I should add that this is often true of teacher education colleges and universities as well. The act of volunteering to work with student teachers frequently serves as the sole quality control in the selection of collaborating teachers (Meade, 1991). In these situations, it is likely that what student teachers learn during the practicum will often conflict with the aspirations of college and university teacher educators for them.

Even if we assume for a moment, however, that collaborating teachers are employed who represent all of the best qualities desired by college and university teacher educators, there are still major obstacles to student teacher learning in the simple apprenticeship approach. One of the most serious is that being a collaborating teacher most often carries very little recognition and reward and usually must be done in addition to handling a full teacher's work load (Beynon, 1990). Typically, no provision is made in the duties of collaborating teachers to enable them to actively carry out their important roles as teacher educators. Even if they want to provide careful guidance to student teachers, there is rarely time to do so. In most cases, colleges and universities provide little formal training for teachers who want to assume these roles; and even when they do, teachers are typically given very little information about, let alone input into determining, the teacher education program curriculum. Consequently, the lessons of experience for student teachers in the apprenticeship are often determined by the luck of the draw, and not as a planned part of a curriculum. In fact, the concept of a practicum curriculum (Turney, Eltis, Towler, & Wright, 1985) is foreign to the sink-or-swim apprenticeship model, and it is often the case that collaborating teachers and student teachers are only vaguely aware, if at all, of the purposes and goals and desired experiences of the practicum and its relationship to the overall teacher education program (Griffin et al., 1983; Yates, 1981).

The most fundamental limitation of the simple apprenticeship approach is that student teachers are placed with individual mentors rather than in schools with a number of different mentors. For even if the luck of the draw is good, and collaborating teachers exhibit many of the characteristics and capabilities favored by the ideology of a teacher education program, it cannot be assumed that the expertise will be acquired by the novice through mere exposure; there is plenty of evidence to the contrary (e.g., Feiman-Nemser & Buchmann, 1987). Nor can it be assumed that the expertise that is exhibited by the collaborating teacher is exhaustively excellent and sufficient for preparing novices for situations different from the one in the collaborating teacher's classroom (Stones & Morris, 1977).

Although there is clearly a great deal of expertise about teaching that resides in the heads and practices of experienced teachers, the apprenticeship model is not, in my view, the way to take advantage of it. Even though I have been critical here of the sink-or-swim apprenticeship model that has characterized the practicum for a long time, I do not mean to minimize the importance of tapping into the knowledge and expertise of collaborating teachers. On the contrary, we need to figure out ways to take better advantage of the knowledge of teachers, both about teaching and about teacher education.

Fortunately, we are beginning to see the emergence of a literature that includes the knowledge of teachers about teaching (Cochran-Smith & Lytle, 1993) and the practical knowledge of collaborating teachers about teacher education (e.g., Feiman-Nemser & Beasley, 1993; Wood, 1991). The problem is not that this knowledge might conflict with what college and university teacher educators might want for their students. A dialogue among teacher educators and their students that includes the voices of diverse perspectives is educative and should be encouraged. The problem is that apprenticeship as it now exists does not encourage collaborating teachers to share any of their knowledge about teaching or teacher education. The simple apprenticeship model encourages collaborating teachers to act as teachers but not as teacher educators (Feiman-Nemser & Buchmann, 1987).

The Applied-Science Practicum

The second major approach to organizing the practicum in initial teacher education is one that places the emphasis on student teachers' *applying* knowledge and theories in the classroom that they have been exposed to in academic courses. Many teacher education practicums are preceded by or run concurrently with academic course work, and student teachers are assessed primarily according to how well they measure up to some external standard of excellence derived from academic course work. These standards derive either from the academic disciplines or from educational research on teaching and learning.

Some educators believe that the key to the development of teaching expertise lies either in a thorough preparation in the academic and foundational disciplines, or in assimilating what is referred to as the "knowledge base of teaching"—research conducted by university academics on teaching and learning. Here, in contrast to the apprenticeship approach, the source of teaching expertise is thought to lie outside of the practices of teachers. It is not uncommon in teacher education institutions throughout the world for the practicum to be viewed as a nuisance or intrusion that diverts students from serious study (Pozarnik & Kotnik, 1988). The purpose of the practicum from an applied-science point of view is for the student teacher to develop the ability to act in ways consistent with the ideology of the courses. The practicum becomes essentially a time to demonstrate things learned previously, rather than a time for new learning. For example, is the teaching sufficiently multicultural, culturally responsive, consistent with conceptual-change theories of learning? Are the integrity of the disciplines maintained in the work of the student teacher?

Schön (1983) has done a very thorough job of critiquing the technical rationality that underlies this approach to the practicum. He points out that in any number of professions, such as architecture or musical performance, the idea of relying on the *application* of scientific theory has never worked very well in solving the messy problems that practitioners face in the "swampy lowlands of practice." A growing body of research in the United States has questioned the idea that more courses in the academic disciplines (as they are now taught in most places) will necessarily remedy the learning deficiencies that are evident in schools. Some of the work of the National Center for Research on Teacher Learning (NCRTL) and the Wisconsin Center for Education Research has demonstrated very clearly that requiring more subject-matter courses in mathematics and biology does not necessarily help prospective teachers become better teachers of these subjects to diverse learners in elementary and secondary schools (e.g., Hewson, Zeichner, Tabachnick, Blomker, & Toolin, 1992; McDiarmid, 1989). Recent research related to the concept of pedagogical content knowledge has also demonstrated the inadequacies of relying almost exclusively on a general academic preparation for teaching that fails to consider the implications for teaching of the subject matter (e.g., see Grossman, 1990; Tamir, 1988).

Although it is obviously important that teachers have more than a superficial understanding of the subject areas they teach, and although it is clear that there is much of value for prospective teachers in some of the findings of research on teaching and learning conducted by academics *and* practitioners, it is a mistake in my view to adopt the technical view of the relationship between theory and practice that is assumed in an applied-science practicum. If we view theory as existing only in the teachers colleges and universities, and practice as existing only in schools, and the task of learning to teach as one of learning how to apply that which is acquired in colleges and universities to the schools, we are missing out on the vast expertise that resides in the practices of teachers and on the potential to generate theory through teaching practice.

The Inquiry-Oriented Practicum

In the third and final approach to the teacher education practicum, the inquiry-oriented practicum, teaching is viewed as a form of research and teachers as reflective practitioners. The process of understanding and improving one's teaching must start from reflection on one's own experience, it is believed, and the sort of wisdom derived entirely from the experience of others, even other teachers, is thought to be less valuable (Winter, 1989). In the inquiry-oriented practicum, teacher educators emphasize helping student teachers develop a greater understanding of their own practical theories[3] and tacit knowledge of teaching, and on learning how to develop new knowledge about teaching through their reflection in and on their teaching practice. Here the source of teaching expertise is thought to lie in part in the practices of teachers. Whether the emphasis is on collaborative discussions about teaching in practicum seminars, on action research, or on storying experience through journals or other forms of narrative, the goal is to help prospective teachers develop the disposition and capability to take responsibility for their own professional development.

While I have been closely involved with furthering the cause of inquiry-oriented practicums, I do not see this approach as necessarily helpful in answering the three questions posed by Feiman-Nemser and Buchmann (1985). What it is that student teachers reflect about, and how they do so, will help determine whether the reflection helps them become more capable of assuming the full scope of the teacher's role, of accomplishing the central purposes of schooling with all students, and of continuing to grow as teachers throughout their careers (Zeichner, 1993).

Before moving on to what I think can be done to capitalize on the strengths of each of the three approaches and to avoid their pitfalls, I want to briefly discuss several enduring problems of the practicum that have existed no matter which of the conceptual approaches to the practicum has been employed.

COMMON OBSTACLES

Embedded in my comments about some of the obstacles to teacher learning associated with the three different approaches to the practicum are several issues that transcend the different approaches. I've already alluded to two of these problems in my comments about research on the practicum: (1) practicums, no matter what orientation they represent, typically place student teachers in classrooms and ignore the preparation of teachers to work in schools and communities; and (2) few practicums involve the placement of student teachers in schools that serve low-income pupils of color. The practicum in effect serves to undermine the achievement of worthwhile learning by all pupils, by preparing teachers to teach only some pupils.

Another common obstacle to teacher learning in the practicum is the generally uneven quality of practicum supervision or mentoring. Despite the existence of examples of good mentoring practices in some programs (e.g., see Lucas, 1991), for the most part the literature has shown that very little deep thinking about teaching and learning goes on in supervisory conferences with teacher education students; that there is an unwillingness on the part of many collaborating teachers and university supervisors to discuss controversial issues or to offer critical feedback for fear of upsetting the delicate interpersonal balance of the triad (Menter, 1989; Richardson-Koehler, 1988; Zimpher, DeVoss, & Nott, 1980); and that practicum students frequently reject or ignore the comments of college and university tutors who come from the outside and observe them on a periodic basis (Calderhead, 1988). Also, despite the existence of theoretical models of clinical supervision (Pajak, 1993) and of supervision strategies aimed at promoting conceptual change (Handal & Lauvas, 1987), in practice the evaluation of practicum students still seems to be based largely on their personality and social acceptability, rather than on their teaching competence (Guyton & McIntyre, 1990; Kalekin-Fishman & Kornfeld, 1991).

One solution to this, according to some, is to provide better training programs for collaborating teachers and college and university supervisors, so that they will be able to use the best mentoring practices (McIntyre & Killian, 1987). Although it has been shown that supervisory training can improve student teachers' satisfaction with the mentoring they receive (e.g., Smith, 1990), this will not solve the problem of poor mentoring, because one of the main reasons for the uneven quality of mentoring in the practicum is that the practicum is not a priority issue for either the schools or the colleges and universities. More and better training for mentors does nothing at all to alter the context in which mentoring takes place.

Earlier I alluded to the problem that in few places are collaborating teachers given the time and the support to carry out their important roles. In most places, being a collaborating teacher is something that is done in addition to a full workload. College and university tutors also have very little institutional incentive for providing high-quality mentoring, because of the low status of this work in their institutions. Often there are inadequate resources for the practicum and inadequate time spent in the schools by supervisory staff. Unless we do something to alter the structural context in which the practicum exists, efforts to reform the practicum curriculum will be insufficient. None of the different approaches to the practicum curriculum can provide an acceptable answer to Feiman-Nemser and Buchmann's (1985) three questions within the current institutional climate for the practicum.

WHAT IS TO BE DONE?

Because of the interrelationship of the practicum with the other components of a teacher education program, some of the changes I will suggest go beyond the practicum itself. Any practicum that relies exclusively on any of the three approaches I have discussed thus far will not be educative in the sense that I have defined it: helping teachers assume the full scope of the teacher's role, helping them accomplish the purposes of schooling with all students, and helping them develop the capacity to learn from further experience. Because of their pitfalls, none of these three approaches—the apprenticeship, applied-science, or inquiry-oriented practicum—can be relied on uncritically as the path to enlightened teacher education practice. Despite the existence of much recent literature that celebrates particular instructional practices, the answer to the problems of the practicum is not to be found in merely having student teachers write journals, construct cases, tell teaching stories, or conduct action research. All of these practices have a place, but not as ends in themselves.

Negotiating the Practicum Curriculum

The first thing that must be done is to treat the practicums in our teacher education programs as seriously as we treat any other college or university course, with a well-thought-out curriculum plan that articulates the kinds of experiences student teachers are expected to have in the classroom, in schools, and in communities. This means that in many places the practicum should be coordinated and directed at the department level and within program areas, rather than by some centralized administrative office that coordinates practicums for many different subject areas.[4] It is a rare teacher education institution that places as much emphasis on designing, monitoring, and supporting practicums as it does on campus-based courses.

Ideally, this practicum curriculum should be negotiated with the collaborating teachers who work with our students. In my own program, this curriculum negotiation takes place both at the program level through the development of program-wide requirements and evaluation criteria and at the level of each student teaching triad, as individual statements of expectations are drawn up for each student teacher (Liston & Zeichner, 1991). Collaborating teachers must be treated as equal participants in the practicum and not as second-class citizens. Unless we treat collaborating teachers like colleagues and teacher educators, they will not act like teacher educators.

Also, as is probably clear by now, I think that this plan for the improvement of the practicum should conceptualize the student teachers' work in a much broader way than is now common. Student teachers should be prepared for work in classrooms, for collaborative work in schools as part of learning communities, and for developing positive relationships with the external communities served by schools. Very little if anything is happening right now in the practicum beyond preparing teachers for working by themselves in classrooms, even in many of the emerging professional development schools. A student teacher's practicum work must include work in a variety of school situations, including schools serving poor children, so that the practicum helps prepare teachers to teach everybody's children, and not just children like themselves.

My criticisms of the sink-or-swim apprenticeship, applied-science, and inquiry-oriented practicums are not intended to imply that there is nothing much to be gained from the wisdom embedded in the practices of experienced teachers, from a thorough grounding in the subjects to be taught, and a good general education, or from the knowledge that has been generated by the research of academics and practitioners on teaching and learning. All of these things are obviously important, but it is the way in which they are utilized that will determine their contribution to making a practicum educative or not. The collaborative development of a practicum curriculum, although important, will help overcome only some of the pitfalls of the practicum, not all of them.

Encouraging Examination of Personal Theories

Although one purpose of the practicum should be to give student teachers access to the thinking and practices of experienced teachers who are selected for representing certain qualities aimed for by the teacher education program (e.g., the way that they connect the curriculum to children's lives or promote active learning), and for their skills as mentors, the primary purpose of the practicum should not be to have the student teachers become like their collaborating teachers.

Student teachers need to learn from the wisdom of practice possessed by their collaborating teachers, from the wisdom of educational research, and from the academic disciplines, but they must be selective and critical about the externally generated knowledge that informs their practice, and they must *transform* this knowledge as they attempt to solve particular problems in their daily work in schools (Shulman, 1986).

The most important thing that we can do in the practicum in initial teacher education is to help prospective teachers become clearer about their own personal theories, which inform and are informed by their practice, and to help them establish themselves as researchers of their practice. Helping student teachers to become clearer about their personal and practical theories, and to critique and reexamine them in light of different points of view, as well as their own practice, will help them be selective and critical about how they use externally generated theories and knowledge. Ideally this reflection about teaching should take place in collaborative settings so as not to contribute further to the isolation of teachers from their colleagues. Paired placements and peer supervision have been used in a number of programs recently to help build the disposition and skill to work collaboratively (Ashcroft, 1992; Skuja, 1986).

Ideally, to avoid the pitfalls associated with "reflection for the sake of reflection," this reflection should also be guided by a vision of schooling and the social order existing in the teacher education program, and not viewed as an end in itself apart from the achievement of worthwhile ends. Whatever particular vision of schooling and the social order exists in a teacher education program, at least in societies that aspire to be democratic, the learning of worthwhile things by all students must be an important part of the practicum curriculum. This is not now the case in many programs.

Restructuring Subject-Matter Courses

Another important part of improving the way in which the practicum contributes to the development of teaching expertise must be to change the manner in which subject-matter knowledge and research on teaching and learning are taught to prospective teachers. Much more attention must be paid, in the teaching of subject-matter courses, to helping students understand the key concepts in their disciplines rather than just memorizing lots of information. More emphasis on the kind of detached subject-matter courses that now dominate teacher education programs across the world will not help solve the obvious deficiencies in teachers' subject-matter competence. One way in which this restructuring of subject-matter instruction can occur is through the development of new partnerships that involve team teaching of subject matter and methodology courses by academic and education faculty (e.g., see Fallon & Murray, 1991). However it is done, academic faculty must become more concerned about the pedagogical implications of the subject-matter knowledge they teach to prospective teachers.

Choosing and Presenting Educational Research

Changes in the way in which the so-called knowledge base for teaching is presented to prospective teachers are also necessary to the reform of the practicum. Instead of continuing to present educational research in an uncritical way, as is done in many programs ("you need to do so and so because research says that it is good"), we ought to help students become critical consumers of research, even that research we hold most dear. In addition to helping our students become critical consumers of educational research, we must help them see themselves as potential generators of new knowledge about teaching. It will be hard for them to see themselves as producers of educational knowledge if the only research they read or discuss is that which has been conducted by college and university academics. We must make special efforts to include the research of teachers and other school practitioners, which has become readily available in recent years.

Changing the Institutional Context

Finally, let me reiterate that none of these things related to the practicum curriculum can be accomplished very well without major changes in the institutional context of the practicum. Neither the schools nor colleges and universities place a high priority on the teacher education practicum. Teachers are expected to assume key roles as school-based mentors without any provision for this in their work and often with only token remuneration, and college and university faculty in most cases lack the institutional incentives and resources to mount and sustain high-quality programs. In my program in Wisconsin, cooperating teachers are paid approximately $.14 per hour for their work with student teachers during a 20-week semester. The minimum wage in the United States right now, for jobs in places like McDonald's, is $4.25. This situation simply has to end. You cannot run good teacher education practicums on the cheap.

Carefully guiding the learning of prospective teachers from firsthand experience in schools is an expensive proposition that requires more resources than conventional academic courses on campus. In most places, teacher education practicum courses are less well supported than practicum courses in other fields such as medicine, nursing, social work, and engineering. In Britain and in the United States, with the implementation of government requirements related to teacher education, the amount of time in teacher education programs devoted to practicum work has increased a great deal in recent years, while the actual resources for these programs have decreased (e.g., Gilroy, 1992; Guyton & McIntyre, 1990). In the end, you get what you pay for. But even in countries like Australia, where collaborating teachers are paid well for their work as teacher educators (around $28 per day in some cases), the overall commitment to the practicum is not necessarily greater than in countries like my own that openly exploit collaborating teachers. The money to pay collaborating teachers in countries like Australia comes from limiting the practicum to very brief periods of time.

I want to share a few specific examples of what I think can be done to alter the structural context of the practicum. First, I think that government bodies responsible for teacher education like state departments of education and school boards must recognize the special status of collaborating teachers on the promotion ladder and in the definition of their work. Collaborating teachers should be provided with time to do the important work of mentoring (Borko, 1989) and accorded the status and recognition they deserve for doing this work. This support should include some released time to meet with student teachers and some formal preparation and continuing support for mentors. Because most teacher education colleges and universities cannot afford to pay for this restructuring and staff development with their current resources, new resources will have to be provided by the government bodies responsible for teacher education. We can also reallocate some of our existing resources, perhaps shifting a portion of the tuition money paid by student teachers to the schools where their work is done, to provide some released time for collaborating teachers.[5] Also, some of the funds now used for micromonitoring teacher education programs by government agencies can be redirected toward stimulating innovative practice.

THE PROMISE OF PROFESSIONAL DEVELOPMENT SCHOOLS

It is hard to envision creating school environments supportive of the practicum and of teacher learning if we think only about placing student teachers with individual collaborating teachers. Much work going on right now throughout North America is directed at situating the teacher education practicum within new institutional partnerships, created in schools that have adopted teacher education as a central part of their missions: professional development schools (PDS), professional practice schools, or partnership schools (e.g., see Abdal-Haqq, 1991; Darling-Hammond, 1993; Levine, 1992). Similar work is going on elsewhere under different names (e.g., see Ashcroft, 1992). These schools, which have made a special commitment to the preparation of teachers and to the learning of all adults who work in them, are usually part of the public school system and are often jointly controlled by school authorities and colleges and universities.

Situating the practicum in professional development schools, or in subcultures within schools where a special commitment has been made to teacher education (Cochran-Smith, 1991), could be the kind of structural change in the practicum that would help us deal with some of its enduring problems. Much of the literature on professional development schools does not discuss how the creation of these new partnerships has affected the teacher education practicum; the process involved in building new kinds of relationships among school staff and college faculty; the links of PDS work with school-improvement projects; and how becoming part of a PDS affects the lives of individual participants (Brennan & Simpson, 1993; Murray, 1993).

The few papers that have discussed the relationship between these schools and the teacher education practicum have argued that professional development schools adopt a distinct philosophical approach to the practicum, associated with particular practices that address obstacles to teacher learning.

For example, Teitel (1992, 1993), Neufeld & Boris-Schacter (1991), and Worth (1990) have all included analyses of the impact of professional development school partnerships on the preparation of teachers in their discussions of Massachusetts PDS projects. A recent report of the seven sites involved in the Ford Foundation–sponsored Clinical Schools project has also included some descriptions of innovations in the practicum that have resulted from professional development school partnerships (Anderson, 1993; Yerian & Grossman, 1993). Teitel (1993) argues, for example, that professional development school partnerships "represent a philosophical approach that values lessons of practice, and invites experienced teachers to help prepare aspiring teachers, both on site and at the college" (p. 80).

In both the institutions studied in Massachusetts and the Ford project sites, school personnel clearly became more actively involved in the total teacher education program, often participating in the teaching of seminars and courses that were taught previously by college and university faculty. Conversely, the college and university faculty, or at least the few involved in the PDS projects, become more involved in schools and in some cases in teaching in schools.

The mentoring of teachers in these schools has typically shifted from the use of external supervisors to the use of school-site-based supervisors, and has overcome some of the problems characteristically associated with the use of external supervisors, such as lack of accessibility, lack of trust, and lack of influence. The placement of student teachers has typically been with teams of teachers rather than with individual collaborating teachers, and has addressed some of the problems of single-class placements. Despite these and other pluses that have come with the professional development school model, I think that we should be very careful about embracing professional development schools and school-based supervision as stand-alone solutions to the enduring problems of the practicum.

For example, there is some evidence that merely shifting the student teaching seminar and supervision to the school does not address some of the problematic aspects of student teacher supervision discussed earlier, such as the lack of discussion of controversial issues like racism (Gillette, 1990). It is also the case that the placement of student teachers with teams rather than with individual teachers does not necessarily address the narrowness of the practicum and its lack of attention to the school and community contexts. Little is said in the professional development school literature about helping student teachers to become knowledgeable about the community served by their schools, to learn how to use this knowledge in their teaching, or to understand about the organizational and political processes of schools. There is also no guarantee that multiple classroom placements will prepare teachers any better for the stewardship of schools, or that a professional development school model will necessarily do a better job of preparing teachers to teach all students (Pugach & Pasch, 1994).

What we have in this new movement in teacher education[6] is a structure that offers much promise in addressing some of the enduring problems of the practicum. It has the potential to raise the status of practicum work both in schools and in colleges and universities. It has the potential to give school personnel a greater role in the total teacher education program, to create greater coherence in the teacher education curriculum, and to create a greater role for mentoring. But if we focus only on the structural change of forming new partnerships and ignore the curricular questions related to teacher learning posed to us by Feiman-Nemser and Buchmann (1985), we may find ourselves, 10 years from now, in the same position we are in today. The most important issues are those related to what student teachers are learning during the practicum, regardless of its organizational structure.

NOTES

1. This chapter is a revised version of a keynote address presented at the annual meeting of the Massachusetts Association of Colleges for Teacher Education and the Commonwealth Teacher Education Consortium, Marlboro, Massachusetts, October 1993.

2. I will use the term *collaborating teacher* to describe the classroom teachers in whose classrooms teacher education students work. Other terms used throughout the world for these school-based teacher educators are cooperating teachers, supervisor teachers, supervising teachers, and mentor teachers.

3. See Handal & Lauvas (1987), Chapter 2, for an excellent discussion of the concept of teachers' practical theories.

4. This does not mean that I am calling for the abolishment of dean's office–level positions of director of school experience, director of field experiences, etc. These administrative offices have an important role to play in assisting program areas in making placements and in university-school relations. My point is that with or without the existence of these offices, the intellectual and curricular aspects of the practicum should be designed by faculty and teachers who work within particular programs.

5. This shifting of tuition money to the school site has recently been done in a limited number of schools by Michigan State University (S. Feiman-Nemser, personal correspondence, September 1993).

6. Although the idea of the professional development school is not new (Stallings & Kowalski, 1990), the extent to which these partnerships have grown in use is new.

REFERENCES

Abdal-Haqq, I. (1991). *Professional development schools & educational reform: Concepts and concern.* Washington, DC: American Association of Colleges for Teacher Education.

Anderson, C. R. (1993). *Voices of change: A report of the clinical schools project.* Washington, DC: American Association of Colleges for Teacher Education.

Ashcroft, K. (1992). Working together, developing reflective student teachers. In C.

Biott & J. Nias (Eds.), *Working and learning together for change* (pp. 33–46). Milton Keynes, UK: Open University Press.

Beynon, C. (1990). Relationships in the practicum: Toward an understanding of the role of the cooperating teacher. In *Proceedings of the Stoney Lake conference.* Toronto: The Joint Centre for Teacher Development, Ontario Institute for Studies in Education.

Borko, H. (1989). Research on learning to teach: Implications for graduate teacher preparation. In A. Wollfolk (Ed.), *Research perspectives on the graduate preparation of teachers* (pp. 69–87). Englewood Cliffs, NJ: Prentice-Hall.

Borko, H., & Mayfield, V. (1993, April). *The roles of the cooperating teacher and university supervisor in learning to teach.* Paper presented at the annual meeting of the American Educational Research Association, Atlanta, GA.

Brennan, S., & Simpson, K. (1993). The professional development school: Lessons from the past, prospects for the future. *Action in Teacher Education, 15*(2), 9–17.

Buchberger, F., & Busch, F. (1988). The role of the practical element in initial teacher education. *European Journal of Teacher Education, 11*(1), 5–7.

Calderhead, J. (1988). The contributions of field experience to primary teachers' professional learning. *Research in Education, 40,* 33–49.

Calderhead, J. (1991). The nature of knowledge growth in student teaching. *Teaching & Teacher Education, 7,* 531–536.

Cochran-Smith, M. (1991). Reinventing student teaching. *Journal of Teacher Education, 42*(2), 104–119.

Cochran-Smith, M., & Lytle, S. (1993). *Inside out: Teacher research and knowledge.* New York: Teachers College Press.

Darling-Hammond, L. (Ed.). (1993). *Professional development schools.* New York: Teachers College Press.

Dewey, J. (1965). The relation of theory to practice in education. Reprinted in M. Borrowman (Ed.), *Teacher education in America: A documentary history.* New York: Teachers College Press. (Original work published 1904)

Dewey, J. (1938). *Experience & education.* New York: Collier Books.

Fallon, D., & Murray, F. (1991). *Project 30: Year two report.* Newark: School of Education, University of Delaware.

Feiman-Nemser, S., & Beasley, K. (1993, June). *Discovering and sharing knowledge: Inventing a new role for cooperating teachers.* Paper presented at the Workshop on Teachers' Cognition & Pedagogical Knowledge, co-sponsored by the U.S./Israel Bi-National Science Foundation & the James S. McDonnel Foundation, Tel-Aviv, Israel.

Feiman-Nemser, S., & Buchmann, M. (1985). Pitfalls of experience in teacher education. *Teachers College Record, 87,* 49–65.

Feiman-Nemser, S., & Buchmann, M. (1987). When is student teaching teacher education. *Teaching & teacher education, 3*(4), 255–273.

Gillette, M. (1990). *Making them multicultural: A case study of the clinical teacher-supervisor in preservice teacher education.* Unpublished doctoral dissertation, University of Wisconsin–Madison, School of Education.

Gilroy, P. (1992). The political rape of teacher education in England & Wales. *Journal of Education for Teaching, 18,* 5–22.

Goodlad, J. (1990). *Teachers for our nation's schools.* San Francisco: Jossey-Bass.

Griffin, G., et al. (1983). *Clinical preservice teacher education: Final report of a descriptive study.* Austin, TX: Research & Development Center for Teacher Education.

Grossman, P. (1990). *The making of a teacher: Teacher knowledge & teacher education.* New York: Teachers College Press.

Guyton, E., & McIntyre, D. J. (1990). Student teaching and school experiences. In W. R. Houston (Ed.), *Handbook of research in teacher education* (pp. 514–534). New York: Macmillan.

Handal, G., & Lauvas, P. (1987). *Promoting reflective teaching: Supervision in action.* Milton Keynes, England: Open University Press.

Hewson, P., Zeichner, K., Tabachnick, B.R., Blomker, K., & Toolin, R. (1992, April). *A conceptual change approach to science teacher education at the University of Wisconsin–Madison.* Paper presented at the annual meeting of the American Educational Research Association, San Francisco, CA.

Kalekin-Fishman, D., & Kornfeld, G. (1991). Construing roles: Cooperating teachers and student teachers in TEFL. An Israeli story. *Journal of Education for Teaching, 17*(2), 151–163.

Koetsier, C. P., Wubbels, T., & van Driel, C. (1992). An investigation into careful supervision of student teaching. In J. H. C. Vanonk et al. (Eds.), *New prospects for teacher education in Europe II* (pp. 245–254). Amsterdam: University of Vriso.

Lamm, Z. (1988). Teacher education in Israel: The present situation. *European Journal of Teacher Education, 9*(3), 233–245.

Levine, M. (Ed.). (1992). *Professional practice schools: Linking teacher education and school reform.* New York: Teachers College Press.

Lieberman, A. (1989). *Building a professional culture in schools.* New York: Teachers College Press.

Liston, D., & Zeichner, K. (1991). *Teacher education and the social conditions of schooling.* New York: Routledge.

Lucas, P. (1991). New practices and the need for flexibility in supervising student teachers. *Journal of Further and Higher Education, 15*(2), 84–93.

McDiarmid, G. W. (1989). *What do prospective teachers learn in their liberal arts courses?* Issue paper 89-8. East Lansing, MI: National Center for Research on Teacher Learning.

McIntyre, D. J., & Killian, J. (1987). The influence of supervisory training for cooperating teachers on preservice teachers' development during early field experience. *Journal of Educational Research, 80*(5), 277–282.

Meade, E. (1991). Reshaping the clinical phase of teacher preparation. *Phi Delta Kappan, 72*(9), 666–669.

Menter, I. (1989). Teaching practice stasis: Racism, sexism and school experience in initial teacher education. *British Journal of Sociology in Education, 10*(4), 459–473.

Murray, F. (1993). "All or none" criteria for professional development schools. *Educational Policy, 7*(1), 61–73.

Neufeld, B., & Boris-Schacter, S. (1991). *Professional development schools in Massachusetts: Maintenance & growth.* Boston: Massachusetts Field Center for Teaching & Learning.

Pajak, E. (1993). *Approaches to clinical supervision.* Norwood, MA: Christopher Gordon.

Pozarnik, B. M., & Kotnik, N. (1988). Practical components in teacher training programs in Slovenia (Yugoslavia). *European Journal of Teacher Education, 11*(1), 41–48.

Pugach, M., & Pasch, S. (1994). The challenge of creating urban professional development schools. In R. Yinger & K. Borman (Eds.), *Restructuring education: Issues & strategies for schools, communities & universities* (pp. 129–156). Norwood, NJ: Ablex.

Richardson-Koehler, V. (1988). Barriers to the effective supervisor of student teaching. *Journal of Teacher Education, 39*(2), 28–34.

Schön, D. (1983). *The reflective practitioner.* New York: Basic Books.

Shulman, L. (1986). Those who understand: Knowledge growth in teaching. *Educational Researcher, 15*(2), 4–14.

Skuja, R. (1986). Paired teaching: A Singapore alternative. In V. Bickley (Ed.), *Re-exploring CELT: Continuing education for language teachers.* Hong Kong: Institute for Language in Education.

Smith, D. (1990). Intern satisfaction with cooperating teacher supervision. *Alberta Journal of Educational Research, 36*(2), 133–140.

Stallings, J., & Kowalski, T. (1990). Research on professional development schools. In W. R. Houston (Ed.), *Handbook of research on teacher education* (pp. 251–266). New York: Macmillan.

Stones, E. (1984). *Supervision in teacher education.* London: Methuen.

Stones, E. (1987). Teaching practice supervision: Bridge between theory & practice. *European Journal of Teacher Education, 10*(1), 67–79.

Stones, E., & Morris, S. (1977). *Teaching practice: Problems & perspectives.* London: Methuen.

Tamir, P. (1988). Subject matter and related pedagogical knowledge in teacher education. *Teaching & Teacher Education, 4*(2), 99–110.

Teitel, L. (1992). The impact of professional development school partnerships on the preparation of teachers. *Teaching Education, 4*(2), 77–86.

Teitel, L. (1993, April). *The impact of professional development schools on colleges and universities.* Paper presented at the annual meeting of the American Educational Research Association, Atlanta, GA.

Turney, C., Eltis, K., Towler, J., & Wright, R. (1985). *A new basis for teacher education: The practicum curriculum.* Sydney: Sydney University Press.

Winter, R. (1989). *Learning from experience: Principles & practice in action research.* London: Falmer Press.

Wood, P. (1991). The cooperating teacher's role in nurturing reflective teaching. In B. R. Tabachnick & K. Zeichner (Eds.), *Issues and practices in inquiry-oriented teacher education* (pp. 186–201). London: Falmer Press.

Worth, K. (1990, April). *The Wheelock/Brookline collaborative: The internship program.* Paper presented at the annual meeting of the American Educational Research Association, Boston, MA.

Wubbels, T. (1992). Taking account of student teachers' preconceptions. *Teaching & Teacher Education, 8*(2), 137–150.

Yates, J. W. (1981). Student teaching in England: Results of a recent survey. *Journal of Teacher Education, 32*(5), 44–47.

Yerian, S., & Grossman, P. (1993, April). *Emerging themes on the effectiveness of teacher preparation through professional development schools.* Paper presented at the annual meeting of the American Educational Research Association, Atlanta, GA.

Zeichner, K. (1993). Connecting genuine teacher development to the struggle for social justice. *Journal of Education for Teaching, 19*(1), 5–20.

Zeichner, K., & Gore, J. (1990). Teacher socialization. In W. R. Houston (Ed.), *Handbook of research on teacher education* (pp. 329–348). New York: Macmillan.

Zimpher, N. (1990). Creating professional development school sites. *Theory in Practice, 29*(1), 42–49.

Zimpher, N., & Ashburn, E. (1992). Countering parochialism among teacher candidates. In M. Dillworth (Ed.), *Diversity in teacher education* (pp. 40–62). San Francisco: Jossey-Bass.

Zimpher, N., DeVoss, G., & Nott, D. (1980). A closer look at university student teacher supervision. *Journal of Teacher Education, 31*(4), 11–15.

About the Contributors

Elizabeth Bondy is Associate Professor of Education at the University of Florida. Dr. Bondy teaches and conducts research in the area of elementary teacher education. She also coordinates "Bright Futures," a multiagency project in which university students provide tutoring for youth at risk for academic failure. She is co-author of *Reflective Teaching for Student Empowerment: Elementary Curriculum and Methods*.

Robert Floden is Co-Director of the National Center for Research on Teacher Learning and Professor of Teacher Education and Educational Psychology at Michigan State University. He has been active in the design and conduct of teacher education programs at both preservice and doctoral levels. Floden has written on a wide range of topics, drawing on his expertise in philosophy, statistics, psychology, program evaluation, research on teaching, and research on teacher education. He is currently working on studies of the connections between professional development and education reform.

Mary Louise Gomez is an associate professor of literacy education and teacher education in the Department of Curriculum & Instruction at the University of Wisconsin–Madison, where she co-directs Teach for Diversity, an experimental master's degree program (offering teacher certification in grades 1–6) grounded in issues of social justice and equity. Her research, which focuses on teachers' perspectives and how these challenge, inhibit, and enhance teaching for literacy, has been published in book chapters and journals such as *Teaching and Teacher Education, Language Arts, The Journal of Negro Education*, and *The Journal of Education for Teaching*.

Susan Melnick is an associate professor and assistant chairperson in the Department of Teacher Education and senior researcher in the National Center for Research on Teacher Learning at Michigan State University. A former secondary school English and Spanish teacher, Melnick has been actively involved for more than two decades in the education of both prospective and experienced teachers. Her primary research interests are reflected in her scholarly writing on policy issues in teacher education and in learning to teach; professional knowledge for teaching; and concerns of race, class, gender, and educational equity, both domestic and cross-national.

Dorene Ross is Professor of Education and Coordinator of Elementary Teacher Education Programs at the University of Florida. Dr. Ross conducts research in the areas of diversity, teachers' perspectives, and teacher reflection. She is co-author of *Reflective Teaching for Student Empowerment: Elementary Curriculum and Methods.*

Trish Stoddart is Associate Professor of Education at the University of California, Santa Cruz. She is a cognitive psychologist who conducts research on teacher learning and development. Her research focus is on the teaching and learning of science and mathematics and the utilization of advanced technology in instruction. She has published extensively in the areas of science and mathematics teacher education, teacher certification, and school restructuring. In 1992, she was the recipient of the Award for Outstanding Scholarship in Teacher Education presented by the Association of Colleges and Schools of Education in State Universities and Land Grant Colleges. In 1992 and 1994, she was presented with the Award for Outstanding Contribution to Technology Education presented by the Association for the Advancement of Computing in Education.

Alan R. Tom is Professor of Education in the School of Education at the University of North Carolina at Chapel Hill. His teaching, program development, and research interests focus on the initial preparation of teachers and their career development. Tom is author of *Teaching as a Moral Craft* and the upcoming *Redesigning Teacher Education* with SUNY Press.

Ken Zeichner is Hoefs-Bascom Professor of Teacher Education, University of Wisconsin–Madison, and a senior researcher with the National Center for Research on Teacher Learning, Michigan State University. He has codirected a student teaching program in elementary education since 1976, and teaches graduate courses in the study of teacher education. His recent publications include "Beyond the divide of teacher research & academic research" in *Teachers and Teaching*, "Reflections of a teacher educator working for social change" in *Teachers Who Teach Teachers: Reflections on Teacher Education* (F. Korthagen and T. Russell, Eds.) and "Action research: Personal renewal & social reconstruction" in *Educational Action Research.*

Index

NAMES

SUBJECTS